CW00658793

The Empire of Depression

For Laura, River, and Julia

The Empire of Depression

A New History

Jonathan Sadowsky

polity

Copyright © Jonathan Sadowsky 2021

The right of Jonathan Sadowsky to be identified as Author of this Work has been asserted in accordance with the UK Copyright, Designs and Patents Act 1988.

First published in 2021 by Polity Press

Polity Press
65 Bridge Street
Cambridge CB2 1UR, UK

Polity Press
101 Station Landing
Suite 300
Medford, MA 02155, USA

All rights reserved. Except for the quotation of short passages for the purpose of criticism and review, no part of this publication may be reproduced, stored in a retrieval system or transmitted, in any form or by any means, electronic, mechanical, photocopying, recording or otherwise, without the prior permission of the publisher.

ISBN-13: 978-1-5095-3164-6

A catalogue record for this book is available from the British Library.

Library of Congress Cataloging-in-Publication Data

Names: Sadowsky, Jonathan Hal, author.
Title: The empire of depression : a new history / Jonathan Sadowsky.
Description: Cambridge, UK ; Medford, MA : Polity Press, 2021. | Series: History of health and illness | Includes bibliographical references and index. | Summary: "How depression colonized the world"-- Provided by publisher.
Identifiers: LCCN 2020016685 (print) | LCCN 2020016686 (ebook) | ISBN 9781509531646 (hardback) | ISBN 9781509531660 (epub)
Subjects: LCSH: Depression, Mental. | Depression, Mental--History.
Classification: LCC RC537 .S293 2020 (print) | LCC RC537 (ebook) | DDC 616.85/27--dc23
LC record available at https://lccn.loc.gov/2020016685
LC ebook record available at https://lccn.loc.gov/2020016686

Typeset in 10.75 on 14 Adobe Janson by
Servis Filmsetting Ltd, Stockport, Cheshire
Printed and bound in Great Britain by TJ Books Limited

The publisher has used its best endeavors to ensure that the URLs for external websites referred to in this book are correct and active at the time of going to press. However, the publisher has no responsibility for the websites and can make no guarantee that a site will remain live or that the content is or will remain appropriate.

Every effort has been made to trace all copyright holders, but if any have been overlooked the publisher will be pleased to include any necessary credits in any subsequent reprint or edition.

For further information on Polity, visit our website:
politybooks.com

Contents

Figures

Preface

When is sorrow sickness?

The writer Virginia Heffernan had a bad break-up. This happens to a lot of people. It can make you sad, sometimes for a long time. At some point, though, Heffernan began to feel that the grief over lost love was overtaken by something else, an illness. Worse, the depression seemed to grow on its own, to become something separate from the grief, disconnected from the break-up.

Trying to understand what was happening, she wondered if her search for happiness was the problem – was she depressed because she expected too much out of life? Or perhaps, she thought (as many people with depression do), she was simply a bad person. Was the depression an excuse for not having a career – was she simply lazy? Not an easy question to answer, because excessive self-criticism is a sign of depression. Was her depression an excuse for laziness? Or was that very question the depression talking?

These puzzles are not new. What happened next, though, is a product of more recent history – and the history of a recent product. Heffernan got a prescription for antidepressants. Sitting on a train, she poured the pills into her hand and looked at them wondering if the chasm she felt in herself could truly be filled by these chemicals.[1] A lot of people have been asking this question in recent decades. The question holds a mix of hope and fear. Many feel some relief if the answer is yes. Not only relief from the illness, but also from the torment of doubt over whether they have an illness. If a medicine works, that might reassure that the illness is real. Still, many look at these chemicals with worry, and not just because, like all medicines, they can have unwanted side effects. It can also seem weird that your basic outlook – optimistic or pessimistic, self-hating or self-loving – might be a chemical process. While these questions have grown acute in the antidepressant era, the link of body to mood, of stuff to spirit, has been an enigma for centuries. And nothing arouses the puzzlement as much as the terrible pain on which we paste the label: depression.

This book is about that pain. A pain that isolates, but one always set in a social domain. A pain of soul and body that reminds us how hard it is to say where soul ends and the body begins. A pain found in diverse places and times, changing its features to suit the village where it arrives. A pain that devours hope, and leaches pleasure, ambition, and simple ease. One doctor said there is only one worse illness, rabies.[2] Whether he was right or not, few maladies match depression's super power: to drain life of value, to turn what was golden into mud.

It is also a pain with a history. The history lies in its morphing of form and expression, and in the countless efforts to grasp its origin, meaning, and essence – efforts that are necessary and useful, and yet always fall short. And it lies in the changing ways healers have tried, with incomplete success, to provide relief.

I stress several themes. One is that depression is shaped by history and culture, but that comparisons across time and space are possible, and essential. A second is that we do not have to choose between understandings of depression as biological, psychological, or social. This false choice is a product of recent history. We call depression a "mental illness." Critics of psychiatry sometimes complain that the problems named by that term are not really illnesses. I am more concerned about the other half of the phrase – they are never just mental. Depression always involves the body. A third is that there is a politics to depression, a politics of inequality. This is another area where some have posed what I think is a false choice, between a "medical" model and a social model. Health, illness, and healing are always set in a social context, and showing that they are does not make them less medical. As

I am completing this book, the COVID-19 pandemic is unfolding. In addition to its ravages on human health, it is shining a light on many social problems, including class and race inequality, the inadequacy of the public health and medical insurance systems in many societies, and the bigoted blaming of peoples for illness, a scapegoating that medical historians see resurfacing with dismal predictability. Depression also puts a spotlight on many social problems. It does not cease being a medical problem because of that any more than a virus does. A fourth is the classic historian's caution against scorning the past. Much of the history of depression is made of efforts by smart and concerned people, doing their best with the knowledge available, to understand and treat it. As in other areas of medicine, some zealots have pushed their favored approach too far. Many others have sounded cautions, seeing the incomplete state of psychiatric knowledge.[3]

Many books on the history of psychiatry are scathing catalogues of its harms. Psychiatry *has* harmed a lot of people, through imprisonment, stigmatization, invasive physical treatments, or misguided over-reliance on drugs. Even talk therapy, often assumed to be inherently more humane, can be abusive or harmful. Saying this is not to be against psychiatry. It's a matter of empirical fact, amply shown by historians of psychiatry. We should not whitewash this history, but we also have to reckon with how psychiatry has helped people. The vast majority of depression patients are voluntary. They return to their doctors because treatment helps them to feel better and live their lives closer to the way they wish. Many people without access to treatment would dearly like it.

I have written with occasional levity. An entirely somber book about depression might be hard to read, or even depressing. There should be no mistaking, though, the seriousness of the subject. Severe depressions can be ruinous, a threat to livelihood, the most precious relationships, and physical health. They can also be directly life-threatening if they lead to suicidal thinking or suicide. Less severe forms can also be painful indeed, and are too often trivialized.

Many historians have recently stressed the newness of the modern concept of depression. The last 120 years have seen vast changes in its meaning and treatment. Whether what we now call "depression" has existed in all times and places in human history is a hard question, and I give it a lot of attention. One part of the question is whether the illness once called "melancholia," a term that was used from classical antiquity with waning use in the twentieth century, was the same as modern depression. I look at this problem in chapter 2, but to sum up here: no, melancholia and modern depression are not identical. They could not possibly be, because neither has had a fixed, stable meaning. A historical relationship does exist between the two concepts, though. A history of depression that excluded the history of melancholia would be badly incomplete.

Throughout the history of depressive illness, some have noticed, in some cases, a relationship to manic states. Current psychiatry uses the diagnosis of bipolar disorder, formerly known as Manic Depression, to indicate an illness of fluctuating moods, with manic phases alternating with depression. At other times, this has been considered simply one form of melancholia or depression, and sometimes it has been used as the blanket term for all depression. It would be ahistorical to omit any mention of mania or bipolar disorder here, but it will also not be a major focus. Unipolar and bipolar depression overlap, both in symptoms and treatment. Some now believe they are two different kinds of the same illness, others do not. Some even speculate that all the mood disorders *and* psychoses are related on a spectrum, which could turn out to be hundreds or even thousands of discrete illnesses.[4] Some focus is necessary. I am focusing on unipolar depression.

Through history, and also now, many different diagnostic labels have referred to depressed mood. Even within those categories, presentation and experience vary. We might speak of "depressions," just as some claim schizophrenia is not a unitary condition and prefer the term "the schizophrenias." I prefer to state the diversity here, and treat it as a given from here on. The unity of these diverse illness descriptions does not come from a core feature one can find in all of them. It comes from their shared inclusion in the centuries of debate about their meaning.[5]

I look at the history of many treatments. Treatments for depression are often divided into two main types: (1) the physical, or somatic treatments, and (2) the psychological treatments, most of which are talk therapies.[6] Both physical and psychological treatments for illnesses of mood have been around for centuries. Current physical treatment is dominated by antidepressant drugs developed in the last 70 years or so.

In the middle of twentieth century, the first drugs called antidepressants came into use, most importantly a class of drugs called the tricyclics, and another called monoamine oxidase inhibitors (MAOIs). A bit later the selective serotonin reuptake inhibitors (SSRIs), such as Prozac, fully ushered in the antidepressant era. Also important is electroconvulsive therapy (ECT), invented in Italy in the 1930s. ECT is used on a far smaller number of people, mostly people for whom other treatments have failed. I look at physical treatments, those used widely now, those discarded, and some that may have a promising future, in chapter 5.

The talk therapies are now dominated by two major strands. One is a tradition of depth psychology, also called "dynamic," or psychology of the unconscious. Depth psychology is based on insight into, and "working through," inner conflict. A majority of depth psychologists are loosely or strictly Freudian, but some follow other strands, such as the Jungian. Many people are unaware of how much psychoanalytic thought has changed since Freud's time. I will show these changes in chapter 3. Another major talk therapy is Cognitive-Behavioral Therapy (CBT), which works to correct logical errors in the thoughts of the depressed person, and encourages changes in behavior. Treatments addressed to the thoughts and behaviors of people with depressive illness have been practiced since antiquity (see chapter 2), but they were vigorously thought out and applied in the second half of the twentieth century (see chapter 4). Some talk therapists – possibly most – in practice combine insight, cognitive work, and behavioral advice.

None of these treatments, physical or psychological, lack vigorous critics. I examine the treatments and their critics, and have opinions about them. My job as a historian includes placing developments in context, and weighing evidence carefully; it does not include neutrality or objectivity, if they were possible, which they are not. One opinion I will get to now: sweeping attacks on either physical or psychological treatments are unpersuasive to me. Specific criticisms, of specific physical or talk therapies, can have value. But I am wary of arguments that physical treatment is inherently bad, toxic, or abusive, or that talk therapy is unscientific because it is not biological.[7] These judgments are usually driven by unfounded philosophical dogma. Or worse, by turf wars between psychotherapeutic and pharmaceutical clinicians.

Many treatments for depression are effective for many people, even though none are effective for all people, and some people struggle to find a solution that works for them. I am not shy about assessing how well treatments work, or about noting their drawbacks – and they do all have drawbacks. Depression is a monster, and we need an array of weapons to fire on it.

Depression has an "empire" in two senses. First, in Western psychiatry and societies, it became a dominant way of interpreting mental distress, upending other language, in a gradual process that gained powerful momentum starting in the later twentieth century, though it began before then. Second, this linguistic shift then began to spread globally. Older names and conceptions of distress are increasingly competing with the label depression. We will see, however, both that illnesses of great sorrow may not be new to many areas adopting this turn in language, and that older cultural and medical models do not simply give way to new ones, but interact with them in complex ways. One thing this book is not is a long lament on the over-diagnosis of depression, and the turning of life's normal suffering into a medical problem. Lots of books make this complaint now, and most of them make valid points. The danger of over-diagnosis is real. I give the issue attention, but also some pushback and alternative views. Increasing diagnosis rates of depression in recent decades is a fact, but its cause and meaning are not obvious. There are three possible reasons for it. There could really be more depression. Or, we could be having about as much depression as before, but catching more of it – better detection. A third possibility is diagnostic drift – the relabeling of states that were considered different illness, or not considered illness at all. Two or all three of these possibilities could be at work.

Many laments about the over-diagnosis of depression, and the medicalization of ordinary suffering, are data-poor. They look at widening criteria for diagnosis, or the sheer numbers in treatment, and assume too many people are being diagnosed. They rarely show directly that a lot of people with depression diagnoses do not meet a threshold for real illness – whatever that threshold may be. Greatly increased rates of diagnosis over a short time is grounds to *wonder* about over-diagnosis, but not, by itself, *proof* of over-diagnosis.

Psychiatric diagnosis draws a lot of valid criticism. It can stigmatize people and behaviors. It increasingly calls any problem in life a disease.

Depression has an unusual status in these debates. With the exception of a few people on the antipsychiatric fringe, most people agree that certain mental disorders, such as severe psychoses, count as illnesses. And many, including many psychiatrists, also believe that we have gone too far in taking normal problems of living and calling them illnesses. In the case of depression, it is a matter of degree. Most people think serious and moderate cases of depression warrant medical treatment. Many also question whether everyone in treatment reaches that threshold. Where should we draw the line? I do not answer this question, but I do hope to show how hard it is, and that it is not as new a question as it might seem. The history of depression is in part a history of the tug-of-war over where the line should fall.

Some argue that depression, or other mental illnesses, are not true medical conditions. They will often point to the lack of a clear physical lesion, or the shifting and imprecise definitions. Fewer say *why* there needs to be a physical lesion, or a precise and unchanging definition, for something to count as a medical problem. Instead, they treat these measures as self-evident. They are not. Others stress that depression is a social and cultural problem. This is correct, but does not mean depression is not also a medical problem.

Sometimes I look at a major problem or controversy in the science of depression and say the truth is unknown. One job of the humanities is to nurture tolerance of uncertainty. Granting uncertainty is not the same as a cynical nihilism which declares all knowledge bankrupt. Where I think the knowledge about depression is sound, I say so. The social and cultural aspects of depression may yield more certain knowledge than the physical ones, despite progress in understanding the biology over the past century or so.

I have taught a course on depression for years, and I have found that many people who take it are people who have a depression diagnosis, or are wondering if they should have one. Many people who have picked up this book may be in the same situation. The course, I tell students, is not, should not, and cannot be therapeutic, and neither can the book. It will cover debates over whether depression is "really" an illness, and about whether treatments for it are effective. But before we get into the nuances of these debates, I want to say that I think "yes" is the most convincing answer to both questions, as well as the safest. If you feel like you may need help, you should try to get it. Doubting whether you have an illness or not is unlikely to help you feel better. And yes, we have effective treatments for depression, and there is a good chance that one of them can help.

Depression touches a problem all people face.[8] We all know sadness, and we all can feel the loss of interest in things, the disturbed sleep, and appetite changes sorrow can cause. Yet most people think that the misery sometimes seems – because of its severity, longevity, or apparent disconnect from reality – like an illness. But when? Other illnesses, probably all, vary in their meaning and appearance across time and cultures. Susan Sontag vividly showed, for example, that tuberculosis and HIV, both caused by known infectious agents, have been shadowed by culture, by metaphors and image associations that influence how they are understood and experienced.[9] These associations have a power beyond what science can tell us about the physical effects of disease. Illnesses are always embedded in society and culture, and subject to change according to time and place. Still, few are as changeable as depression.

The plasticity reflects a hard problem: deciding what is a proper reaction to life's inevitable distress. Most of the world's religion and philosophy – our accumulated wisdom – assume human life is filled with anguish. As Paul Simon sang in "The Coast," sorrow is every-where you turn. But when is sorrow sickness?

Acknowledgments

Thanks to my family above all. My father, for 57 years of support, encouragement, and wisdom. It's common to think your father is the best man in the world when you are a child, but I still think it now. River Sadowsky, Julia Sadowsky, Nina Sadowsky, and Richard Sadowsky all cheered me on, and cheered me up. My wife, Laura Steinberg, a psychiatrist and psychoanalyst by profession, and a skilled copy editor as well, is my greatest support and best reader.

Three people at Case Western Reserve remain especially vital. Alan Rocke, now retired, continues his unbroken streak of reading everything I write, on this project from the embryonic proposal to the full draft manuscript. Eileen Anderson-Fye, always there for me, helps me in too many ways to list. And no one could ask for a better friend and intellectual partner than Ted Steinberg has been to me.

Two colleagues elsewhere also deserve special mention. David William Cohen, my mentor in graduate school, has left a lasting imprint even as my research focus has diverged from his. My intellectual north star, I still seek him out during his retirement when I need advice on a knotty problem. My interests have grown to overlap with those of my other main inspiration, Liz Lunbeck, a crucial support to me at so many times, and so many ways, over the course of my career.

Thanks to other Case Western Reserve colleagues who helped with the project in various ways: Mark Aulisio, Francesca Brittan, Nese Devenot, Kimberly Emmons, Sue Hinze, Tina Howe, Peter Knox, Andrea Rager, Maddalena Rumor, Catherine Scallen, Renée Sentilles, Maggie Vinter, Ann Warren, and Gillian Weiss.

Also thanks to the many colleagues elsewhere who helped in concrete or less tangible ways: Ana Antic, Hubertus Büschel, Stephen Casper, Carolyn Eastman, Marta Elliott, Jeremy Greene, Matthew Heaton, Vanessa Hildebrand, Nancy Rose Hunt, Sanjeev Jain, Richard Keller, Barron Lerner, Beth Linker, Amy Lutz, Sloan Mahone, Sarah Marks, Elizabeth Mellyn, Emily Mendenhall, Randy Nathenson, Daniel Pine, Hans Pols, Sharon Schwartz, Trysa Shulman-Shy, Nina Studer, and Catherine Sullivan. Elizabeth Durham and Katie Kilroy-Marac get special mention for helpful reading at unconscionably short notice.

I had the help of a number of research assistants at various stages, helping me identify and get sources, and reading drafts. Thanks to Beth Salem, Matthew Yoder, Sufia Bakshi, Riley Simko, Kat Retting, and Sherri Bolcevic. Maia Delegal was especially invaluable down the final stretch of writing.

Two anonymous reviewers read the initial proposal for the book and the book itself, and I owe them a lot. One was more sympathetic to my overall approach than the other, but they were both constructive and thoughtful, and their comments made the book better.

Parts of this book were presented at various conferences and seminars, at: the Department of the History and Sociology of Science at the University of Pennsylvania; the conference "Global Histories of Psychiatry," Groningen University, The Netherlands, November 2018; the conference "Decolonising Madness," Birkbeck, University of London, April 2019; a joint meeting of the Carl Jung Institute of Cleveland and the Cleveland Psychoanalytic Center, May 2019; the conference, "Psychiatry as Social Medicine," The Johns Hopkins University, November 2019; and the Bioethics Work-in-Progress group at CWRU. Thanks to those who commented and inspired in those venues.

Thanks to Meghan Gallagher and Katie Nabors for keeping everything running smoothly, and especially to the amazing Bess Weiss who always goes above and beyond.

Thanks to Bill Claspy, Jen Starkey, and Erin Smith at Kelvin Smith Library, who always made sure I got what I needed.

Thanks to Pascal Porcheron at Polity for his interest, encouragement, and suggestions, and to Ellen MacDonald-Kramer for her help with logistics. I've so enjoyed working with this team.

Students in my class on social and cultural aspects of depression have helped me think through many of the issues over the years, but thanks especially to Carolyn Slebodnik, and Tarun Jella. Students in Foundations of Medicine, Society and Culture did the same, but especially, Disha Bhargava, Dami Oshin, Karthik Ravichandran, and Sarah Siddiqui.

"Depression is a thing in which one seems to be dead in life."[10]

1

Depression is a Thing

"People who don't have depression have a lot of difficulty understanding it, but people who have it are also often befuddled by it."
                                        – Chimamanda Ngozi Adichie[1]

Imagine a young woman in Philadelphia, a foreign student attending college and far from home for the first time. She is in a phase of sadness, close to despair. She feels isolated, but rebuffs people who invite her to social events. She lacks motivation, letting her room get messier by the day. Is this a case of clinical depression?

Imagine further that the student herself says no, rejects the label of depression when it is suggested by her aunt, a Nigerian doctor who is also a recent immigrant to the United States. She tells her aunt to stop using this American way of naming her distress. She does not have an illness at all, she says. Ifemelu, the main character in Chimamanda Ngozi Adichie's novel *Americanah*, believes she is having a normal reaction to her situation. She is poor, her undocumented status has made it hard to find a job, and she is far from loved ones. Who wouldn't have sadness, maybe some lethargy and social withdrawal? Uju, her aunt, believes she has a *real disease*, though one not talked about much in Nigeria. Americans, Ifemelu responds, have a disease for everything. Ifemelu's "symptoms" melt away without much comment once she finds a good job and makes friends.[2]

The conflict between Ifemelu and Uju might seem to be a new one, peculiar to modern America's impulse to give medical names to life's problems. Yet the troubled distinction between depression and normal sadness runs through the history of the ailment. Can the border between the two be drawn sharply? Do they have the same sources, or distinctly different ones?

According to the World Health Organization, depression is now – newly – the single biggest contributor to the global health burden.[3] They estimate that there are more than 300 million people worldwide living with depression, with an 18 percent increase between 2005 and 2015. Between 2011 and 2014, about one in nine Americans said they took an antidepressant.[4] Many of them took drugs named "antidepressants" for other problems, such as insomnia and pain management, but the diagnosis of depression has swollen massively.

The meaning of the swelling is not obvious, though. Are more people getting depression? If so, what is causing this epidemic? Doctors, though, may simply be diagnosing depression more. If so, are they catching more of the cases that were always there, or changing the norms for diagnosis? Or is the rising currency of the label "depression" influencing how people interpret their mental distress, whether it is profound psychic pain, or moderate unhappiness? How much does the mere presence of antidepressants influence the rates of diagnosis? *Counting depression is a vexed project.*

The different explanations for rising rates of diagnosis all have smart advocates. Those who think we are having more depression point to alienating or distressing aspects of contemporary life, from wealth inequality and violence, to social isolation brought on by social media.[5] Whether the world is any more depressing or alienating than it was 75 to 125 years ago, when the diagnosis was less common, is not obvious, though. We had lower rates of depression diagnosis during the First and Second World Wars, Western imperialism, Jim Crow, and the Holocaust. Early twentieth-century sociology is rife with laments about the alienation of modern, urban societies. The era's philosophy gave us elaborate arguments that life was absurd and without ultimate purpose.

So perhaps we are not living through an epidemic of depression but of *calling things* depression. This view usually goes with criticism of the pharmaceutical industry – which certainly does have a financial interest in a broad definition of the illness. As inviting as this argument is, though, consider that before the era of rising diagnosis rates, mental health advocates sought better detection of depression, an illness they thought was *under*-diagnosed, and a terrible and needless contributor to human misery.[6] From their point of view, we are only now finding all the depression they believed was there all along. They were urging more diagnosis before drug companies were making money on block-buster antidepressants.

Put more systematically: whenever any illness is diagnosed more than before, there are three possibilities. The first is what epidemiologists call "*rising true prevalence*" – an actual increase in the number of sick people. The second is *better detection*. If, for example, you use hospital admissions to count the number of people with a sickness, you only count the people who come in to the hospital. You might get a better count if you go door to door in a community. Better detection can also come if doctors and the public grow more aware of the condition, so more patients come into treatment. But what if what you are count-ing is itself changing? This is the third explanation, *diagnostic drift*. A diagnosis may be naming distress that before would have been covered by a different illness label, or perhaps not be an illness at all. In debates about mental health, these possibilities are often treated as competitors but two of them, or even all three, could be working in tandem.

Knowing the prevalence of a disease is challenging when its defini-tion is stable and has a clear sign, such as a blood test. With an illness like depression it is even harder. *Counting depressions is a vexed project*, partly because depression is hard to define.

Depression, in a clinical sense, is a diagnostic term. The prefix "dia" means apart and "gnosis" is knowledge. To diagnose means "to know apart," to distinguish from something else. Doing this for depression has not proven easy.

What Is Depression?

Many have a loose sense of what clinical depression is – an illness of unusually low mood. That simple definition hides a lot of complexity and change.

Let's look at Major Depressive Disorder (MDD) in the current

Diagnostic and Statistical Manual of Mental Disorders (DSM-5). MDD is the central diagnosis for depressive illness in the current manual, though other illnesses include depressive symptoms. The DSM-5 will not be the last word on what depression is. If the past is any guide, the category of depression will continue to transform. Discontent with MDD has already emerged. Some clinicians and researchers think MDD embraces too many subtypes of depression.[7] According to one recent textbook, "no clinician or researcher believes that MDD is a single 'illness.'"[8] More precision might lead to better treatment plans. For now, though, we lack a widely-agreed upon subdivision.[9] DSM-5 calls for MDD if five of nine symptoms have been present for a two-week period. The nine symptoms are:

1. Depressed mood most of the day, nearly every day.
2. Markedly diminished interest or pleasure in all, or almost all, activities most of the day, nearly every day.
3. Significant weight loss when not dieting or weight gain, or decrease or increase in appetite nearly every day.
4. Change in sleep – sleeping too little or too much
5. A slowing down of thought and a reduction of physical movement (observable by others, not merely subjective feelings of restlessness or being slowed down).
6. Fatigue or loss of energy nearly every day.
7. Feelings of worthlessness or excessive or inappropriate guilt nearly every day.
8. Diminished ability to think or concentrate, or indecisiveness, nearly every day.
9. Recurrent thoughts of death, recurrent suicidal ideation without a specific plan, or a suicide attempt or a specific plan for committing suicide.

One of either of the first two listed symptoms must be present, but none of the rest are required, as long as four others are present. The manual also says that the symptoms must cause significant distress or impairment, and must not be caused by substance abuse, or by another illness.

Time is key. Symptoms have to be lasting for a diagnosis. But the time given is arbitrary. I am not saying that the authors of the manual erred when they set the duration. They had to pick something, or else people could get a diagnosis after being in a bad mood and losing appetite for a few hours because of something the President tweeted. (This happens to me sometimes.) The right length of time, though, cannot be settled scientifically. Future research may refine our knowledge of depression to a point where the amount of time could be settled objectively. I doubt it.

We also frequently ask if the symptoms seem justified by events. Although not a factor in current DSM diagnosis, in much of Western history many definitions of depressive illness have insisted that the distress must be out of proportion to the life situation.[10] As early as the time of Hippocrates in Greek antiquity, some said melancholia was present only if the symptoms were not normal reactions to life events. A few centuries later, the physician Aretaeus wrote of melancholic patients being "dull and stern, dejected or unreasonably torpid, *without any manifest cause.*"[11] Freud's classic work on the subject started with the premise of the difference between normal grief and melancholia without cause. One psychiatrist wrote in 1976 that depression differs from normal sorrow if it "seems exaggerated in relation to the supposed precipitating event."[12] This *proportionality criterion* – the mood must be out of proportion to the life situation to be called sickness – has had a deep mark on Western concepts of depressive illness, and continues to influence debate, even though it is not now an official part of diagnosis. It also likely influences paths to treatment – people undergoing clearly stressful losses may be slower to conclude they have an illness and need medical attention than people having the same feelings in the absence of those events. Ifemelu reminded Uju that if she was sad, she had reason to be. Ifemelu did not add that such sadness might be depression if her life situation were sunnier. That would, though, seem to save the label from the charge of making every bad feeling an illness. The proportionality criterion often poses challenges in practice, though. The fifth edition of the DSM removed the "bereavement exclusion" from the diagnosis of major depression. In previous editions, the symptoms didn't count toward a diagnosis if they came during mourning. Some psychiatrists worried that this change to the manual took a normal, if painful, part of life and turned it into an illness.[13]

Consider heartbreak. Say you were deeply in love with someone who dumped you. You might have five of the nine symptoms above. Both medical and lay opinion usually say that we should not medicate heartbreak. But what if the symptoms last a long time, or become especially severe? If the heartache lasts for years on end, is it then an illness? At what moment does it become so? What if the heartbroken person becomes suicidal? We then might want to intervene medically. But exactly how far short from suicidality is normal enough to be out of the range of medical attention?

The questions lack objective answers. Both the time and proportionality criteria shift with cultural norms, historical moments, and even from person to person.

What Makes Something an Illness, Anyway?

The tacit question in the conversations between Ifemelu and Uju is, what makes anything an illness? How do we decide?

One option, often favored by people who dislike psychiatry, or want to reject a "medical model" is to say a physical lesion must be present. This is appealing. We like to have something we can see. But this is not how most societies have decided on illness states through human history, and it's arbitrary. Many lesions now known for illnesses were once unknown – was Alzheimer's Disease not an illness before Alzheimer identified the brain pathology? If we someday do find a clearer biological measurement of depression, would depression magically transform into an illness then, after being not an illness now?

Another option is to use illness to refer to atypical states or conditions, but atypical states are not always bad. We would not want to say that someone with unusually high ethical standards has "Excessive Morality Syndrome." We might, though, if it was causing undue suffering. So perhaps we should add that the condition must cause pain or limitations in daily life. But this could include everything from being left-handed in a world built for right-handed people, or being gay in a society that persecutes gay people. Psychiatry tried labeling being gay as an illness, partly with the hope it would diminish the stigma. The results were terrible.[14]

Psychiatrist Nancy Andreasen has argued that no one has developed "successful, logical, and non-tautological definitions of . . . disease, health, physical illness, or mental illness."[15] She's right.

Attempts to separate "real" from made-up illnesses open a bottomless pit of philosophical debate. Some conditions are easily agreed upon – cancer (an illness), and left-handedness (not an illness), for example. More ambiguous cases can be tough. With agreement, the suffering person gets "the sick role," with the associated exemptions (such as missing work) and obligations (such as trying to get better). Medical care is appropriate.[16] But the agreement is the outcome of a social process. Even when a known physical marker is present, a social process decides whether it is a sign of illness.

People sometimes try to change the social agreements by adding or subtracting illnesses. In an effort at subtraction, libertarian antipsychiatrist Thomas Szasz – a fan of the "physical lesion" yardstick – excluded all of mental illness, and sought to take psychiatry out of medicine. Given how much of human history, all over the world, has seen things like psychotic symptoms, or disabling distress, as signs of illness, Szasz had a lot of success. But just as Szasz was free to question the medical status of mental illness, others were free to re-assert it. They had even more success. A more complete success in subtracting an illness came when gay activists challenged the label of homosexuality as an illness. They were not, they said, suffering from their same-sex attraction. They may have been suffering from lack of social acceptance, but calling their sexuality "illness" was not helping. It did a lot of documented harm.

As for addition, new illness states are being named all the time. I'm surly when I first wake up in the morning. Not an illness, right? But if I want to say I have "Morning Surliness Syndrome (MSS)," I can, and if a lot of people start to agree, then its status as an illness will be a social fact. Others can object, by saying we didn't always have this newfangled MSS, or asking where is the physical lesion. Ifemelu might say, how American this is, to call something an illness because the culture values morning perkiness. What would matter is how many people I convince, especially if they include doctors and insurers. If a drug could make you more perky in the morning, my success is more likely. This sounds like a fanciful scenario. But it is close to what happened with Erectile Dysfunction.[17]

If you think social agreement is a bad way to decide on what an illness is, you are free to propose objective criteria. But you will have to get everyone to agree to them. Best of luck!

Psychiatric diagnosis causes more division than those in most areas of medicine. Labels change their meaning, drop out of use entirely, are occasionally revived. The history of psychiatry is strewn with labels with no real clinical purpose, and others that were well-meaning, but failed, attempts to dispel stigma. It is child's play to show that a DSM diagnosis is a "social construction." You can teach a class of college freshmen how in under ten minutes. And, psychiatric diagnoses are always to some extent a reduction. Using them can hide context, complexity, and subjective experience. The potential for harm, especially stigma, is always present. These drawbacks are not unique to psychiatry, though. Any diagnosis in medicine can stigmatize, even if stigma is greater for some than others. And any diagnosis is reductive if it draws attention from the larger context. Saying someone has tuberculosis does not reveal the social roots of the medical problem, in poverty or occupation, for example.[18] It can also miss cultural context; tuberculosis has had changing meanings and associations.[19] As I write, we are vividly seeing the dreadful effects of COVID-19. The virus is exploiting existing social inequalities and inflaming existing stigmas. These social dimensions are not captured by diagnosis alone. They also do not make the illness less real.

Psychiatric diagnosis is fraught, but that does not make it useless. Diagnosis provides a pathway to practical things like treatment and insurance coverage, and can also be comforting.[20] A vague sense that something feels bad can be a burden. Naming the feeling as an illness helps people make sense of pain, and can be a first step toward seeing it as a solvable problem. People may feel less alone, to know that their distress is something others know and recognize.

Many people write critiques of the DSM. These critiques often – and I mean *really* often – call the book psychiatry's "bible." By calling it a sacred text, these critics show their irreverence. The analogy is bad, though. Few psychiatrists regard the *DSM* as sacred, and most recognize its weaknesses.[21] Psychiatrists know the *DSM* fails to capture all the nuances of mental illness.[22] Criticism of the *DSM* is necessary, but not all that contrarian. Perhaps instead of using a manual we should let clinicians use their judgment, based on experience, to make individualized treatment plans. This is what many do anyway, whatever they write on the insurance submission. Much would be lost without some standard manual, though. Clinicians would find it hard to communicate about patients, and research comparing patients would be hard to design. Many patients are dependent on third-party payment, and insurers want a classification system.

Critics of psychiatric diagnosis point to discredited diagnoses to claim the whole enterprise is flawed. Homosexuality is one example, but there are lots of others. In the nineteenth century, a racist White doctor said that escaped slaves in the American south suffered from "drapetomania," an illness whose symptom was the desire to be free.[23] Hysteria was a diagnosis that stigmatized women and was used to control them. Psychiatric labels often do have political and cultural bias. But these examples do not show that psychiatric labels have no possible value. To say they do is as dogmatic and uncritical as saying that they have perfect validity.

So, What About Depression? Is It an Illness?

The word "depression" refers to a sickness, but also to a mood everyone experiences. The mood ordinarily passes, and is often driven away with simple changes like going for a run, cleaning up your room, or taking a shower. Even when it lasts longer, it may pass in time, and fade as life gets better. Ifemelu's mood changed as she got a job and made friends. This does not mean she never had a clinical depression, and the novel never says for sure either way. But people who have not had the illness often struggle to see that it cannot be easily shaken off, and may require medical treatment.

Deciding whether depression is an illness would be easier if it were a less amorphous category. The number of symptoms that have been called symptoms of depression is huge. I began keeping a list of every symptom I found, in any context past or present, to be a symptom of depression (see figure 1). I have grouped them into three domains: (1) affective/behavioral – having to do with mood and actions, (2) psychotic – having a break with reality, and (3) somatic, or physical. Almost all depression diagnoses include affective and somatic items. Psychotic symptoms

Affective/Behavioral
- Depressed mood
- Loss of interest in things
- Guilt
- Sadness
- "Excessive" sadness
- Expectation of bad things to happen
- Rumination
- Social withdrawal
- Feelings of worthlessness
- Suicidality
- Trouble concentrating
- Cognitive dysfunctions
- Indecisiveness
- Agitation
- Anhedonia (the inability to feel pleasure)
- Irritability
- Hopelessness
- Labile mood
- Tension/nervousness
- Frequent crying
- Agoraphobia
- Hypochondria
- Existential angst
- Low motivation
- Suppressed emotion
- Feeling of "emptiness"

Psychotic
- Delusions
- Extreme paranoia
- Imagined poverty
- Hallucinations

Somatic[a]
- Digestive problems, including flatulence, constipation, stomach pain
- Motor retardation
- Insomnia
- Reduced sex drive
- Decreased or increased appetite
- Literal downcast eyes
- Low energy
- Sensation of bodily heaviness
- Reduced or absent menstruation
- Tension, especially in head or neck
- "Pins and needles"
- Heart, chest pain
- Paleness
- Sweaty palms
- Labored breathing
- Dizziness
- Bitter taste in the mouth
- Tinnitus
- Experience of darkness or mist in front of the eyes
- Cold hands and feet
- Trouble swallowing

There are overlaps in this list. To make the list as comprehensive as possible, I deliberately included possible redundancies. Many of these symptoms are also features of other mental illnesses, or of illnesses that are not considered "mental." A similar list appears in Ryder et al. (2008); I drew on it while composing this one. See Andrew G. Ryder, Jian Yang, Xiongzhao Zhu, Shuqiaou Yao, Jinyao Yi, Steven J. Heine, and R. Michael Bagby, "The Cultural Shaping of Depression: Somatic Symptoms in China, Psychological Symptoms in North America?" *Journal of Abnormal Psychology* 117 (2008), 300–13.

[a] Some of these are "reverse somatic," meaning a symptom that is the opposite of the expected symptom. For example, if being unable to sleep is a somatic symptom, sleeping too much would be the reverse somatic symptom.

Figure 1   *A (futile) attempt at a comprehensive list of depression symptoms in all contexts, past and present, sorted into domains*

belong, in most twentieth-century psychiatry, to particular subtypes, though they were more dominant in descriptions of melancholia.

With all the variability shown in figure 1, are we really talking about the same illness in all times and places? And yet, there are human universals: of body (brains, hearts, hormones, genitals, for example) and experience (hunger, pleasure, intimacy, grief, awe, and so on). They vary in form by culture, but even with immense variation, translation across cultural frontiers can be possible.[24] Virtually all human societies have a concept of mental sickness, or madness.[25] Does that include depression? Depression seems to fail the "physical lesion" test. In the absence of the clear physical lesion, the possible universality of depression as an illness might seem to do the same work: if it is an illness everywhere and at all times, then it must really be an illness – and if not, it might seem to be less real. But before getting into the question of depression's universality in detail, a caution: this criterion is no more definitive than a physical lesion. If an illness exists only in particular places and times, we can only conclude exactly that. We cannot conclude it is a fake illness. Illnesses particular to cultures are as real as any other.

Do They Have Depression Everywhere?

If the debate between Ifemelu and Uju was tacitly about what makes something an illness, it was explicitly a debate about the role of culture in deciding. Mental health research has had much the same debate for at least a century now. Depressed mood happens everywhere. Whether depression as an illness is also everywhere is less clear. Depression has been called the single most fraught psychiatric diagnosis for cross-cultural study.[26] This is a strong statement, since they are all fraught.

Two main questions have animated this fraught inquiry. The first is whether depression is a "culture-bound" syndrome of the West.[27] A "culture-bound syndrome" is an illness only found in certain cultures. Examples include *koro*, found especially in parts of Asia; people believe their sex organs are retracting and will disappear; and *ataque de nervios*, common in some Latin American contexts, often showing uncontrollable shouting, and a sensation of heat rising in the chest, among other symptoms.[28] Depression, Ifemelu argued, was a North American culture-bound syndrome.

If depression is not a culture-bound syndrome, it may vary in form. This raises the second question is: Do some cultures express depression in a more physical way, and less in terms of mood – and if so, what is the ground for calling it "depression"?

My own view is, first, that depression is probably not confined to the West, though it does seem that Western medical culture may have been historically more preoccupied with it than some others. Second, it may not be so much Western culture in general that is distinctive, but psychiatry itself. Psychiatry is a cultural system, with a set of beliefs about depressive illness that are not universal, but growing more global in their influence every day.

Looking at how views of depression in Africa have changed shows how knotty these questions are. In the early twentieth century, in colonial Africa, Western psychiatrists said that depression was rare to non-existent. In the 1960s and 1970s, the early independence period, more cases were found, and some began to say rates were as high as in the West, or higher.[29] Rise in prevalence, better detection, or diagnostic drift?

Better detection played some role. Early reports came from asylums, who admitted people upsetting social order, not people with the social withdrawal or lethargy often found in depression. Colonial asylums were not for therapy. They were more like prisons for the mad. The numbers probably changed during independence because people started looking at suffering people in other contexts, out of asylums.

But racism also had a role in the low numbers found in the early reports. Claims that depression is uniquely Western are tied to the history of Western imperialism. During the Atlantic slave trade, European slavers created stereotypes of carefree Black people, immune from melancholy and mental illness.[30] These images co-existed with, and soothed, an awareness by slave owners and slave traders that slavery could cause severe melancholy. On slave ships, slave traders saw that among captives even in this horrific setting, extreme cases of melancholy stood out. The captors sometimes took some modest medical measures to address it.[31] The image of Africans as immune to depression remained sturdy, though. It served a purpose. It allowed a denial of the inhumanity of slavery by diminishing the full humanity of the enslaved. The image influenced later colonial observers, biasing them against finding depression in Africa.[32] Depression, these observers thought, was not just an illness, but a *capacity* held by more civilized people. Mental illness was not alone in this prejudice. White physicians once thought cancer was rare among Black people because it was a disease of more advanced races.[33]

The idea that depression was rare in Black people survived into racist North American science well into the twentieth century. In 1914, a doctor at the Georgia State Sanatorium claimed that "The Negro mind does not dwell upon unpleasant subjects; he is irresponsible, unthinking . . . Depression is rarely encountered even under circumstances in which a White person would be overwhelmed."[34] A 1962 account of American Black people and depression shows the mental contortions racist science makes to avoid rethinking its assumptions. The report granted that there was no evidence of less depression in Black than White people. The authors then offered possible reasons why rates *might* be low among Black people anyway. Then, they used these speculations to confirm that the rates were indeed low![35]

While Western racism influenced the perception of depression, the question of its prevalence in Africa puzzled African observers, too. Nigerian T. A. Lambo, one of the first African psychiatrists, changed his mind, first thinking depression was rare, then wondering if it was being under-counted, and finally deciding it was being misdiagnosed.[36] Depressed patients, he decided, had been given a wrong label: neurasthenia. Neurasthenia was an illness made famous by American neurologist George Beard in the nineteenth century. Like depression, it had many symptoms, including depressed mood, mania, anxiety, irritability, impaired intellect, indigestion, malnourishment, insomnia, weakness, nerve pain, loss of faith, and fear of poverty.[37] Most of these symptoms could be a part of a depression diagnosis in current Western medicine. Depression, though, is classed as a mental illness that can have physical effects. Neurasthenia was the opposite: Beard thought it was a physical illness that could have mental effects. He thought it was a loss of nervous energy, and urged physical cures.[38] Neurasthenia started to decline as a diagnosis in the West in the early twentieth century, but went on to be used in African and Asian countries, and still is in some.

In the early 1960s, Lambo worked with an international team to compare concepts of mental illness among the Yoruba of Nigeria with those in Western contexts. No Yoruba word translated exactly as depression.[39] Many symptoms of depression, though, came up in Yoruba accounts of distress. They included "sapped vitality . . . crying continuously, extreme worry, loss of appetite," and lost interest in life.[40] The research team didn't decide whether depression was a defined illness for the Yoruba, though they found depressive symptoms just as common as in the Western context. Many Nigerians continue to believe their country has no depression, that depression is a Western thing. Many are also challenging this view, though (see figure 2).[41]

The changing African figures show that debates about the rates of mental illness are never only about numbers. They are also about how definition, culture, and politics shape the collection of the numbers.[42]

Many languages, like Yoruba, lack a medical word for depression.[43] As Kenyan writer Ted Malanda wrote after actor Robin Williams's suicide, "I can't wrap my mind around the fact that depression is an illness. We are stressed and depressed all the time! In fact, it is such a non-issue that African languages never bothered to create a word for it. Anybody who knows what they call depression in their mother tongue, please step forward."[44] Does this settle the case? Maybe not. If a society lacked a specific word for malaria, and only had a word for fever, we would say they had malaria if we could find the microbe in them, even if they did not have the specific word. But depression has no specific microbe, and in the case of malaria, the person is considered sick. Do depressive symptoms only become an illness state if the society groups them into a diagnosis?

Ifemelu might say that this grouping happens because of the Western expectation of happiness. Societies that expect suffering from life might have depressive mood, but not the illness. This might, for example, include Buddhist societies. In Buddhism, the first of the four noble truths is that existence is suffering. Perhaps it makes no sense, in such a context, to call depression an illness.[45] If so, however, I do not see how any state of distress, whether mental illness, infectious disease, or chronic physical disease, could be an illness. Buddhist societies certainly have illness. Some Buddhist societies have also had long histories of seeing extreme sorrow, or loss of interest in life, as signs of illness.[46] So do other societies without a special expectation of happiness. In Iran, sadness is a mark of seriousness and maturity, but is separate from depression, the illness.[47]

Figure 2   *This image was brought in to a class on depression by a Nigerian student. It's not clear that the artist meant to depict depression; the student said it represented depression to her.*
Source: Peju Alatise, "The Unconscious Struggle."

Sorrow and loss of interest are emotional signs. Depression has physical signs, too, and cross-cultural debate has also asked whether any apparent lack of depression in a place only means that depression's physical aspects are the focus. This is called "somatization," to make something physical, related to the body.[48] The idea of somatized depression is not new. Western psychiatry has known it as "masked depression," depression without obvious sadness, since the early twentieth century.[49] It's important to stress – people often miss this point – that no one is saying that a person has depression just because they have a backache or an upset tummy. Both psychiatrists and anthropologists usually say that if depression is suspected because of body problems, it is only confirmed if depressed mood or related emotional signs are found after a closer look.

Anthropologists have found depression somatized in Asian, African, and Latin American societies.[50] But in the United States, rural people, non-White people, and lower-class people often also somatize depression.[51] People come to primary care physicians with physical complaints and leave with a diagnosis of depression if other depressive symptoms are found in the exam.[52] Urban, White, affluent people are a minority in the United States, let alone globally. If so many places somatize depression, perhaps somatizing is the norm. The term itself may be misguided. It assumes that the primary state of depression is emotional, and the physical aspects secondary.

Can pain ever be purely physical or purely psychic? Do we ever feel physical pain without it affecting our minds? Do we ever feel psychic pain without some sensation in our bodies? After many years of reading accounts of depression, I recall none where the depression lacked any physical aspects. DSM 5, with its requirement of five out of nine symptoms, requires at least one somatic symptom for a depression diagnosis. Emotional ones alone won't tally to the threshold of five. Western psychiatry, then, insists on a physical dimension. *Depression is always a bodily experience.*[53]

The harder problem is not whether depression has physical symptoms, but the opposite: can a diagnosis of depression be made without signs of sadness? Without sadness, a depression diagnosis may stretch the term until it becomes incoherent.[54] Perhaps later evidence could confirm depression. One psychiatrist gave the example of a woman who complained only of headaches, and then hung herself.[55] The psychiatrist inferred depression from the suicide. Another psychiatrist had patients with symptoms including anorexia, insomnia, impotence, and menstrual irregularity, but little evidence of sadness.[56] Some of the patients improved after electroconvulsive therapy. If a patient with no apparent sadness improves after a treatment for depression, is a diagnosis of depression warranted?

Treatment gives the cross-cultural questions practical urgency. It seems wrong to deny a suffering person a treatment that works because their culture expresses or names the suffering differently. Concerns about the spread of Western psychiatry as a form of cultural imperialism are also valid, though. Using labels from one culture in another one always risks veiling local experience.[57]

One possible solution is to use local categories, or "idioms of distress," that are used by particular cultures, instead of supposedly universal diagnoses. The hope is to capture nuances of meaning in different settings.[58] For example, a Punjabi idiom called "sinking heart" has some overlap with the English word "depression," including weakness and unhappiness.[59] Physically, "sinking heart" manifests in the chest. In the words of afflicted people:

> When I have sinking heart my heart goes fast. One minute it goes up and the next minute it goes down. It is as if my heart is shrinking and my whole body is going wrong.

> I used to get this in my heart all the time and it felt like shaking . . . or shrinking . . . in my heart. This feeling made me walk up and down. I could not sit still and I felt great agitation.[60]

Other expressions of sinking heart include dry mouth, faintness, headache, and trouble breathing. Some of this picture is suggestive of depression, but some of it less so. If you simply call it depression, you lose aspects of how Punjabis see the problem. Their medical model revolves around the heart. The heart distributes food, breath, and blood, and is a reservoir for emotions and drives. Western psychiatry roots emotion more in the brain. Loss of control of the heart is loss of control of the self for Punjabis. This loss of control can happen when people pay too much attention to their emotions.[61] By contrast, many Americans might say you "lose yourself" when you pay too *little* attention to your emotions.

When symptoms in local idioms overlap a lot with those of depression, it's possible that the idioms capture local ways of thinking about depressive illness more than they show absence of depression. One idiom of distress found in numerous places translates as "thinking too much."[62] In some contexts, this idiom does not look much like depression, but in many others it does. Perhaps many of the languages without a word for depression are calling it "thinking too much."

Referring to depression as a "Western" illness raises other problems. What even is "Western culture"? American society has numerous sub-cultures, and depression patients do not share the same concepts of sickness, even if they are evaluated using the same manual. Europe is a multicultural continent, with differences in how low affect and distress are seen.[63] And what are the boundaries of "the West"? Much of the tradition regarding melancholia during classical antiquity was adopted by Islamic writers during the Middle Ages. The great Persian scholar Avicenna had a section on melancholia in the *Canon of Medicine* (completed in the eleventh century). Like much of classical antiquity, this tradition was transmitted to Europe during the Renaissance.

One thing *not* at stake, to me, in the depression and culture debates is the realness of depression. Culture-bound illnesses are as real as any other. We often treat things that are (in the tired academic phrase) "socially constructed" as less real. But our houses, tax codes, and the internet are "socially constructed." They are not found in nature before human action, but they are real.[64]

Arguments for the absence of depression, anywhere, pose the question of whether one was looking in the right way. Arguments that depression is universal pose the question of whether the suffering could be better captured in local terms. One thing is certain, though: depression is fast becoming a universally-used label. As the reach of Western psychiatry grows – to the point where it might be better called "cosmopolitan psychiatry" – people all over the world are using its language to understand distress.

Cultural differences concern more than the existence of or rates of depression. Western psychiatry often treats anxiety and depression as separate things that often occur together.[65] In many places, though, anxiety and depression are seen as part of one thing.[66] Cultures also differ in how they explain depression. In the West depression has recently been treated as an illness with physical causes, such as genes or neurochemistry. Critics point out that this can cover up psychological and social aspects. Most cultures do not do this, though. Globally, it is more common to consider depression to be at once psychological, social, and physical.

The model of depression in Western psychiatry is not best seen as a norm from which others depart, but as a set of cultural assumptions of its own. Western psychiatric views of depression stick out in four ways. First, Western psychiatry emphasizes emotional over physical symptoms. Second, it separates anxiety and depression.[67] Even in the West, the separation of anxiety and depression is new.[68] Third, Western medical tradition has stressed the proportionality criterion. Most cultures consider hardship in life an obvious cause of depression. Fourth, even though Western psychiatry highlights mood over physical symptoms, it ironically puts unusual stress on physical *causes*, at least in recent decades.[69] The Western stress on individual biology treats suffering individuals apart from their social context. Globally, depressive illness is usually considered something that happens because of social conditions, not something caused mainly by biology.

As Western psychiatry's assumptions and practices spread globally, we may see important gains and losses. One gain may be the spread of effective treatments outside their culture of origin. To the extent, though, that the conception of depression is biological and individual-istic, socially sensitive views may be lost.

The question of the newness of depression poses similar challenges. Some believe clinical depression has been around for all of human history. One Assyriologist, struggling with depression herself, sees evidence for her ailment in texts from the ancient Middle East that are thousands of years old.[70] Perhaps the guilt-ridden despair that disabled King Saul in the Hebrew bible was clinical depression.[71] Many histo-rians in recent years stress instead the ways depression is a new illness category. [72] The argument for newness can also sow doubt about the reality of the illness. It shouldn't. Depression can be new and culture-bound and still be an illness.

Is It a Gift?

When aunt Uju pushed the illness label, she did not think she was describing a gift. Some though, believe that for all the wretchedness of depression, it confers certain assets. Lots of creative people in history seem to have had depressive symptoms. Abraham Lincoln's melancholy may have added to his political gifts, by helping him to understand other people better.[73]

Three questions caution against making a grand conclusion about this. One, how many other illnesses have a lot of gifted people had? If any illness is common, a lot of the people who get it are going to be gifted. Second, how many people with depressive symptoms were *not* especially creative, and we have never heard of them, because they had no special gift? Third, how many creative people were lost to history because depressive illness kept them from using their talents?[74] Depression may shape the kind of creativity a person has, but I doubt that it gives more creativity.

Creativity aside, some say that people with depression have a better grasp of reality.[75] In research this is called "depressive realism." As Susanna Kaysen, the author of *Girl, Interrupted* puts it, "My main objection to optimism is that it's incorrect. Things are somewhat more likely to turn out badly."[76] Some depressed people do say they value the insight the illness yielded. If this is a gift, it comes with a curse.

Mind and Body

Repeat as Necessary: Biological and Psychological Models Are Complementary, Not Incompatible.

Far too many people have tried to argue that depression is purely biological, or purely psychological. Biological understandings of depression do not prove that psychological or sociological understandings are wrong. Psychological and sociological understandings do not undermine biological understandings.

The media will often report new research showing that genes, or inflammation, or gut bacteria, or some other biological factor causes depression. However good this research is, it is not inconsistent with psychological approaches. The inflammation might be caused by stress. Or, genes may create a vulnerability that is pricked by personal history. When put that way, doesn't it seem obvious? Yet many say, in response to new research on biological factors, "well, there goes Freud!" This is a logical fallacy. Put another way, it is wrong. Biological and psychological models are complementary, not incompatible.

Apart from cause, depression always has psychological content – problems in families, or work, obsessive thoughts, etc. Psychology can have insight into these problems, no matter how much biology may have caused the illness. Biological and psychological models are complementary, not incompatible.

A biological treatment can work, even if the cause of illness isn't biological. Efficacy of electroconvulsive therapy, antidepressants, or other physical treatment does not allow firm conclusions about cause. A treatment of the brain can work for a problem with a psychological origin. Biological and psychological models are complementary, not incompatible.

People can benefit from physical and psychological treatments at the same time. Antidepressants and psychotherapy have greater efficacy when combined, for example.[77] They may act on different aspects of the problem, but that may be exactly why they are most effective together – different aspects of the problem require different work. Biological and psychological models are complementary, not incompatible.

Let's look at two memoirists of mental illness, Kay Redfield Jamison and Elyn Saks.[78] Jamison suffers from bipolar disorder, Saks from schizophrenia. Jamison and Saks both came to appreciate that their illnesses were both psychological and physical.

Jamison began having extreme mood swings as a young adult. She was hesitant about medication – the illness had elevated states she did not want to give up. After facing the wreckage of excessive spending and self-destructive behavior several times, she came to see that the medicine was essential, life-saving. As a scientific researcher on bipolar disorder herself, Jamison is steeped in the genetic science of the illness. Neither this, nor her reliance on medication, stopped her from finding insight-oriented psychotherapy helpful for her recoveries.

As a law student, Saks began to have scary psychotic episodes. She sought the help of psychoanalysis, which she found helpful in decoding the source and meaning of her delusions. She was resistant to drugs, however, fearing they would suggest that she was *really* ill in a way that she did not want to be. The psychoanalysis did not do enough. Like Jamison, she accepted drug therapy, with some resignation. The combination of treatments, together with strong social supports, enabled her to become a law professor. The efficacy of the psychoanalysis was not enough to keep her from trying drugs. The efficacy of the drugs did not lead her to abandon her support for psychoanalysis, and she became a psychoanalyst herself. The importance of the social supports did not lead her to discount or discard her need for medical treatment.

The evidence that depression has both biological and psychological dimensions is so vast it is beyond questioning. For all the enigmas that surround the ailment, one proven thing is that it is not entirely mental or physical. The only thing strange about this is how people struggle to see it. Efficacy of physical treatments for depression never seems to sway people skeptical of them, who continue to insist that psychotherapy or social reform is the only way forward. Nor does the efficacy of psychotherapy, or our knowledge of the social causes of depression, seem to sway many who reduce depression to biology.

Reductionists of various kinds have had their day, especially over the last century. Depression is a complex problem. It has multiple causes – which makes it unlikely only one kind of response will do.

This is a way depression does differ from melancholia. The medical ideas underpinning the idea of melancholia were never just mental or just physical. They assumed mind and body constantly influence one another. How did we lose that?

2

Too Dry and too Cold

"How weary, stale, flat and unprofitable,
Seem to me all the uses of this world."

– Hamlet

Melancholy: An Early Modern Epidemic

In staging melancholy, Shakespeare presented his audience with something it knew well. Melancholy gripped the attention of much of Renaissance Europe. It posed many of the same puzzles that depression poses now. For example, where is the line between sickness and normal sadness? Is Hamlet's melancholy proportionate to events? Is Ophelia's? Their mental anguish expresses itself in such different ways. Hamlet does not have delusions. His melancholy, though, is severe, causing a general disgust with life. He gives "suicidal ideation" its most famous language. Hamlet has real problems. He is mourning his father, and is upset about his mother's scanty grieving. The instructions the ghost of his father give him plunge him into hard dilemmas about what to do. He is a haunted man. He is well enough to *feign* madness, yet he has struck many audiences as not just a man with problems, but a man with a sickness. Some have seen sickness as the only way to make sense of his lethargy.[1] Ophelia also has real problems – she feels spurned by Hamlet, and later she also has a father to grieve. Ophelia, though, shows not only sadness, but disordered thought – her disjointed speech and odd behavior are more clearly "mad." The play is unsettled about the ultimate cause.[2]

Macbeth seems at least as melancholy as either of them, at least by the end of his drama. His weariness, despair, and inability to find anything of value in life sound like the words of deep melancholy:

> Tomorrow, and tomorrow, and tomorrow,
> Creeps in this petty pace from day to day,
> To the last syllable of recorded time . . .
> Life's . . . a tale
> Told by an idiot, full of sound and fury,
> Signifying nothing.

Macbeth, though, has committed terrible acts. A life drained of meaning seems fitting.

In her searing account of life on Prozac, Elizabeth Wurtzel wrote, "I can't escape the icky feeling I get every time I'm sitting in a full car and everyone but the driver is on Prozac."[3] Since she wrote, the perception that depression is everywhere has only grown. Yet when English writer Robert Burton published his epic volume on melancholic sickness in 1621, he thought much the same, and so did many people in his time.[4] One sixteenth-century writer said that melancholics were too numerous to count. Another said few people did *not* have the malady.[5] The perception was not limited to England, but was widely held across Europe.[6]

Then as now, perception may not have matched reality. Renaissance obsession with melancholy was a cultural trend, apart from the real incidence of sickness, which we have no way of knowing. Some blamed the social upheavals of the Protestant Reformation, or a rise in witchcraft and demonic possession. Others worried about the loosening of morals.[7] (People always worry about the loosening of morals.) No one blamed the drug companies for disease mongering, because there were no drug companies yet.

Burton's *Anatomy of Melancholy* sought to explore all sides of the illness – causes, experience, and treatments. His framework was the humoral theory of the body which had dominated European medical thought since antiquity, and continued to well after Burton's time. Most European thought about melancholia, from the ancient Greeks into early modernity, was stamped by humoralism. Health was maintained by the balance of four bodily humors: blood, phlegm, yellow bile, and black bile.[8] The word "melancholy" comes from humoralism. The Greek *melankholia* means an excess of black bile. Medical writers differed on the reasons why some people had the excess. They also differed about what should be done. But the premise, that melancholia was caused by humoral imbalance, held for most. As one historian of humoralism says, "A human being who was not constituted of humours would have been unthinkable, just as someone who is not constituted of cells is inconceivable today."[9]

Humoral theory declined starting in the eighteenth century. More mechanistic conceptions of the body challenged it in the Renaissance, and the rise of the germ theory of disease in the nineteenth century dealt a decisive blow. Modern conceptions of the body, its nature, and what makes it sick are fundamentally different from the ones shared by Burton and his peers.

Melancholia and Depression

Melancholia was an illness marked by dejection, fear without cause, and sometimes a delusional break with reality. Was it what we now call depression?[10] The question itself is new, though, dating roughly to the coming of Prozac. Before the 1990s, almost every author on the subject, whether psychiatrist or historian, assumed that depression was a new name for melancholia.[11]

If melancholia and depression have no relationship, then depression is a new thing that emerged around the turn of the twentieth century, and this chapter has no business being in this book. Please keep reading. I hope to persuade you otherwise. But melancholia and depression cannot be identical, because neither has had a perfectly stable meaning. For all the fuzziness and flux of the modern depression diagnosis, melancholia may have had more.

Sometimes melancholia included delusional states, with a radical break from reality, not just a gloomy assessment of it. In modern psychiatry, delusions *can* be symptoms of some depressive disorders, such as psychotic depression.[12] Melancholia had many – very many – symptoms grouped in it. But fear and sorrow run through most descriptions.[13]

Melancholia was associated with men, modern depression with women (see figure 3).[14] Men may not have really suffered from melancholia more. We do not have anything close to reliable numbers for any century before the twentieth, but in rare instances where some figures for melancholia exist, they show about even division by sex.[15] Tallies of depression in recent decades show higher numbers of women, though the meaning of these numbers is disputed. The cultural image of the melancholic, though, was male, that of the depressed person female. The melancholic man was a heroic, romanticized figure, a figure of genius. The less exalted term "depression" came into favor just as women dominated in the cultural imagery of the ailment.[16]

We cannot say that melancholics "really" had depression. We can look, though, at family resemblances between the descriptions of the two. Some portrayals of melancholia contrast starkly with modern depression. Others look similar. Comparisons do not require the two to be identical. Some continuity between melancholia and depression may be found, even if they lack perfect overlap. Seeing that historical eras differ is a beginning of historical wisdom. It is not the only end.

We know the two terms are related historically, because doctors began to use "depression" on purpose to replace melancholia. Psychiatrist Adolf Meyer urged the change in 1904 because melancholia implied a known cause for a sickness with uncertain causes. His suggestion was gradually adopted by more people in the profession in the decades after. Also, the *debates* about melancholia, its cause, meaning, and cure, are similar to those about depression. Many of them relate to Western mind-body dualism – the idea that the mental is not physical, the mind is a separate thing from the body.[17] In this dualism, mind and body can interact with each other, though exactly how can get murky. Social and humanistic studies of the body, sickness, and healing have shown how this dualism is a cultural artifact, far from a human universal.[18] In any context, mental activity is embodied, and in my view the mind is better thought of as something the body does, rather than as something separate from the body.

Figure 3 *This image is usually considered the most iconic representation of melancholia. Note that the illness entity is gendered female, but that for most of Western history, the illness sufferer was gendered male*
Source: Albrecht Dürer, "Melancholia", 1514, via Wikimedia Commons

But the separation is deeply ingrained and shows itself in science, clinical settings, and popular imagination.

For most of European history, "melancholia" and "melancholy" were used interchangeably, to refer to an illness.[19] Depression came into use in the eighteenth century, but originally referred to a mood. Then, around the turn of the twentieth century, "melancholy" and "depression" began to trade places. Depression could still refer to mood, but often meant illness. Melancholy came more often to refer to mood. "Melancholia" was sometimes used by psychiatrists for a specific kind of depression – severe, often involving psychosis, and of apparent biological origin. In this chapter, I use melancholia to refer to the ailment, unless discussing a context where the term melancholy was used for it.[20]

A Substance Too Gross Even for Flies: Black Bile in Antiquity

If you have been alive any time starting in the 1980s, you have likely heard that depression is caused by a "chemical imbalance."[21] This phrase was not a nuanced rendering of what the science showed, but it was widespread in popular press and TV commercials for drugs. The substances have changed, but this was the idea behind the humoral theory of medicine. Sickness was caused by imbalance. In the case of melancholia, the imbalance was too much black bile, the humor associated with dryness and cold. Purging, in hope of expelling the excess substance, was a common treatment. Not all premodern observers of melancholy were humoralists, but it was the most influential paradigm for centuries, particularly from the time of Galen in the second century onwards.[22]

Each of the humors had a natural purpose in the body. Ill-health was caused when they were out of their correct proportion.[23] Each of the four humors corresponded to a temperament: yellow bile with the choleric, blood with the sanguine, phlegm with the phlegmatic, and black bile with the melancholic.[24] Each was also associated with one of the four seasons, one of the four elements, and one of the four stages of life. In each person, a humor could be dominant because of inborn constitution, or acquired because of habits and environment. The physician's job was to put the humors back in balance.

Galen devoted a whole book to proving the existence of black bile. He thought it came into the bowel and intestines through the liver.

Appearing in vomit and feces, causing anthrax and cancer, it was so vile that "No fly or other creature would wish to have a taste of it . . ."[25]

For much of antiquity, all of madness was divided into three parts.[26] "Phrenitis," a delirium with fever, was caused by inflammation of the brain. Mania was delirium without fever. Melancholia was the third. The term had the same ambiguity depression does now, referring both to a mood or temperament in the normal range of life, but also a sickness under certain conditions, such as when it was severe, or lacking apparent cause.[27]

In early Greek literature, melancholia was often an illness of anger. Later antiquity put more stress on dejection.[28] The Hippocratics developed the humoral approach about 400 BCE. Too much black bile caused several symptoms now associated with depression, such as low mood, low appetite, insomnia, and a feeling of being tired of living.[29] Anything that dried out or cooled the body could cause the imbalance. Maintaining balance was not easy. Aging would cool the body and lead to melancholia. The arrival of autumn, and eating certain foods, could do the same.[30] From the time of Hippocrates onwards, many writers on melancholia stressed the proportionality criterion – the emotions must seem unwarranted by the outer context.[31]

The *Problemata*, a work written by Aristotle or one of his students, described black bile as a mixture of hot and cold, the hot corresponding to a manic phase of the illness.[32] The symptoms listed in the *Problemata* were many, including despair, sluggishness, social withdrawal, mania, and suicidality, but also epilepsy, skin sores, varicose veins, inexplicable cheeriness, and overconfidence. The *Problemata*'s lasting influence was linking melancholia with genius. According to the *Problemata*, ALL great men were prone to the ailment.

The less-famous Rufus of Ephesus left a deep mark on ancient thought about melancholia. Through his influence on Galen, he was important for European thought as long as humoral theory had status.[33] Rufus also used melancholia to refer to a temperament, a mood, and an illness.[34] Some people were prone to it by innate nature.[35] Anything that cooled or dried the body contributed.[36] Heating of bile, though, could also lead to illness, because it would be followed by its blackening. The physical basis could explain the content of delusions. A person who imagined himself to be a ceramic urn was expressing bodily dryness.[37] Another "risk factor" for melancholia was important to later writers: too much study, too much time with books.[38] This belief echoed through the Renaissance.[39] Melancholia caused social withdrawal, or even hostility to company.[40] It caused physical sensations, such as a feeling of heaviness in the body.[41] Sleeplessness, decreased appetite, and memory disturbance were also symptoms. But two symptoms feature frequently in melancholia, despite other shifts in emphasis, and they are moods: dejection and fear.[42]

Since melancholia was both a sickness of the body and of the mind, ancient doctors had both physical and mental treatments.[43] Some ancient psychological treatments were what we call "cognitive," pointing out errors in thought, such as gently suggesting to the melancholic that the sorrow was without cause.[44] Others we would now call "behavioral" – Galen suggested exercise, and avoidance of dark wine and aged cheeses.[45] Physical treatments included herbal remedies and massage. Rufus recommended wine in moderation; it would warm the body and cook raw humors.[46] Sex was also good. Coitus was a remedy for several ancient writers; one said that it was "evacuative and calming."[47]

As is the case with depression now, those who stressed psychological causes favored treatments involving talk and behavior, and those who thought of melancholia more as a physical ailment favored physical treatments.[48] But discussion of the mental aspect did not stress introspection. A deep look into the afflicted person's psyche was not a feature of diagnosis or treatment.

Sickness and Sin: The "Most Oppressive of Demons" in the Middle Ages

Melancholia was a matter of the mind and body, but was it also a matter of morality? In the Christian Middle Ages, melancholic symptoms were called "acedia," and were associated with sloth. Sloth, of course, is a sin, and a deadly one. Melancholy also violated the Christian command to be cheerful,[49] though St. Paul thought some sadness was good if it led to penance.[50] The humoral and physical basis of the sickness was still assumed. Observers began to wonder more, though, about what blame the sick had for their suffering. That question has survived, often in subtle ways, into the modern era of depression.

Acedia was a temptation, according to a father of Egyptian monasticism named Evagrius Ponticus. Late in the third century of the common era, he settled in deserts southwest of Alexandria, and spent the next 17 years with hermit colonies.[51] Acedia, he said, was a demon, the most oppressive demon of all. It would attack a monk's soul between the fourth and eighth hours, and would make the sun "appear sluggish and immobile, as if the day had fifty hours."[52] The demon's force could be strong enough to drive him away from the monk's life. One influential monk, John Cassian, connected acedia especially to sloth.[53] Despondency was also a feature, though. Cassian described acedia as a "weariness or distress of the heart," and "akin to dejection."[54]

In the Middle Ages, lists of sins proliferated, and they included acedia. The sin was also considered an affliction. Confession was a form of healing, and penance a medicine for the soul.

The term melancholia did not disappear. The Jewish philosopher Maimonides wrote about melancholia, influenced by Rufus. He saw a link between melancholia and digestion, and thought the illness was related to dry stools.[55] He also noticed that melancholia could turn into mania.

St. Hildegard of Bingen, a visionary of the eleventh century, wrote a lot about medical matters, and provided a theory about how sin and the humors were related. The bile was changed by the sins in Eden, which turned it to darkness. The "black bile . . . first originated from Adam's semen through the breath of the serpent, since Adam heeded its counsel in taking food."[56] Black bile is in everyone, and a reason for humanity's sorrow and wickedness, our inability to find joy in this life, or even hope for the next one.[57]

As a humoralist, Hildegard did not think everyone had the same problem with this forlorn substance. Some were innately melancholy, men whose

> brains are fatty. Both the membranes encasing the brain and their blood vessels are turbid. The color of their faces is dark, even their eyes are firelike and viperlike. They have hard, strong blood vessels containing black, dense blood.[58]

Her descriptions of such men were filled with animal imagery: "With women they are without restraint like asses," their embrace of women is "hateful, and deadly, like that of ravaging wolves." Others shun the female sex "but in their hearts they are as violent as lions and they behave in the manner of bears." The melancholic were lustful and sex could relieve the malady.[59]

The reciprocal effects of mind and body, and the combining of supernatural and natural understanding, continued in the later Middle Ages. The Flemish painter Hugo van der Goes experienced madness featuring dejection and suicidality before entering a religious house near Brussels in 1477.[60] A colleague thought the madness may have been a natural result of eating foods that caused melancholia, and perhaps also what we would now call "stress." But he also thought that it may have been a divine punishment for his pride in his fame and achievement. These were not opposed, since "illness was . . . a two-way traffic between soul and body."[61]

In the later Middle Ages, commentators put growing emphasis on the body and declining stress on sin.[62] In language, melancholia began to displace acedia. Acedia was rarely mentioned during the Renaissance. Melancholia, however, became big.

An Epidemic of Early Modernity

"For if the heart is troubled and sad, physical weakness follows too . . . Diseases of the soul are real diseases."

-- Martin Luther[63]

The early modern period, between the Middle Ages and the modern industrial era, saw many social changes – the growth of mercantile capitalism, the renewed interest in writers of antiquity in the Renaissance, the Protestant Reformation, and a new willingness to question authoritative texts. The treatment of madness, though, did not change much between the Middle Ages and the early modern period.[64] Most early modern writers fused their spiritual or psychological explorations of melancholia with humoral assumptions about the workings of the human body.

By the end of the sixteenth century, melancholia was becoming a signature sickness of the time, prompting several learned books, the most famous by Burton.[65] In England, Elizabethan and early Stuart literature was filled with melancholy characters.[66]

Many writers on both melancholia and depression have been people with the illnesses. Marsilio Ficino, a Catholic priest of the fifteenth century who was an important figure in the Italian Renaissance, was an example. He thought melancholia was a condition of the soul, seated in the body, with astrological influences creating a temperament that life habits could ease or worsen.[67] Ficino was a humoralist, but his work shows that humoralism was a flexible set of ideas. Those (like him) born under Saturn, were born prone to melancholia. But scholars were especially prone. Saturn and Mercury were cold and dry, and pulled people toward scholarship. But coldness and dryness were also brought on by the scholar's lifestyle. Philosophers were at special risk.[68]

Food was a problem. Anyone frustrated by the long list of foods modern nutritional science tells us to avoid will also want to avoid Ficino's dietary advice for melancholics. Black bile, he said, was worsened by rich, dry, or hard foods that cooled the blood, as well as by too much food and wine. Melancholics should avoid salted food, bitter or stale food, burned food, roasted or fried food, rabbit, beef, old cheese, pickled fish, beans, lentils, cabbage, mustard, radishes, garlic, onions, leeks, blackberries, and carrots.[69] Fortunately, some foods could relieve melancholy, such as fruits and other sweets.[70]

Food and scholarship were not the only dangers. Ficino warned against anything else that cools or tires a person. But things that warmed were also a problem, because they could dry you out. He warned against dark emotions: anger, fear, misery, and sorrow. Also, literal darkness. And anything that dries the body, including lack of sleep, worry, purging, urinating, physical exertion, fasting, cold dry air, and frequent sex.[71] You may begin to wonder how anyone kept from becoming melancholic, but wait until we get to Burton.

Sixteenth-century German views of madness, including melancholia, can be seen through comparison of two famous figures, Martin Luther and Paracelsus.[72] Luther was fascinated with madness. He used charges of madness against theological opponents (who returned the favor) and had a lot to say about melancholia. Luther thought melancholia caused inattentiveness. This helped make sense of strange stories in the Hebrew bible. Lot absent-mindedly had sex with his own daughters. Isaac bestowed his birthright blessing on the smooth-skinned Jacob instead of the hairier Esau, while Jacob was wearing some lambskin in order to deceive their father. How could these things happen? For Luther, Isaac's poor eyesight did not explain enough. He thought both Lot and Isaac must have been melancholic.

For Luther, melancholia mingled the physical and the spiritual. He called it an "essentially physical disorder."[73] But physical problems could have spiritual causes, and their cures a spiritual basis. Luther did not think melancholia was entirely bad, though. He mistrusted the spiritually content. Inner conflict was a mark of mental vitality and wisdom. Low spirits showed that one knew the deeply wrong state of the world and humanity, and sadness showed conscience. Perhaps he felt consolation in this, as he often felt attacks of doubt and deep sorrow.

Paracelsus was a Renaissance physician and philosopher who was proud to have broken with Galenic humoralism.[74] In his early work, he emphasized reason and materialism, but he turned to a more Christian, biblical outlook later in life. He grouped madness into five principal kinds, including melancholia. Like the humoralists, he thought that melancholia came from both inborn temperament and life changes. His sensibility differed from Luther's, but they shared certain beliefs about melancholia. Both believed, for example, that it could be the result of demonic possession. They also shared an ambiguous view of the moral aspects. They thought sin was a disease, but they also thought that disease could be a punishment for sin. And they both thought that mind and body were meshed. Neither could be changed without changing the other.

Intending to comfort a friend, clergyman and physician Timothy Bright published a popular book about melancholy in 1586. Bright wanted to sever any connection between melancholy and sin. Melancholia had physical, psychological, or even Satanic sources, but was not the result of divine judgment.[75] He recommended good diet, exercise, grooming, rest, and sleep as antidotes.

Burton was motivated to write by his own melancholy, and found writing therapeutic.[76] *The Anatomy of Melancholy* was a popular book, going through six editions in Burton's lifetime.[77] *The Anatomy* was a bookish book. Burton read everything he could find on the subject. Symptoms of melancholy for Burton included anxiety, fearfulness, sadness, gloom, restlessness, dissatisfaction, emotional instability, suspicion, weeping, complaining, aggressive behavior, social withdrawal, lethargy, an inability to experience pleasure, insomnia, suicidal tendencies, delusions, and hallucinations.[78]

When looking at Burton's views of the causes of melancholy, his mimicry of earlier writers needs to be kept in mind. He lists a lot of causes, because he probably listed every one anyone had ever proposed. Modern medical students can get "Medical Students' Disease," where learning so much about sickness and its causes can lead to hypochondria. Many of Burton's readers may have had similar experiences, knowing how many things caused melancholy. I will name many of them, but not all. My book contract has a word limit.

Like Hildegard, Burton rooted human misery, including melancholy, in the sins of Eden and saw some melancholy as a part of being human that no one could avoid.[79] Causes also included God's intervention, or the supernatural acts of other beings, such as angels, saints, witches, and magicians.[80] But Burton was a humoralist, too. Lots of things caused the imbalance – the planets, the climate, other illnesses, too much study, social isolation, old age, and autumn, for example. Burton thought that men more often got melancholy, but that women would be more deeply affected – think of the contrast between Hamlet and Ophelia.[81]

Then, the foods. Burton had a long list of dangerous ones: beef, pork, goat, venison, hare, and polecat. Peacocks, pigeons, ducks, geese, swan, herons, cranes, "all those . . . fowls that come hither in winter out of Scandia, Muscovy, Greenland, Friesland, which half the year are covered all over with snow and frozen up . . ." Possibly all fish, but perhaps only some, such as eel, lamprey, crawfish, and any bred in muddy and standing waters. Milk, and all that comes from it – butter, cheese, curds. But not whey, or ass's milk, for some reason. One did not want to be cool, as a cucumber, which was disallowed along with gourds, melons, and "especially cabbage." Roots: onions, garlic, scallions, turnips, carrots, radishes, parsnips. Fruits: pears, apples, plums, cherries, strawberries. Beans and peas were a problem, because they bred thick, black blood. Spices caused heat in the head, pepper, ginger, cinnamon, cloves, and mace. Also honey and sugar. Though, perhaps not honey. Black wines, and strong thick drinks. Also cider, and hot, spiced, strong drinks. Beer was ok, but only if it was not too new or too stale, smelling of the cask, sharp, or sour.[82] One might be left asking what, exactly, was ok to eat. A few items, such as lettuce, were safe.[83] Diet was not made easier by Burton's further caution that eating too much, or too little, could also cause melancholy.[84]

With food, Burton was only getting started on causes. Bad air, cold air, thick air, foggy air, misty air, air from fens.[85] In an anticipation of our modern Seasonal Affective Disorder, too much darkness: cloudy days, night, underground vaults.[86] Exercise was good, but only if moderate.[87]

Burton said that the label of melancholic sickness should be restricted to cases where it seemed unwarranted by life circumstances.[88] Yet he was paradoxically mindful of life situations that could lead to the malady: Idleness and solitude. Insults and slanders. Loss of liberty, servitude, imprisonment. Poverty. Loss of friends. Bad marriage. Disgraces. Infirmities.[89] Burton asserted the proportionality criterion, but followed it without discipline.

Activities and lifestyle mattered. Life should not be too hedonistic or too ascetic. Extreme love of gaming and too much sensual pleasure were worrisome.[90] He followed Ficino in warning against too much study.[91] He knew from experience.

Remedies were plentiful too. They included prayer, changes in diet, changes in air, exercise, music, and cheerful company.[92] But Burton did not think melancholy could be cured. He thought it could be relieved, but relapses were likely. He urged melancholics to constant vigilance over their health.[93] He also believed, as so many modern therapists have said, that the patient must *want* to improve.[94]

For Burton, melancholy was definitely a physical condition. But it caused, and was caused by, emotions. The responsible emotions included sorrow, naturally, which cools the heart, inhibits sleep, and thickens the blood. Sorrow could make people "weary of their lives, cry out, howl and roar for the very anguish of their souls."[95] But other emotions, too: shame, anger, worry, covetousness, pride, and self-love.[96] Burton explained that

> as the body works upon the mind by his bad humours, troubling the spirits, sending gross fumes into the brain . . . disturbing the soul . . . with fear, sorrow, etc. . . . so on the other side, the mind . . . works on the body, producing . . . melancholy, despair, cruel diseases, and sometimes death itself.[97]

The Anatomy of Melancholy was the fullest flowering of the humoral view of melancholy. Soon after, humoralism slowly lost ground. William Harvey's discovery of the circulation of the blood (seven years after the first edition of *The Anatomy*), and growing conceptions of the universe and the body as governed by mathematical and mechanical laws undercut much of humoral theory.[98] For mental illness, the brain attracted growing focus.[99]

New medical models yielded big gains for human health – most dramatically, from the second half of the nineteenth century, the success of germ theory in accounting for, preventing, and treating infectious disease. Many hoped for similar success in mental illness, but the path to such success may be different.

Trading Places: From Melancholia to Depression in Modernity

The slow transition from melancholia to depression started in the eighteenth century. The famous British writer Samuel Johnson, one of the afflicted, used both terms in the eighteenth century, referring to his "vile melancholy."[100] By the nineteenth century, "depression" referred to a general decline in functioning. By the middle of that century, "mental depression" was used for mental illness. The modifier "mental" gradually fell away.

As humoral theories of melancholia declined, the symptom profile changed little: dejection and fear without cause, and no accompanying fever.[101] An important nineteenth-century British textbook named melancholia as one of the major forms of mental illness, and listed disinterest, listlessness, idleness, social isolation, suicidal inclinations, fearfulness, gloominess, tearfulness, sleeplessness, disturbed dreams, disordered "uterine function" in women, and lack of interest in sex for men as the symptoms.[102] When you look at this list, it is hard *not* to see similarity with modern depression.

The French physician Philippe Pinel saw melancholics as quiet, suspicious, and loving solitude.[103] The proportionality criterion held.[104] Pinel's student, Jean-Étienne Esquirol, stressed that the fear lacked apparent cause, but also that patients had insight – they knew that their fears might not be well-grounded.[105]

Some grew uneasy with the term melancholia before Adolf Meyer.

Esquirol objected to the term for two reasons. The first was its ety-
mology; Esquirol was a posthumoralist. The other was that the term
melancholia was also used loosely to refer to melancholy mood, and
thus lacked precision – though the same would later be said of the term
depression.

George Beard did not think neurasthenia was a new term for melancholia, but a new ailment, caused by modernity. As we saw, neurasthenia
often included typical symptoms of depression.[106] Many clinicians saw
the overlap at the time.[107] Freud, before he founded psychoanalysis,
considered neurasthenia to be a type of depression. Already alert to the
role of sex, he thought that lowered sexual energy caused by too much
masturbation caused neurasthenia.[108]

The influential German Emil Kraepelin, working in the late nineteenth and early twentieth century, provided the foundations of modern
psychiatric diagnosis. For all the changes since Kraepelin, much of
current diagnosis is based on his distinction between manic-depressive
disorder (now known as bipolar disorder) and dementia praecox (now
known as schizophrenia). Kraepelin described symptoms and course
of illnesses in detail, without speculation about the causes. He used
manic-depression as an encompassing category for mental illness
involving problems of mood.[109] He also coined the term "involutional
depression," referring to depressions that came later in life, often with
paranoid features.[110] He separated anxiety states from depression, as
well.[111] Whether this was a gain for diagnosis is questionable, given how
often anxious and depressive moods occur together.

After about two centuries of decline in humoral theory came the
address by Kraepelin's younger contemporary Meyer in 1904. Meyer
thought both "melancholia" and "depression" were large categories,
and suggested speaking of "depressions," instead of depression. He
preferred the term depression to melancholia, because he thought that
depression was more "unassuming."[112] Like Esquirol, he thought that
the term melancholia carried too much cultural baggage.

The term "melancholia" did not die out right away in clinical
description. It was used interchangeably with depression well into
the middle of the twentieth century, though depression gradually
became more common. Some psychiatrists drew on the older term's
associations with delusions, and used melancholia, or sometimes "mel-

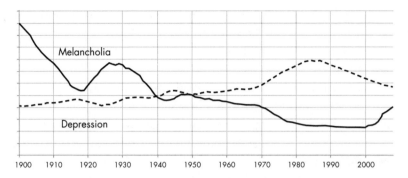

Figure 4 *This Ngram shows the change of frequency in the use of the terms
"melancholia" and "depression"*
Source: Google Ngrams

ancholic depression," to refer specifically to psychotic depression.[113]
By the 1950s, melancholy and depression had largely switched places.
Melancholy had been a clinical syndrome and depression a mood.
Depression became a word for a clinical syndrome, and melancholy
became a word for a mood. An Ngram showing the change of frequency in the use of the terms "melancholia" and "depression" is
presented in figure 4.

The diagnostic shuffle – ditching or re-defining old labels, garnering
support for newly-coined terms – used to be a process that took decades
or even centuries. Now it seems to happen every few years.

Does Stealing Office Supplies Make You an Evil Person?
A Note on Guilt

Taking some office supplies home from work without permission
is naughty. Few would say it makes a person evil. If that person is
depressed, though, they may be hard to convince.

This example comes from a sketch of clinical depression in a psychiatry book for lay people. A secretary had an injury that made it hard
to do her job well. Soon, she had weight loss, insomnia, loss of interest
in the activities she used to like, anxiety and restlessness, and a sense of
worthlessness.

One symptom puzzled her husband: guilt. She used to take home
office supplies for her personal use, and felt deep remorse. Her husband

figured her boss wouldn't think it was a big deal, and he was right –
when she confessed, the boss said he knew employees sometimes took
supplies home, and he didn't care. Even after this, she obsessed over
her great sin.[114]

While the husband may have found this puzzling, people familiar
with depression would not. Relentless self-accusation, out of scale to
what others think is fitting, is a common symptom of depression. Was
it for melancholia? Is it a symptom of depression in all contexts where
depression is found?

We saw that some think depression is a modern and Western malady,
while others think it is more universal. A similar question arises with
this symptom – is it a part of Western modernity?[115] By Freud's early
twentieth-century writing on melancholia, guilt was a defining feature.
As with the presence of depression, though, the presence of guilt as a
symptom may depend on how you look for it, and what you call it when
you see the signs.

If guilt in depressive illness is particular to Western modernity, why?
One culprit could be a "guilt culture," a culture where people's moral
orientation is guided by internal sanctions more than by fears about
public reputation.[116] Some have proposed that a "guilt culture" arose in
modern Western society in the early modern period.[117] With a broader
culture filled with guilty thought to begin with, it might be pronounced
in mental illness. Anyone suffering from depressive illness might
amplify the guilt, and engage in severe self-accusation over something
as small as lifting some office supplies.

Guilty feeling in melancholics may not really be so modern, though.
In the Middle Ages, penance was considered one possible remedy for
acedia.[118] Hildegard associated guilt and melancholia.[119] Hugo van der
Goes' dejection and suicidality were accompanied by the conviction
that he was eternally damned.[120] If this is not guilty thinking, what
is? Somewhat later, but still fairly early, Timothy Bright's purpose
in writing about melancholia was to distinguish the guilty conscience
of a melancholic from that of a well person, and the Dutch physician Johannes Weyer wrote in 1598 of melancholics tormented by
conscience.[121]

What about guilt as a symptom peculiar to Western depression?
This is a fraught question, the same way the question of depression as

Western illness is. Just as some colonial psychiatrists in Africa thought that depression was rare on the continent, some thought that guilt was rare as a symptom. Here again, the claim was folded into racist images of the untroubled native mind. Other observers – the same who found more prevalence of depression in Africa – did find guilty thoughts as symptom.[122] Margaret Field, an anthropologist and psychiatrist who did fieldwork in a healing shrine in Ghana, found depression common, with guilty obsessions in most of the cases. These thoughts appeared with other depressive symptoms: frequent weeping, insomnia, lethargy.[123] The patients were self-accused witches. They were at fault, they said, for the death of all their deceased kin, blight on crops, and traffic accidents, for example. Field thought this was similar to patients she had seen in London hospitals, who were also convinced, without good reason, that they were guilty of terrible crimes. Field's idea was not new. In early modern England, some people thought that self-accused witches were really melancholics.[124]

Researchers in India in the 1970s expressed surprise at the low level of guilt as a symptom, because Indian cultures had many cultural inclinations to guilt.[125] But guilty thoughts might not emerge in an impersonal medical interview, and only come out in a deeper therapy.[126] Other scholars did find guilty obsessions in Indian depressives, often attributed to bad acts in past lives.[127] Guilty feelings in depression seem not so rare outside the West, but the content of the guilt varies culturally.[128] Perhaps we should speak of "idioms of guilt" as we do of "idioms of distress."

The "guilt culture" concept is Western self-congratulation. Like depression itself, excessive guilt was oddly touted in colonial thought – seen as a crippling symptom of sickness, but also a sign of cultural accomplishment. Anticolonial theorist and psychiatrist Frantz Fanon observed that his French colleagues thought that Algerians were not capable of true melancholia, but only a "pseudo-melancholia."[129] The psychiatrists thought that Algerians did not feel guilt as a symptom, because they turned all their aggression outward. Saying that Algerians were capable of only a "pseudo-melancholia" was an indirect way of saying: these are not civilized people.

False Choices and Their History

Doctors, therapists, patient advocates, and others continue to argue over physical versus mental, genes versus trauma, drugs versus therapy. These debates often pose false choices. Both psychological and physical treatments can be helpful. Genetic inheritance and events in life can both play a role in causation. Dogmatic claims on either side of these three debates keep appearing. We should not allow them.

Treating depression as a physical state might seem now – at least to its ardent advocates – as an enlightened departure from moralistic or psychological views of earlier eras. But discussions of melancholia usually assumed both physical and mental aspects. An arch moralist like Luther saw the physicality of madness. Earlier eras had a wisdom we now fight to keep in view – that physical does not have to mean *just* physical any more than mental has to mean *only* mental.

The humoralists can seem quaint and unscientific. Their insight and observation can be underestimated. One powerful tool of science is *reductionism*, as in the search for a single cause for diseases. This tool yielded much progress in the case of infectious disease once germ theory was verified. But this doctrine of single cause was a sharp tool that cut too neatly. It never accounted for the social sources of sicknesses – and they all do have social sources – including infectious diseases. The doctrine of single cause never captured the complex interplay of the physical and the psychological, an interplay with a role in all sickness, including those illnesses we call "mental."[130]

The humoralists did not know all we know now. They did not know of neurotransmitters. They did not know of double helixes and genomes. They had not imagined the rigor of randomized trials. Despite these handicaps, they observed that some people seemed to have an inborn tendency to melancholy, but also that life and lifestyle mattered. They saw that lifestyle changes, such as increased physical activity, could help. Some saw the role of social factors. Without sophisticated social analysis of class, Burton could see that poverty was a factor in depression.

Psychoanalysts and other explorers of the unconscious mind have had an ambiguous role in the struggle over the primacy of mind or body. A few have taken a rigidly psychological approach. More, though, believed that psychology and physiology interacted.

When Freud and his followers turned their attention to depressive illness, they paid close attention to guilt as a symptom. For Freud, guilt was not just any symptom, but the core symptom. His starting point was the distinction between melancholia (an illness) and grief (a normal response to events). He asked if we could use grief to understand melancholia. Perhaps the outward similarities might be a clue to deeper ones. Those deeper ones would only be found by probing the unconscious mind.

3

Turned Inward

How many psychiatrists does it take to change a lightbulb?
Only one, but the lightbulb must want to change.

Yes, it is an old one, but why is it funny? It spoofs a cliché about therapy, but it also speaks to something counter-intuitive about therapy: why wouldn't people want to change? People go to psychotherapy voluntarily, in order to change. Depressed people are in a lot of pain. Surely, they want it gone? Surely, they want to change – or at least they think they do.

The nub here is that they "think they do." Yes, someone who seeks a therapist consciously wants to change. But not everything is conscious. Every therapist has known patients who say they want to change but seem devoted to staying the same. The unconscious mind explains this. The tradition of dynamic or depth psychology provides a way of probing it.

For Freud, the unconscious solved the puzzle of guilty feelings – why *do* depressed people consider themselves evil for taking home office supplies? Freud had a startling take on guilt in depressive illness. He believed the self-accusations were, in a way, true – though perhaps not in the way the depressive person thought. He and other psychoanalysts thought that the self-accusations came from angry or accusing feelings felt toward other people, which became directed at the self. Depression, then, reflected "anger turned inward." This became a catchphrase of depression in the first half of the twentieth century, just as "chemical imbalance" was in the second. Guilt is then not one symptom among many, but the key that unlocks depression's enigmas.

Psychoanalysis was not alone in underscoring guilt in depressive illness. Guilt is central to descriptions in the work of the pioneering French psychologist Pierre Janet.[1] Kraepelin thought guilt mattered for outcome – depressive illness would be more chronic in patients who had guilt as a symptom. Guilt figured in psychoanalytic thought in particular, though, as a clue to the cause of the illness.

Psychoanalysis began in the late nineteenth century, originally a fringe movement advanced by Freud and a circle of followers. The movement revolutionized how people think about the mind on a global scale, but it came from a small group, meeting weekly in Freud's house in Vienna. Many psychiatrists of the time were skeptical, though many were also curious about the unconscious and the potentials of talk therapy. By the middle of the century, psychoanalysis had vast influence over not only psychiatry and mental health work, but also other medical specialties, such as pediatrics. It also changed popular thinking about the mind, in lasting ways. Every time we say someone is "projecting," or "in denial," for example, we are using psychoanalytic ideas of the unconscious mind.

In some ways, psychoanalysis became too successful for its own good. While many psychoanalysts were open-minded about other approaches to illness, and to challenges to Freud, others believed that psychoanalysis as Freud conceived it was the only path to mental health. This rigidity cost the movement when serious challenges – medical, scientific, and political – gathered force in the second half of the twentieth century. By the 1970s, the influence of psychoanalysis was waning. Some questioned its claim to be scientific. Some second-wave feminists called psychoanalysis a bulwark of patriarchy, and though psychoanalysis also had feminist currents, charges of sexism were fair. Changing structures in medical insurance made psychoanalysis, which was already expensive, even more inaccessible. Statistical measures, drawn from randomized trials, became the standard of proof for medical treatments, and they were hard to apply to psychoanalysis.

Drug treatments had flaws of their own, but they were cheaper and easier to use than psychoanalysis.[2] Drugs, as well as some new forms of talk therapy, were also easier to study in trials. When some of the more extravagant claims of psychoanalysis fell short, disillusionment set in, especially with more alternatives available. The disillusionment led some to the extreme conclusion that psychoanalysis was worthless. A similar dynamic is happening now with antidepressants. Excessive hope was placed on them, and some now say they are worthless. Neither psychoanalysis nor antidepressants are worthless. Being on the defensive has had some healthy effects for psychoanalysis, though. The field has grown more open to other approaches, and less dogmatic.

The death of psychoanalysis has been announced numerous times, but it never really happened. Freudian approaches lost status in the psychiatric profession, and in academic psychology. "Full-blown" psychoanalysis – multiple sessions per week, on the couch – is not so common now. It is costly and time-consuming, though its unavailability is a loss for people with deeply-lodged psychological problems, that take intensive work to "rewire." But psychodynamic therapy – less intensive work, based on the same ideas as psychoanalysis – continues, and those ideas remain influential wherever talk therapy is used. They still inform much of clinical social work, for example.

The thinkers I look at in this chapter are diverse, and not all were loyal to Freud's ideas. All practiced *depth psychology*, which is defined by inquiry into the unconscious. Depth psychologists believe that the unconscious deeply influences us, and its ways can be mysterious; it can become known to us partially and indirectly – through dreams, or slips of the tongue for example. Depth psychology stresses inner conflict as a source of psychological problems. It also works with *transference*, the tendency to relate to other people according to unconscious wishes or fears of what they might be, and less by the reality of who those people are. In therapy, this usually means relating to the analyst in patterns set by the patients' orientation to their parents. Interpreting and working through transference can be a crucial path to the unconscious. Learning about the unconscious allows some control over it, reducing unnecessary suffering. Carl Jung, a follower of Freud who broke from the psychoanalytic movement but remained a depth psychologist, put it this way: "Until you make the unconscious conscious, it will direct your life and you will call it fate."

Most people do recognize an unconscious mind, at least in small things like waking up in the morning suddenly knowing the solution to a problem from the day before. Psychoanalyst Julia Segal gives another example: when we read Jane Austen's novel *Pride and Prejudice*, we realize Elizabeth Bennet is in love with Mr. Darcy before she herself does.[3] We see that people can fail to be conscious of their own minds, in ways evident to outsiders.

"Freud is dead" headlines have run in popular media many times since his literal obituaries appeared in 1939.[4] Many people think that all of Freud's ideas have been disproven and his psychology is obsolete. Freud did get many things wrong. So did Isaac Newton and many other pivotal scientists. Freud's takes on female psychology are famously, and often painfully, bad, for example. The movement might have avoided justified criticism from feminists if it had been more open to the revisions concerning gender roles that psychoanalyst Karen Horney advocated for, starting in the 1920s.[5] But this relates to another problem: Freud often led the movement in a cult-like fashion. Big departures were treated as heresy and their advocates driven out of the movement.[6] Psychoanalysis is a vast field, however, with many insights into personal psychology.

People can be weird about Freud and psychoanalysis. Once I was talking about psychoanalysis with an academic psychologist. She said she used psychoanalytic ideas in her work, but did not use their psychoanalytic names, because she would not be able to publish her work in psychology journals if she did. Think about what this says about academic psychology: the ideas in the work can pass peer review, but only if they are disguised to hide the use of an unfashionable theory – which comes from the most famous explorer of psychology in history.[7] Another time I assigned to a class Freud's "Mourning and Melancholia," his main work on depression, and my class found the ideas strange. Some began to ask why Freud was so "obsessed with mothers." I asked if it was unreasonable to think that people's mental lives were deeply shaped by their relationship with the person who most met their needs in the first years of life, who is most frequently the mother. Then the reading began to make sense to them.

One important question about Freud's legacy is the simple one of whether insight into the unconscious can promote mental health and even treat illnesses. Evidence shows that psychotherapy works, but not all of the many forms of it seek insight into the unconscious. Isolating what is most helpful in the various psychotherapies has proven challenging. Dynamic therapy in the Freudian tradition is at least as effective as other talk therapies, though, and some research has shown longer-lasting benefits.[8] People who say dynamic therapy has been proven ineffective are misinformed.

Psychoanalytic thinking on depression did not really begin with Freud, though. It began with his colleague, Karl Abraham.

The "Abrahamic Tradition" in Depression Studies

"I have often heard it said that depression is anger turned inward. I don't know how true this is, but there is no denying that the events of my childhood played a major role in fostering my vulnerability to depression."
                                                    – Meri Nana-Ama Danquah[9]

The key idea in most psychoanalytic thought about depression has been anger toward others, redirected against the self. Freud created many aspects of psychoanalytic thought – the basics of the theory of dreams, the famous developmental theories involving oral, anal, and phallic stages and the Oedipus conflict, the three-part model of a mind divided into id, ego, and super ego – all of these first came from Freud. Many of them grew out of his work with "hysteria" patients, a term used commonly in Freud's day, as depression is now. The idea of anger turned inward was given its first broad elaboration by Freud's colleague, Karl Abraham, a Berlin-based psychiatrist.[10] Abraham's ideas about depression were based on more clinical experience than Freud's.[11] They may also have more empirical support now.[12]

At first, Freud thought depression was physical in origin.[13] His colleague Wilhelm Stekel did early work about depression, moving the inquiry in a more psychological direction. Stekel thought that guilt in depression came from death wishes toward others. They were turned inward because conscience forbade directing them to the original target.[14] Abraham built on this foundation.

Abraham was the leading figure in psychoanalysis in Berlin, which surpassed Freud's Vienna as the center of psychoanalysis by the 1920s. He analyzed many influential analysts, including Karen Horney and Melanie Klein, two pioneers who were among the earliest analysts to make big breaks with Freud.[15] Horney was among the first to see that Freud's ideas about gender would not do, and is widely credited with founding a feminist tradition in psychoanalysis. Klein was a founder of child analysis and a major and influential innovator in theory and clinical technique. Abraham himself showed some independence of mind from Freud.

Abraham was trained in psychiatry, unlike Freud, who trained as a neurologist. When Abraham was a small boy, his mother suffered some hard blows. Her sister Rosa died in her twenties when Abraham was one year old, and Rosa's husband died the following year. Around the same time, Abraham's mother fell down some stairs and had a miscarriage, a loss she mourned deeply and often for the rest of her life. Abraham's childhood was marked by his mother's grief. His work on depression was haunted by the problems children face when their mothers are unable to focus on them. He may have suffered from depression himself. When he sent Freud his first writing on the subject – a psychoanalytic study of nineteenth-century artist Giovanni Segantini – he warned Freud that the work had "some personal complexes behind it."[16]

Abraham looked at Segantini's paintings, and related them to the painter's life.[17] When Segantini was six months old, his brother died, and his mother became bed-ridden. By the time Segantini was five, both of his parents were dead, and he went to live with a stepsister who treated him badly. He ended up in a reformatory. Abraham said that Segantini suffered lifelong depression.[18] This may not be surprising given Segantini's hard beginning. But Abraham thought more than loss and grief were at work. Abraham thought Segantini was also angry at his abandonment. The anger was turned inward on the self, resulting in the depression. But why?

Many of Segantini's paintings were of mothers and children, but they came in two types. Some of the paintings showed loving, nurturing mothers. Others showed eerie and detached women. One painting in particular, "The Bad Mothers," struck Abraham (see figure 5). A woman is floating by a tree in a desolate and wintry landscape. An infant

Figure 5   *Karl Abraham contrasted this painting with others that showed nurturing mothers. The contrast defended against the pain of aggression toward the artist's mother which, if turned toward the self, could cause depression*
Source: Giovanni Segantini, "The Bad Mothers", 1894, via Wikimedia Commons

is trying to suck at her breast, but her attention is diverted, her head facing away, her eyes closed. She could be dreaming, sleeping, or even dead. She is not holding the child – one arm seems to be reaching to the tree, the other she holds at her waist. Despite the winter setting, she is wearing little, just willowy shreds in the shape of a dress, with nothing covering her arms or breasts. The child seems to be straining to get the mother's milk – certainly not getting maternal warmth.

Why, Abraham wondered, did Segantini paint such different images of mothers, dividing them rigidly into two types? Abraham thought they were two attitudes toward Segantini's own mother, attitudes that needed to be kept separate. The stark difference between the visual images he painted made that separation. Psychoanalysts call psychic division of the mother figure (and anything else) into good and bad *splitting*. Strong ambivalence causes anxiety. Feelings of rage toward someone you also deeply love are hard to tolerate. Splitting manages the anxiety by dividing things into the all-good and the all-bad. You might make a new friend who thinks you are the best person ever, who later gets disappointed, turns on you, and sees you as the worst. This is splitting in everyday life. Another example is people who thought psychoanalysis itself was the best way of understanding the mind, who later saw it as having no merit at all. In reality, most things and people – parents, children, co-workers, political leaders, political parties, religions, intellectual movements – are not all good or all bad, but complex mixtures. Splitting prevents us from seeing the complexity of the whole.

Segantini's paintings reminded Abraham of something he often saw in his depressed patients. Their childhoods were marked by mothers whose attention was compromised by grief or illness. (In seventeenth-century England, Robert Burton also thought that a childhood with too little affection could lead to depression. But then, Burton thought a lot of things could lead to depression.) For Abraham, a mother's inattention placed the children in a tough spot. They love and need the mother, but the mother is also the main person who can withhold needed things. When those things are withheld, a desire for revenge emerges, but such feelings toward such a loved and needed person are hard to bear, and lead to remorse. Abraham thought that all children are born with aggressive tendencies that could be intensified by vengeful feelings caused by neglect. The vengeful feelings are turned inward, causing depressed affect.

This did not, by itself, lead to clinical illness, in Abraham's view. If people later suffer similar letdowns, such as lost loves, they may react in the same way, by turning their rage against themselves. This is why depressed people feel not only unhappy, but unworthy of happiness. They feel guilt out of balance with any real crimes. In the lightbulb joke, patients do not want to change. Abraham's theory explains why. If patients' suffering is caused by unconscious remorse, they may consciously want to end their misery, but unconsciously they think it is what they deserve.

Abraham also believed in an inborn factor to depression, what we now call a "genetic predisposition."[19] Some have accused psychoanalysts of ignoring the physical, but many of them have seen complex interactions between mind and body – often more so than some biological psychiatrists who try to banish psychology from consideration.

The aggression of the child, Abraham thought, was shown in biting at the mother's breast, an impulse he called "cannibalistic."[20] In adult depression, Abraham thought, remorse over this impulse explained the reduced appetite of people with depression. This is one of those psychoanalytic interpretations that may strike skeptics as far-fetched. Darian Leader notes that the apparent weirdness of speaking about cannibalistic drives toward people we love seems less bizarre when we consider how often people who love someone say they could "just eat you up".[21]

Abraham observed patterns in his depressed patients and built them into a general theory of depression. He did not consider multiple paths to depressed states. Abraham also used a small sample to claim that psychoanalytic treatment had high efficacy, at a time when few effective treatments were available.[22] Abraham was a trained psychiatrist, who had observed depression and its treatment outside of his private practice too, so his claim may not have been baseless. Using small numbers of patients to make large claims was common in medicine in the early twentieth century. The people who developed early somatic psychiatric treatments, including ECT, also based their claims of success on small numbers of patients.

Freud used the old word, melancholia, unlike Abraham, who used depression – though the clinical pictures they described were similar. Freud also frequently took subjects first explored by his followers or dissenters, and then wrote his own account, stamped with the authority he had as founder and leader of the movement. If he intended "Mourning and Melancholia" to replace Abraham's work as definitive, he had some success. Many psychoanalysts consider "Mourning and Melancholia" a masterpiece, and it became a touchstone for later exploration of depression.[23]

Freud's melancholia looked much like what we now call depression.[24] Melancholics, he said, suffered sadness beyond what we expect in the normal course of life, and a withdrawal of interest from life and the world. Sources of pleasure and satisfaction seemed empty or futile – "weary, stale, flat and unprofitable," in Hamlet's words. Appetite and sleep were disturbed.[25] Freud started by observing the similarity to mourning. Freud was not the first to notice these similarities. Nor was he the first to note an obvious difference: we consider the sadness of grief normal. It is hard to go through, but it is not sickness, and may be healthy. Freud used the proportionality criterion. The symptoms showed sickness when they did not match external reality. He also observed that the low self-esteem common in melancholia is usually absent in mourning.

Freud wondered if the sadness we consider normal, mourning, could provide insights into the one we consider sickness, melancholia. Might the difference between mourning and melancholia conceal a similarity in their origin? If so, the cause of melancholia might not be truly absent, but hidden. Many of Freud's ideas came from his work with patients and developed from there to his famous theories about dreams, slips of the tongue, and other aspects of general psychology. He often sought insight into healthy minds from mental illness. In "Mourning and Melancholia," however, he sought the reverse. He looked at a normal state, grieving, to understand an illness.

Mourning, Freud said, is an adjustment to the reality of loss. Memories of the lost person are held in the mind, often painfully, but gradually lose some emotional force. Interest in the world is withdrawn. Perhaps melancholia was also caused by loss, but unconscious loss. But of what? Freud wondered if guilt provided the answer.

Freud said it was pointless to refute the guilty thoughts. He thought the self-accusations were valid, though not in the way the person consciously thought. If we listen with care, he said, we will often find that the accusations apply to someone the person loves or loved, but has lost. The loss did not have to be an actual death or departure of the person, but could be a disappointment in the relationship. Freud then took a step Abraham had not. He thought one reaction towards the loss could be to absorb the lost person into the self. This is *introjection*, unconsciously taking an object, such as a loved one, into oneself.[26] Introjection is the opposite of the more familiar term projection. Projection is an unconscious process of denying an unwanted part of our self, by seeing it in others. We might feel badly about our greed, aggression, or other unsavory traits. In order to banish the guilt, we imagine it is others who are greedy or aggressive. In introjection, we are taking on other people and making them a part of ourselves. Introjection is another idea in psychoanalysis that can seem strange, but it resembles what we mean when we say of a departed person, "a part of her will always live inside me."

Freud shared Abraham's view that loved objects were also targets of aggression: the people we feel the strongest emotions toward create ambivalence. After all, the people we love most have the most power to disappoint us. If we think a loved one has taken from us, in introjection we might see ourselves as thieves. This is why stealing office supplies could become a source of deep remorse. The act might seem trivial to others, but the depressed person's feelings come from feeling that something they needed badly was taken from them. Taking office supplies is only a symbolic marker for the truly valuable thing felt as stolen. The original target for punitive feelings, the real thief as it were, has been introjected, a part of the self now. As long as this remains unconscious, it is not a matter for rational debate, which is why Freud thought it was pointless to refute it.

The extent of alleged anti-biological dogma in psychoanalysis has been exaggerated, sometimes wildly.[27] Freud said on the first page of "Mourning and Melancholia" that many cases of depressive illness likely had biological origins.[28] He was trying to explain the psychological origin of those that did not. Though some psychoanalysts wished to ignore biology, the majority did not. Freud, and most of his followers, thought mind and body had complex interactions, but they often focused on the psychological because of the limits of biological knowledge when they were working.

The strongest departure Freud made from Abraham's views was the stress on introjection. Freud told Abraham that eventually he would come to share the views of the master.[29] This prediction came true. A few years after "Mourning and Melancholia," Abraham returned to the subject, adopting the concept of introjection. Abraham's new work was dripping with deference to Freud, despite a dig at his mentor for having grasped melancholia intuitively, not through deep clinical work.[30] Abraham now credited Freud with seeing that depression was not just anger turned inward, but turned inward at the introjected object.

Melanie Klein, who was analyzed by Abraham, was the most important psychoanalytic innovator on depressive illness to follow. Klein pushed Freud's ideas in directions so new that some questioned whether they could be called Freudian. Klein insisted that they were, and managed – unlike some other radical innovators – to preserve her place within the psychoanalytic fold.

Klein was born in 1882 in Vienna, and suffered a lot of personal griefs. She had a brother and a sister die during her childhood, and she married a man who had affairs soon after the wedding. She spent much of her twenties in a depression of her own. Interested in medicine and the intellectual life from an early age, she was first analyzed by Freud's close associate Sandor Ferenczi in Budapest. She moved to Berlin and worked with Abraham, before leaving because of the growing anti-Semitism in Germany. She then moved to Britain, where she became perhaps the most important figure in the history of British psychoanalysis, and founder of the school of psychoanalysis called object relations. She was a pioneer in the analysis of children, and famed for the development of the play technique, where children play in the presence of the analyst, as an alternative to free association on the couch, which is hard for children. Abraham had put more emphasis than many other analysts on the role of the mother in development, as opposed to that of the father. Klein, who was one of the first psychoanalysts who was a mother, took this further.

Klein shared Abraham's interest in the infant's aggressiveness. She thought ambivalence toward the mother was the model for other splitting the person might engage in later in life. Ambivalence toward the mother was both inevitable and intense, because the mother was at once the main provider and depriver of the most needed things, both physical and emotional. This, she thought, was a problem for all of us, but when not resolved successfully, could result in mental illnesses.

Klein developed a theory of psychological positions, called the paranoid-schizoid position and the depressive position. The positions are originally phases in infant development, but unlike the stages in many psychological theories, Klein thought that people do not pass through them in a linear way, but cycle through them continually over the course of life. The paranoid-schizoid position is dominant in the first months of life. It is "paranoid" because infants project their destructive impulses onto the mother and other figures, and thus imagine persecution. Projection of aggression onto the outside world explains things like childhood night fears, such as monsters under the bed.[31] The "schizoid" part is the splitting. The need to manage ambivalence toward caregivers leads, in fantasy, to the splitting of them into all good and all bad versions, an inability to see them as whole and complex people. In the depressive position, children achieve the ability to see the mother as whole. This causes remorse over the destructive fantasies, because of the awareness that they were directed at a loved object. With remorse comes the wish to provide reparation. The paranoid-schizoid and depressive positions have different main anxieties. In the paranoid-schizoid position, anxiety is persecutory, fear of annihilation. In the depressive position, anxiety becomes concern for preservation of the loved object.[32]

The depressive position is depressive in affect, but *the depressive position is not clinical depression*. The depressive position is a normal and healthy part of growth. The aggressiveness, and the remorse that follows, are universal. Depressive affect surrounds weaning especially, experienced as a loss.[33] The mother's breast symbolizes love and security, everything good. If the aggressive impulses are excessive, though, depressive illness can result, if the conflicts are not resolved adequately. Working through the depressive position means tolerating fear and guilt. A mother who can bear the child's occasional hostility and sadness can help with this.[34] She serves as proof to the baby that fantasies of destruction do not cause actual injury.[35] The growth of skills, the flourishing of creative abilities, and an ability to control hostile impulses, all increase children's sense of their constructive capacities, countering the depressive feelings.[36]

Not only is the depressive position not a mental illness, it is a potential path to mental health. It can lead the person to see whole objects (avoid splitting) and engage in creative work. If this development fails, though, clinical illness may result, showing itself in desperate submission to remorse, or frantic efforts to deny guilt. A wish to triumph over the parents can reactivate the guilt from the early aggression.[37] This is why depression can set in at unexpected times, when the person is experiencing success, not setbacks.

Stekel, Abraham, Freud, and Klein each had their own ideas and emphases. Taken together, they form the basis of the theory that depression is anger turned inward. Several later analysts elaborated. One was Otto Fenichel, a follower of Freud's in Vienna who emigrated to the United States. Fenichel accepted the role of aggression turned inward.[38] He thought three other things contributed to depression: (1) childhood loss, (2) a loss in later life, which sparks the depression by its repetition of the early one, and (3) a constitutional factor – that is, some inborn tendency.[39] Psychoanalysts at this time were working in an era when little was known about genetics, but like the humoralists, they observed that illnesses ran in families.

Fenichel lacked Abraham's optimism about psychoanalytic treatment for depression. Writing in the 1940s, a decade before the first drugs called antidepressants came, he defended psychoanalytic treatment only by saying little better was available, given the risks of the shock therapies – whose value he saw for some patients. Some of those who would not be deeply helped, he thought, would at least feel a little better after psychoanalysis because they had a place to unburden themselves of their thoughts.

In the later decades of the twentieth century, French psychoanalyst André Green took Abraham's legacy in a different direction. Green shared Abraham's interest in the effects of mothers who were emotionally unavailable to their children. He referred to them as "dead" – not literally, but in the sense that the children feel the mother's unavailability as a kind of deadness. These are mothers who had terrible losses of their own when their children were small. The mother's sorrow would deny the children the fulfillment in being able to please their mother that other kids might have. As adults, these patients do not always seem depressed when they seek treatment, though depressive tendencies may emerge later in treatment.

Green thought the maternal depression caused a "blankness" in the child.[40] The blankness comes from anxiety the children feel at the loss of the mother's affection. The loss leads the children to withdraw their own. The child will then be vulnerable to the "sinister black of depression."[41] The children may then try compensations. Attachment to the father may be one, though often the father may be no more available. Meaningful activities that are normally healthy may have an overly-driven quality to them. Playing is felt not as freedom to play but compulsion to imagine, and intellectual growth is a severe drive for achievement, not an enjoyable use of creativity. Surface success may come, as jobs are taken and performed, marriages made, and children raised, but all with a certain deadness inside. That is why they end up in the psychoanalyst's office.

The best-selling book *The Drama of the Gifted Child*, published by Swiss analyst Alice Miller in the late 1970s, also has affinities with Abraham's work, though more because of the theme of emotionally-remote parents than through anger turned inward.[42] Miller saw many depressed patients whose parents gave them a lot of attention, and even praise and admiration. This made their depression puzzling, but Miller found that the attention often flowed more from a wish to use the child to make up for the parents' own insecurities than from the needs of the child. Like Abraham and Green, she found the parents often had depression themselves. The children became sensitive to the insecurities of the parents, and performed the roles the parents needed them to, serving as living counter-depressants. This alienation from their own needs causes the depression in the children, which might alternate with grandiosity as a defense against the depression. As we will see in the memoir literature on depression later, this picture resonates with many depressed adults. As one memoirist wrote, when she read *The Drama of the Gifted Child*, "like other middle-class, over-achieving readers I've talked to since, I felt that Miller was writing about me."[43]

Alternatives

Not all explorers of the unconscious workings of depressive illness followed Abraham and Freud's ideas. One of Abraham's analysands, Sandor Radó, thought depressives were people who were too dependent on supplies of love from others. Children will desire love from their parents, but inevitably misbehave, and the penalties they face will be felt as a withdrawal of love. They may learn to fend off punishment with remorse, pre-emptive self-punishment. This may begin consciously, but in time become an unconscious habit. Depression, in Radó's theory, is a way of saying to the world, go easy on me, see how much I am suffering already.[44]

Edward Bibring, another member of Freud's Vienna analytic society who emigrated to the United States, thought that many depressions did not involve self-aggression, and cases of self-aggression did not always cause depression. Instead, Bibring stressed helplessness – the feeling that comes when wishes cannot be fulfilled. This could be anything from failing to woo a love interest to powerlessness in the face of political events. Helplessness was a feeling likely felt deeply by a Jewish psychoanalyst like Bibring, who lived through Hitler's annexation of Austria in 1938. But for Bibring, helplessness leading to depression was not simply a reaction to current events. Depressive feelings acquired power by inflaming infantile frustrations at being denied food – a common experience, since human infants cannot obtain their own food, and often are not, or cannot, be provided with it whenever they want.[45] The theme of helplessness is poignant because Bibring had Parkinson's disease as he was writing. He died from it in 1959, at the age of 64.

A few years later, American psychologist Martin Seligman applied electric shocks to dogs, and found that dogs who had no predictable way to avoid the shocks seemed to display affect and behavior that looked like human depression. He went on to propose, as Bibring did, that depressive illness was a response to a person's powerlessness to control adverse events. He also proposed, as Bibring did, that experiences of helplessness in childhood could predispose adults to depression.[46] He called his theory "learned helplessness," and it became famous in depression studies. Despite its deep similarity to Bibring's,

Seligman presented his model of depression as an act of intellectual daring, a radical break from the psychoanalytic orthodoxy of the time.[47]

Edith Jacobson also thought earlier analytic thought had made too much of guilt and attacks on the self. She thought Bibring went too far in dismissing its importance entirely, though – and that Bibring put too much emphasis on helplessness. Jacobson was a Jew born in Germany in the 1890s, as the field of psychoanalysis was starting to take shape, and became a physician at a time when few women were able to do so. She trained in psychoanalysis in the 1920s and was analyzed by Fenichel. By the 1930s, she was a respected analyst and an active leftist. The Nazis pressured her to reveal the identities of communists she was treating in therapy. She resisted the pressure and they imprisoned her. She managed to escape and emigrated to the United States, where she treated many depressed patients over several decades. Her writings on depression were based on rich clinical experience.[48] When setting depression apart from sadness, Jacobson saw that many depressed patients *wish* for sadness, as a path to fully feeling emotion again, a relief from the "deadness" of depression. She stressed a failure of the mother to understand and accept the child. She also believed many depressions, particularly psychotic ones, likely had biological roots.[49]

In Washington DC in the 1950s, a group led by psychoanalyst Frieda Fromm-Reichmann proposed that envy, and the fear of envy, was central to depression. Referring to the biblical figure, they wrote of a "Joseph Syndrome," in which a parent's favored child might, oddly, be prone to depression. Such children fear the aggressive envy of siblings. Underselling oneself, hiding one's talents, becomes a deep-seated part of their personality. They cannot use their greatest assets, and may even come to believe that they do not have any. Such people will become depressed at counter-intuitive times, such as when they get a promotion at work.[50]

Carl Jung: Depression as an Opportunity

Depression, most agree, is a bad thing. Is there anything good about it? Abraham thought it gratified a need for self-punishment. This is a sad form of "good." Swiss psychiatrist Carl Jung was more generous toward depression. He believed it could spawn growth and creativity.

While working in an asylum – where he was for a time a colleague of Abraham's – Jung developed ideas about the unconscious mind parallel to Freud's in many ways. After the two met, they had an intense personal and intellectual partnership. Partly because Freud feared that the high proportion of Jews in the movement risked making psychoanalysis seem a Jewish psychology, he hand-picked the non-Jewish Jung as his successor to lead the movement.[51]

That did not work out. Jung promoted ideas that Freud considered too different to be psychoanalysis. Jung grew doubtful about the centrality of sexuality in Freud's thought. Libido, which for Freud was a sexual force in people, Jung defined more broadly, as any psychic energy, or emotional investment. It could include sexuality, but also other motivations. Jung was also more open to thinking of a spiritual nature, which to Freud verged on mysticism. While Freud tolerated minor dissent, Jung's departures went too far. Jung went on to develop his own depth psychology, which recognized a debt to Freud, but which found Freud's ideas limited.

Jung started with the ambiguity of depression as both a mood and an illness.[52] When it is a mood, people will want to move past it. It becomes illness, and marked by devaluing of the self, when the motivation to change is lost because of low "psychic energy." He believed people had a finite amount of psychic energy, distributed between the unconscious and conscious minds. In depression, this energy was turned away from the world, and turned inward to the unconscious. "Psychic energy" may seem intangible – can it be seen and measured like, say, electrical energy, and if not, how do we know it is real? As anyone with personal or clinical experience with depression will tell you, though, depressed people do feel a shrinking of energy that seems poorly explained by physical factors such as calories consumed, physical fitness, or amount of sleep. No matter how much depressed people sleep, they feel they need more, and waking hours are always spent feeling tired.

But why is all this energy being consumed by the unconscious? The depression, Jung thought, is a sign that the person needs to pay attention to the unconscious, as though it were waving and saying, "Hey, stop fussing over all those external things, pay attention to me, I have things to tell you." Jung stressed the creativity of the unconscious and saw in depression a chance at personal transformation. The person needs to look within, to see what attracted the psychic energy, which will appear as a fantasy or image.

Depression, then, for all its pain, could lead to growth. Drawn to mythology, Jung compared depression to the hero's journey to the underworld to fight a monster, leading to the symbolic death of the hero. What is dying in reality, Jung thought, are attitudes of the depressive state. Tendencies to always consider oneself a victim, for example, will fall away – but only if one reckons with the darkness in the unconscious. Depressives might be so identified with the ways they act and think that they will be unable to use the opportunity the depression offers. *The lightbulb must want to change.*

Was Jung right to see depression as an opportunity? For a book about people taking antidepressants, sociologist David Karp asked them if they saw anything positive about their illness. Nearly all respondents said it made them more aware, more sensitive, more insightful.[53] For Jung, though, depression by itself was a dead end. It was an avenue to growth and creativity only if overcome.

Jung, like Freud, said little about why depression happened to some people and not others. Like Abraham, he thought an inborn tendency was likely. He thought therapy should not focus on the cause, but address the imbalance in the psychic energy. Looking squarely at fantasies associated with the depression would liberate the patient from the consuming attention of the unconscious, freeing up psychic energy for use in the external world.

Psychoanalysis in the Time of The Broken Brain

If Prozac had been around for Freud, would he have tried it for his patients? In the 1970s, a doctor named Rafael Osheroff was treated for severe depression solely with psychoanalytic talk therapy, in an era when antidepressants were available. He successfully sued the hospital, arguing that he was not getting the standard of care. Psychoanalytic resistance to physical treatments became a hot topic.

It's likely, though, that Freud would have been not only open, but eager to try new physical treatments. He began his career as a neurologist, and was hopeful about the therapeutic powers of drugs.[54] He insisted to the end of his life that science would eventually reveal the biology behind mental illness.[55] It is possible he might have thought, as many of his later followers did, that biology was only a first step, and that deeper change would require dynamic therapy.

Psychoanalysis did, though, face a steep challenge in the 1970s, as the field of mental health shifted to a new emphasis on biology. Psychotherapy, much of it psychoanalytic, continued, of course. But psychiatrists, and later the lay public, increasingly thought that depression was a brain disorder. This will be detailed in the following two chapters, but for now note three major reasons. One was the anti-depressants. Their apparent efficacy led many to think the causes of depression must be physical – though physical treatments for depression had been used for centuries without banishing psychology in earlier eras. A second change was genetics. Some heritability of unipolar depression got more scientific backing. A third factor was the revision of the DSM, to DSM-III. The new manual avoided mention about the causes of depression and most other mental illnesses, focusing instead on description. It stripped psychoanalytic language from the diagnoses, though, and its descriptive nature probably encouraged biological psychiatry. Biological approaches were not new. Strident claims that they were the only relevant approaches were, though.

Psychoanalysts had to respond. Some converted and became biological psychiatrists. Some went the opposite way, focusing exclusively on psychological causes and treatments. But most of the major writing by psychoanalysts on depression from the 1970s onwards took a third path, granting and welcoming the power of biological approaches. They did not think that the new biological approaches disproved psychoanalysis approaches or made it obsolete, but saw the two as complementary.

Silvano Arieti and Jules Bemporad, who co-authored a psychoanalytic textbook on depression in the 1970s, reported good results with antidepressant drugs, though they thought most patients would also need psychotherapy.[56] Psychologist Nancy McWilliams wrote a textbook on psychoanalytic diagnosis which also supported the use of drugs. McWilliams wrote that the most disturbed depressed patients included "delusional and ruthlessly self-hating mental patients who, until the discovery of antidepressive medicines, could absorb years of a devoted therapist's efforts and still believe uncritically that the best way to save the world was to destroy the self."[57] McWilliams also recognized genetic vulnerability to depression. Psychoanalysts held, though, that the meaning of symptoms still mattered, and they faulted purely biological approaches for not grappling with subjective experience.

The presence of biological *processes* in depression also did not mean that the *causes* were purely biological. John Bowlby, a British psychoanalyst who had been influential for decades, published the last volume in a famous trilogy on attachment and loss in 1980. Chemical changes in the brain during depression, Bowlby thought, need not imply that the causal sequence was chemical first, mood second.[58] He found that people with depressive illness often had unstable relationships with parents, may have been repeatedly told they were unlovable or incompetent, or were likely to have suffered an actual loss of a parent during childhood.[59] In their 1978 textbook, Arieti and Bemporad pointed out that studies of genetics and neurochemistry were not at that time conclusive – an argument that looks smart in retrospect, since they are still not.[60] They also argued that the efficacy of drugs does not prove that psychology doesn't matter, but instead that physical changes in depression can be addressed independently.[61] A 2004 psychoanalytic textbook touted the value of short-term therapy, cognitive therapy, and medication, but said that treatment of depression remains challenging (it does). It then argued that psychodynamic treatment can help in mild or moderate cases, and that patients with bipolar disorder and severe major depression can also benefit, if their symptoms are reduced by medication.[62]

Julia Kristeva, a philosopher and psychoanalyst from Bulgaria who has been working in France since the 1960s, applied a psychoanalytic lens to the gender ratio in depression.[63] Mental health workers have been puzzling over the gender ratio in depression for decades. Why do women get diagnosed with depression more than men? Are they really more prone to depression, or simply diagnosed more? If women are more prone, why? If more diagnosed, why?[64] Some feminist psychoanalysts, drawing on the idea of introjection, have proposed that depression in women might be related to identification: boys are less vulnerable to the introjection of the mother because their sex is different.[65] Girls identify with the mother, take her more deeply inside the self, and direct anger toward the introjected object.

The central dilemma for young children, Kristeva said, is achieving autonomy.[66] In Kristeva's view, this requires a psychic "matricide." But this is harder for girls because of their identification with the mother. The melancholic girl, having not killed the mother, must kill herself. Put another way, the lost object, the mother, is not lost enough. Kristeva sees psychoanalysis – the chance to render experience into language and have it interpreted – as a counter-depressant. This may sound like a purely psychological theory, but Kristeva, whose book on depression came out the same year Prozac was approved, also advocated for the use of medications for mood disorders.[67]

The most ambitious attempt to integrate psychoanalysis and biology is the new and innovative field of neuropsychoanalysis. The leading figure has been South African neuropsychologist and psychoanalyst Mark Solms. The core of Solms's thinking is that psychoanalysis and neurology are two ways of looking at the same thing: mental activity. Neurology looks at the objective, physical processes, and psychoanalysis at the subjectivity.[68] In this way of thinking, mind and brain are not exactly different things with a relationship to one another, but different ways of looking at and thinking about the same thing.

Neuropsychoanalysis of depression presumes that emotions have functions. Solms and his colleagues argue that the brain has a "seeking" mechanism, pushing animals to look for food, sex, and other pleasures. The emotions that spark the seeking are necessary to get animals to engage with the world. Specific pleasures associated with social connection are highly developed in mammals. Drawing on Bowlby, they argue that with lack of attachment, or social loss, a "protest" behavior will ensue. The animal will seek reunion with the lost object. But if the reunion fails, the animal will give up, causing a muting of the seeking system in the brain, leading to feelings of emptiness, deadness, and hopelessness. Antidepressants might not fix the social losses, but they work because they address what is happening in the brain. The reason some people respond to loss with healthy grieving and others with depression may be that the loss repeats unresolved early ones, leading to a sense of hopelessness. Many of these ideas echo those of early analysts like Abraham and Bibring, who lived before the antidepressant era.[69]

Otto Kernberg also applied neuropsychoanalysis to depression. Kernberg, one of the most prominent psychoanalysts in America, is another whose family fled Vienna because of Nazism. Kernberg considered depression in evolutionary terms, and also drew on Bowlby. Depression evolved to end separation distress. Such distress, if prolonged, would be dangerous for infant mammals. Like most psychoanalysts, Kernberg saw early experience as formative. Prolonged separation of the infant from the mother causes rage first, and despair later. These emotions cause higher levels of cortisol in the blood, which has been shown to accompany depression. Genetic factors, Kernberg thinks, dominate in severe depression, and life situation is more relevant to the milder forms. Kernberg thinks that medication and ECT are best for treating severe depressions, and psychotherapy, perhaps combined with medication, for the milder ones. Psychoanalysis, Kernberg says, offers for neurobiology a way of looking at "higher symbolic functions that cannot be reduced to neocortical circuitry," and neurobiology offers psychoanalysis a way of grounding its theories in biology.[70]

A Painful Case: The Lessons of Osheroff

Rafael Osheroff was a successful doctor. In 1978, he became severely depressed. He was first treated with a tricyclic antidepressant. The prescription was from Nathan Kline, a key figure in the development of antidepressant medication. Accounts differ on whether the tricyclic helped.[71] Osheroff decided to change the dose on his own, and then had some worsening of his condition. In early January of 1979, he was admitted to Chestnut Lodge, a respected mental health facility in Rockville, Maryland, near Washington, DC.

Chestnut Lodge had an exclusively psychoanalytic orientation. Two famous psychoanalysts, Fromm-Reichmann and Harry Stack Sullivan, had worked there. Both took the unusual view that psychodynamic methods could succeed for severely ill patients, even those with psychosis. Freud himself had doubted this. Chestnut Lodge did not use shock therapies when they became available. Drugs were regarded as a form of coercion, chemical straitjackets that would only mask the psychic conflict causing the illness.[72] The doctors at Chestnut Lodge thought Osheroff's symptoms came from an underlying narcissistic personality disorder.[73] They treated him with dynamic talk therapy only, for months. His condition worsened. Meanwhile, his hospitalization kept him from a lucrative medical practice. Osheroff had a contract that would be void if he did not return to work in six months. A doctor at Chestnut Lodge dismissed Osheroff's concern about the contract, saying it symbolized "a giant breast that was going to restore the scenes of adoration that he had with his mother."[74] Osheroff asked for medications at Chestnut Lodge, but was denied them.

After a while, Osheroff lost patience with Chestnut Lodge, and his mother arranged a transfer to Silver Hill, a facility in Connecticut that provided antidepressants.[75] He improved rapidly, but his life had been wounded. During his hospitalization, he had been declared legally incompetent. His privileges at the hospital he worked at had been suspended, and his children forbidden to see him. In 1982, he sued. He won the case on appeal and received an out-of-court settlement. In a symbol of the changing times, Chestnut Lodge eventually closed and was converted into condos, and finally razed.[76]

Ghosts, however, outlive the buildings that spawn them. The Osheroff case haunted psychiatry long after the legal proceedings. A divided profession had to decide, what were the lessons of the case? Gerald Klerman, a prominent psychiatrist who advocated for Osheroff, thought the case was about evidence – specifically, what counted as evidence for what works. Klerman was not opposed to talk therapy, and was a key figure in creating a new psychotherapy called Interpersonal. But, he said, the standard for judging a treatment had to be a randomized controlled trial, as it was for the rest of medicine. Chestnut Lodge was guilty of malpractice, he thought, because its treatment was not evidence-based, and therefore was below the standard of care.[77]

Another possible lesson from the Osheroff case was that biological psychiatry is right, and psychoanalysis wrong. Certainly, many psychoanalysts were worried about this conclusion.[78] The better lesson, though, may be that dogmatism is wrong. The big mistake at Chestnut Lodge may have been less the decision to treat Osheroff psychoanalytically than to treat him *solely* that way – particularly since he had the kind of severe depression many psychoanalysts have always been wary of treating with talk therapy alone. Chestnut Lodge's failure to consider a physical aspect of his illness ran against the major psychoanalytic theories of depression. Klerman was right that the decision to treat Osheroff with psychoanalysis alone was below the standard of care for general psychiatry. But it was also below the standard of care within psychoanalysis.

The interpretation of Osheroff's career as a fantasied breast seems wildly misguided. Money and success do have symbolic meaning, in addition to their practical ones. Understanding these meanings might be therapeutic. In this case, the analyst seems to have used the interpretation to dismiss the patient's concerns, not to understand them.

What about Osheroff's path to Chestnut Lodge in the first place? He decided to change his dosage of the tricyclic against Kline's advice for a reason. Was he having trouble tolerating adverse effects? Patients often feel ambivalent toward antidepressants – partly because of adverse effects, but also because they can fail to help the patient make sense of the illness. Osheroff decided to go to Chestnut Lodge for a reason. Perhaps he was seeking more insight into the reasons for his illness and his symptoms? Much of this might well have been explored psychoanalytically. That exploration might be more effective with physical treatments giving relief from the symptoms.

The Osheroff case yields yet another lesson. The diagnosis of depression has exploded since the 1970s. Many critics are alarmed, seeing an epidemic of over-diagnosis. The Osheroff case shows another side of the issue, though. Chestnut Lodge saw depressive symptoms, but insisted that a personality disorder – universally regarded as hard to treat by any method – was the main diagnosis. Whether Osheroff had a personality disorder or not, naming his suffering *as depression* was key to effective treatment.

Whatever strengths biological approaches have, and whatever weaknesses the psychoanalytic tradition has shown, some loss occurs when it is abandoned. The felt experience of depression, the exploration of trauma and loss and the sources of guilty obsessions, all get pushed to the background. Psychoanalysis provided a method and a space for these explorations. These explorations do not matter if the psychological content of depression does not matter. But it does matter, to people with depression. Some may be uninterested in working through their inner conflict and simply want medications or ECT. Many do not share that disinterest. Psychoanalysis continues because the subjective world of the patient continues to matter.

Depression was not a major concern of early psychoanalysis. In

Freud's vast writings, depression forms a small part. The attention paid to depression by later analysts like Green, Jacobson, and Kristeva is a sign of the growing attention paid to the diagnosis. In the century following "Mourning and Melancholia," depression gradually became a major preoccupation of mental health work – and for the lay public.

The task of defining depression, setting its boundaries, building a consensus about what it was and was not, became more pressing. A related challenge was finding ways to measure depression, in both individuals and populations, even as the definition of the illness was in flux. At the same time, medicine was growing reliant on randomized trials to measure how well a therapy worked. Klerman's complaint that Chestnut Lodge's treatment was not evidence-based came when he, and others, were creating new psychotherapies that were less open-ended than traditional psychoanalysis, and thus more easily studied in trials. Medical knowledge was becoming less about case histories and more about numbers, and efforts to carefully define and carefully measure depression became urgent. The results were mixed.

4

A Diagnosis in Ascent

"There is no more bloated category than 'depression,' threatening to all but expunge the nuances of language denoted by 'distress,' 'sadness,' 'despair,' 'gloominess,' 'pessimism,' etc."

– Derek Summerfield[1]

"Psychiatrists do not always agree with one another on how and where the line demarcating depression from unhappiness should be drawn."

– Nancy Andreasen[2]

Blurry Borders

In 1961, the painter Mark Rothko was a star. An obscure artist of modest means for much of his adult life, that year he had his own show at the Museum of Modern Art (MOMA) – days before he was an invited guest at the inauguration of President John F. Kennedy, where he was seated next to the economist Walt Rostow. (The seating was alphabetical. Tragically, no record exists of the conversation between Rothko and Rostow.) Rothko had developed a signature style of stacked, rectangular color fields with blurry borders, and his paintings had become instantly familiar as "Rothkos." After years of working at insecure teaching jobs, he was now selling individual paintings for thousands of dollars and getting commissions from the likes of the Tate Gallery and Harvard University. At the opening to the MOMA show, he seemed pleased and expansive. But at 5:00 the next morning, he showed up at a friend's house in a state of despair. He was convinced the show had exposed him as worthless and empty.[3]

Impostor syndrome is common. Success can be as stressful as failure and loss. And Rothko always had a gloomy side, whether because of his childhood as a Jewish refugee from eastern Europe in an era of pogroms, his outsider status as an immigrant, or his innate temperament. While he always had friends and could be outgoing, he often felt lonely. People close to him said he fell easily into states of despair. He could be a hypochondriac. He had a sharp temper and was prone to gloomy ruminations. He thought he was an artistic genius, but had grim doubts about his work anyway. A close friend spoke of a "great vacuum at the center of his being."[4]

In the 1960s, people close to him started referring to his "depressions." In the weeks before the MOMA show, he had been drinking heavily, gaining weight, and his blood pressure grew alarmingly high. Exactly when Rothko and others began to see a clinical problem, rather than bad moods, is hard to know. In this enigma, he mirrored the trend in the wider society: we were seeing more clinical depression, but were we *having* more, or simply learning how to see it?

In these late years, his paintings, which had dazzled viewers with their lustrous use of color, began to darken. Some of the last ones used mostly black and grey (see figure 6). Some people saw this as an expression of depression. Rothko denied that his paintings expressed his inner state. He hated easy interpretations of his work – maybe all interpretations of his work. One woman who wanted to purchase a painting was upset when Rothko offered her one with dark tones. She wanted happy colors, like red, yellow, and orange. Rothko replied: "Red, yellow, orange – aren't those the colors of an inferno?"[5] The late paintings, he said, were not windows into his darkening psyche.

By the late 1960s, Rothko faced several new stressors. The new movement of Pop Art was drawing attention away from Rothko and painters of his generation. Rothko did not think much of these new artists, but he knew they were the next big thing. In 1968 he was found to have an aneurysm, probably related to hypertension. His physician

Figure 6 *Mark Rothko's later paintings avoided lush colors. Many wondered if these late paintings expressed depression, a speculation that shows the growing awareness of depression in the second half of the twentieth century*
Source: Untitled, 1969 (acrylic on canvas), Rothko, Mark (1903–70)/Saint Louis Art Museum/Gift of the Mark Rothko Foundation/Bridgeman Images

advised him to stop smoking and drinking, and to watch his diet. These were hard changes for Rothko, who had a large appetite and was a heavy smoker and drinker. He grew sexually impotent, and later that year, separated from his second wife. By early 1970, a psychiatrist named Bernard Schoenberg thought Rothko was seriously depressed and urged psychotherapy. Rothko refused.

At the height of his fame, Rothko's midtown Manhattan studio was two blocks away from the office of psychiatrist Nathan Kline. Kline was not as famous as Rothko, but he was also doing well professionally. Born in New Jersey to a family that owned a chain of grocery stores, and to a mother who was a physician at a time when few women were, Kline studied psychology at Harvard before getting his own medical degree in 1943. Where Rothko was dour, Kline's temperament was upbeat. One historian has said that "in the often gray world of academic psychiatry, Kline cut an unusually colorful figure." He stood out like an early Rothko, then, in a world of late ones. One of Kline's colleagues said that his private practice seemed "like something from a Hollywood movie."[6] His high energy level was matched by a therapeutic optimism, spurring him to key roles in the rise of both antipsychotic drugs and antidepressants. Seeking alternatives to both the dismal state of large mental hospitals and lengthy psychoanalysis, Kline was hopeful about the power of drugs. He became one of the towering figures in the history of psychopharmacology.

Kline – like Carl Jung – thought that depression stemmed from a depletion of "psychic energy." Jung thought this depleted state was an opportunity for people to turn inward and confront their demons. Kline had no objection to therapy or introspection, but he wanted easier paths to health. When he heard that a tuberculosis drug was causing euphoria in patients, leading to dancing in the wards, Kline thought this might be the remedy. He contributed to the creation of one of the first classes of antidepressants drugs, the monoamine oxidase inhibitors (MAOIs). Kline treated many depression patients with these, and with the other newly developed class of antidepressants called tricyclics. By 1974, Kline had treated 5,000 depression patients, claiming a success rate of 85 percent.[7]

The MAOIs did not become cultural sensations like Prozac, but awareness of depression was growing. Clinicians and lay people learned to see its signs. Depression came to be as recognizable as a Rothko, and as marketable.

Psychiatry had to undergo some introspection of its own. The question of who exactly was clinically depressed grew more pressing, without yielding easy answers. The borders between sick and normal were as blurry as those surrounding a classic Rothko rectangle. If a person feels overtaken in his professional life, and then suffers an aneurysm, is a gloomy mood simply the sadness one expects? If medications help people feel better, does that prove that they "really" had depression all along?

The MAOIs and tricyclics have some serious adverse effects but they did help people feel better. Some experts think they work as well, and possibly better than, Prozac and the other SSRIs that came later.[8] Rothko was not one of the success stories, though. Multiple doctors urged him into psychiatric treatment, and one prescribed a tricyclic, which Rothko stopped using. One February morning in 1970, he was found dead by suicide in his studio. He cut his arteries after taking a massive dose of the tricyclic. It was prescribed by Nathan Kline.[9]

A Weak Word Conquers the World

In his memoir *Darkness Visible*, novelist William Styron complained about the weakness of "depression," a word he found unequal to the monster it names.[10] However lackluster it may seem, though, it has become over the past century one of the most commonly used in medicine. The word Styron thought was weak became an unstoppable global force.

Adolf Meyer was not a native English speaker. A Swiss psychiatrist and an immigrant to the United States, as the head of psychiatry at Johns Hopkins University he became one of the most influential psychiatrists in the country. He advocated a multi-dimensional approach to patients. Their biology, personal psychology, and social milieu all needed attention. When he urged clinicians to stop using melancholia, and start using depression, Meyer sparked a momentous, though gradual, change in clinical language. By the late twentieth century, melancholia was a marginal term.[11] After its success rooting out "melancholia" in Western discourse, "depression" burrowed its way into clinical and lay language in contexts as diverse as Iran and Japan, inflecting (or infecting?) medical, moral, and religious idioms globally.

Many started comparing depression to the common cold, to stress how widespread it is.[12] This was a bad comparison. For one thing, depression – *by definition* – lasts more than a few days. And while it can have mild forms, it causes immense suffering and debility in its severe forms. Anyone who uses the comparison hoping to raise awareness of depression may have worsened the confusion between mood and illness that troubles the word in the first place.

The rising rates of depression are, as we have seen, subject to differing interpretations. With an illness subject to frequent and contested criteria for diagnosis, the task becomes harder. This chapter traces some of the processes that accompanied the rising diagnosis rates and the increased attention to depression. The invention of new physical treatments for depression, in particular the rise of the antidepressants, was connected to these changes, but that story is mostly left to the next chapter. Here, I look at a diverse group of practices connected to *manualization*. They included the creation of numerical rating scales for depression, new psychotherapies that were more easily studied with statistics, and research on what populations have greater risk for depression and why. All of these were efforts to contain this hazy sickness, whether within the confines of diagnostic manuals, assessment tests, or statistical measures – as if taking a permanent marker to the blurry borders of Rothko rectangles and trying to make the separations strict.

After Meyer: Depression in Ascent

Despite the rise in depression diagnoses since the middle of the twentieth century, depression was a known, and increasingly used, category in the decades before. Abraham used it in his psychoanalytic work. The wider profession of psychiatry gradually followed Meyer's lead in starting to adopt it. This may be partly why Abraham did. Freud, who was not a psychiatrist, used melancholia to discuss the same symptom cluster. In some usage melancholia was reserved for particular types of depression – usually, severe and of apparent physical origin – but some doctors continued to use it interchangeably with depression well into the twentieth century.

In 1925, John MacCurdy, a doctor trained at Johns Hopkins, described depression much as we do now: sadness, sluggishness, feelings of personal inadequacy, and intense guilty feelings that seem baseless to others.[13] "The sun does not shine as it used to, the woods are not so green, even bodily functions have lost their acuity, their legs and arms are wooden . . ."[14] MacCurdy saw a spectrum between ordinary low spirits and a medical problem. Clinical depression, he thought, had more hopelessness, and a lack of will to change. MacCurdy also distinguished between psychotic depression, with delusions, and neurotic depression, where the grasp of factual reality is intact but clouded by gloomy interpretations. He complained that depression did not get enough research attention. He died in 1947. The decades after would see precisely the attention he hoped for.

Kraepelin, and most others in the early twentieth century, focused on severe forms. He developed several different ways of grouping severe mood disorders.[15] He also coined an influential term, "involutional melancholia," which meant serious depressive illness acquired later in life, not inborn.[16] Styron may have lamented the drabness of "depression," but here is a tip for people who want their coinages to become juggernauts adopted in numerous cultures around the world, and well known in lay culture: do not use a term like "involutional melancholia." Plainer language works better.[17]

With increased interest in depression came new attempts to classify subtypes. One common distinction made in the middle of the twentieth century was between "endogenous" depression – biologically based, probably genetic – and "reactive" depression – a response to external events.[18] Suicidal thoughts and insomnia were often thought to be features of endogenous depression.[19] The distinction lives on, but without the status it had 70 years ago. I doubt it was ever easy to know how much any particular case of depression was endogenous or reactive.[20] Even in its heyday, the distinction was questioned within psychiatry.[21]

Abraham Myerson, a prominent psychiatrist in Boston, wrote a book about the mild form. He called it neither depression nor melancholia, but "anhedonia," a lost ability to enjoy life. The word anhedonia now sometimes refers to this loss as a symptom of depression. By twenty-first-century measures, though, Myerson's anhedonia would be depression. The symptoms included loss of interest in activities, loss of appetite, insomnia, poor concentration, and a feeling of lack of purpose.[22] He omitted sadness, though.[23] He thought that anhedonia was caused by the strain of modern life but his remedies were as old as Hippocrates: more exercise, better rest, and better diet. Myerson said he was not talking about a "disease," requiring medical treatment, though he also warned that severe forms were true medical conditions, needing a doctor's attention.[24] He tried using amphetamines to treat it, and was also one of the first American psychiatrists to use ECT.

When the increased interest in depression began is hard to pinpoint. In 1980, the third edition of the DSM came out, and seven years later, Prozac was approved for sale. As important as these were, depression was a subject of growing interest in the decades before. In the 1950s, the MAOIs and the tricyclics were the first drugs to be called "antidepressants." Perhaps psychiatry started to find a lot of nails once it had a hammer. In 1954, though, before any antidepressants were in wide use, two prominent psychiatrists named anxiety and depression as the era's major psychiatric challenges.[25]

One likely factor was the rise of private office practice. When psychiatric work was mainly in asylums, most of the patients doctors saw had severe disorders, including disabling depressions with psychotic delusions or catatonia. Many patients were involuntary, brought to the asylums by their families or law enforcement. Out-patient psychotherapy became common, a voluntary and popular consumer good, over the course of the twentieth century. The success of psychoanalysis played a big part in this, although psychoanalysis was never the only talk therapy. Psychiatrists were seeing more people who had symptoms of depression, but were too well to commit to asylum care.

These changes are too easily dismissed as treating the "worried well." Certainly with more demand for therapy, some of the people seeking it might not have been considered ill before. Some of them may not have been sick at all, even by broad definitions, but seeking help working on serious life problems. Some may simply have been seeking personal growth, what psychologist Abraham Maslow called "self-actualization." There is nothing wrong with that, of course, if people are being helped. But many others were suffering from severe symptoms. The cases presented by Karl Abraham or Edith Jacobson, for example, were patients in a lot of pain. It is good they did not have to choose between an asylum and no care at all.

Rating Scales and Therapies: Depression Quantified

In the late 1950s, as antidepressants were coming into use, British psychiatrist Max Hamilton developed the Hamilton Rating Scale for Depression.[26] A patient would give a numerical score for the severity of various symptoms. The numbers were used for comparisons of the patients before and after treatments, as well as statistical analysis. Hamilton had served in the Royal Air Force, where he knew men who had suffered breakdowns during combat and were thought to have "lowered moral fibre."[27] This stigma may have motivated his search for precise measurement. Hamilton meant the scale to be a measure of severity only, but it came to be used for diagnosis as well.[28] Other scales followed, but the Hamilton scale remains widely used.

Hamilton conceded some flaws in his scale.[29] He wanted it to focus on the clearest, easily identified symptoms.[30] Severity measured by the scale may not match severity measured in a global clinical judgment. With large-scale comparisons among patients becoming more important for medical research, though, measurement became more necessary.

New psychotherapies also had to adapt to the reshaping of what counted as clinical evidence. Many new forms of psychotherapy were developed from the 1960s on, many of them as alternatives to psychoanalysis. Psychoanalysis is open-ended – it does not target a completion date in advance, and the criteria for completion are not always clear. This can be a strength in some ways, allowing deep exploration of conflicts after some symptom relief is achieved. It can also be daunting, though, and it did not fit well in a medical culture driven by statistical measures, or a third-party insurance payment system that sought limits on the number of sessions. These changes helped spur new therapies, including humanistic therapy, which focused on the person's needs to self-actualize, and Gestalt therapy, which sought to focus on the person's situation in the moment, rather than as a result of long-buried inner conflicts. The psychotherapies are too numerous to cover all of them. Two that were important for depression were Cognitive-

Behavioral Therapy or CBT, and Interpersonal Therapy, or ITP. A snappy acronym is always a plus.

Cognitive-Behavioral Therapy merged two approaches, one focused on changing patterns of thought, and one on changing patterns of behavior. CBT's promoters often emphasized its newness.[31] Modifications of thought and behavior to treat depressive illness go back to antiquity, though. CBT gave it newly systematic study.

Aaron Beck, a psychiatrist who had trained as a psychoanalyst, created cognitive therapy.[32] In the late 1950s and early 1960s, he began to think depression stemmed from faulty reasoning, logical errors. Typical examples include all-or-nothing thinking, where the patient thinks they must be perfect or else they are worthless; over-generalization, where they conclude that a single episode of failure defines them; mind-reader error, where they assume people are thinking poorly of them; and disqualifying the positive, where they overlook good that they have, or have done. A student might fail a test and say to the therapist "I'm a failure, and my teacher must have lost all respect for me." The therapist could then point out that a single test does not make one a failure, and that they did not yet know anything about the level of the teacher's respect. Why the depressed person made these errors in logic may interest the cognitive therapist, but the focus of therapy is to help patients learn to correct their errors.[33]

Beck wanted defined measures of depression, clear evidence that a therapy worked, and testable theories. He created his own scale for severity, the Beck Depression Inventory, which is still used today. He disliked how psychoanalysts often turned to the authority of founding figures in the field, rather than using experiment and observation to settle questions. He tried to put the main psychoanalytic theory of depression – anger turned inward – to an empirical test and, with a colleague, studied the content of depressed patients' dreams.[34] They found that the dreams were filled more with loss and rejection than with anger, and they called the dreams "masochistic." This was supposed to refute psychoanalysis, but from a psychoanalytic point of view, that is what masochism *is*: anger or aggression turned inwards.

Psychoanalysts opposed Beck's tests, which they thought left out complexity and individuality. He was denied admission into the American Psychoanalytic Association. He resented this, but he never gave up on Freudian theory entirely. American psychiatry departments were drifting from psychoanalysis, though. At a time of upheaval in his personal and professional life, he worked on cognitive therapy by using it on himself – much as Freud developed early psychoanalysis by analyzing his own dreams. By the 1970s, Beck had refined his ideas and was promoting them. At the same time, a number of behaviorists were finding the strict stimulus–response model of behaviorism wanting, but disliked psychoanalysis. They found Beck's approach attractive, and the merger produced CBT.

CBT came at a time primed for it. The prestige of psychoanalysis was fading, and so was patience for its length and expense. The entire culture of medicine was changing, too. After World War II, medical research came to rely on randomized controlled trials (RCTs), where large numbers of patients get a treatment and are compared to a group given a different one, or no treatment at all. RCTs have flaws, and exclusive reliance on them has downsides. The appeal of these large comparisons is easy to see, though. They have a particular attraction for depression, which can get better over time without any treatment at all. The case for a treatment seems stronger if the number of people who get better with treatment is much larger than the number who get better without it. RCTs became the standard for clinical evidence. CBT fit this changing culture, because it was a talk therapy that could be standardized, though Beck also insisted that CBT was a learned skill and "You can't do cognitive therapy from a manual any more than you can do surgery from a manual."[35] CBT also fit the culture of randomized trials because it had clear goals, and a scale to measure success by.

CBT also had a pragmatic optimism, very American, unlike Freud's bleaker vision. Freud thought all people were plagued by inner conflicts. The work of psychoanalysis was not to purge demons, but to get some control over them. The suffering caused by the conflicts could be reduced. CBT had a sunnier outlook: correct thinking will lead to happier feeling.

Beck understood the appeal of this, and used it to convert people to his view. He privately continued to work with psychoanalytic ideas, trying to understand *why* people had negative thoughts, and retaining some Freudian pessimism about how completely they could be overcome.[36] In canny marketing, though, Beck kept lingering ties to psychoanalysis to himself.

Some critics of antidepressant medications have called them a quick fix that does not address underlying psychological or social causes of depression. Some add that these medications fit well in contemporary capitalism – antidepressants are a commodity you can buy, and improvement in mood will lead to improved workplace performance and less absenteeism. Society gets a better worker *and* a better consumer. No confrontation with alienation or social inequalities needed! If you think this might apply to CBT as well, consider that this is what some of its *proponents* say. In 2014, the UK government announced that people on disability would lose their benefits if they refused to attend CBT sessions.[37]

But while CBT can be seen as a form of managerial control, we should not reduce it to that. All forms of psychiatric treatment have an element of social control, but they can also have true therapeutic value.[38] CBT may fit our current cultural, political, and economic moment. It can still be helpful therapy. It has been over-hyped, though, and may not be more effective than other psychotherapies.[39]

CBT may seem harmless at worst, though some have alleged adverse effects, such as increased anxiety and deteriorating relationships.[40] CBT's promise of quick action is attractive in a culture of quick fixes and cost-conscious corporate insurance. But depression can be a stubborn problem, often needing more than a quick fix. Correcting logic may help many people, but what about those whose illness creates a resistance to logic? Freud thought that rational persuasion would have limited power if the negative thoughts were caused by unconscious conflict. Whether he was right about the reason or not, rational persuasion will not always prevail with a depressed person. In a memoir of her depression, author Tracy Thompson wrote that doctors' attempts to reason with depressed patients might be futile: "This is one of the least understood aspects of depression, this tenacity with which severely depressed people cling to the very perceptions that are most distorted."[41] To psychoanalysts, this is one of the most understood aspects of depression.

Interpersonal Psychotherapy developed in the late 1960s and 1970s. Like CBT, it is meant to be time-limited. Rather than focusing on illogical thoughts, it stresses interpersonal relationships.[42] Depressive symptoms, according to ITP, come when relationships are damaged or threatened. This was a part of Abraham's theory – he thought that frayed relationships in the present re-activated older feelings of loss. ITP aims to help patients develop better communication and social support, in order to have better relationships.

Gerald Klerman started ITP at Yale University in 1969. Klerman had earlier contributed to research showing the efficacy of a tricyclic antidepressant, and would later work on a large study that seemed to show that the incidence of depression was rising.[43] He was Raphael Osheroff's champion, arguing that the treatment provided at Chestnut Lodge was not evidence-based. In the late 1960s, Klerman was working with colleagues to see how well tricyclic antidepressants worked alone, compared with their performance when combined with psychotherapy.[44] At the time, clinical trials for psychotherapy were rare. Klerman and his colleagues wanted a time-limited psychotherapy with clear goals. They used CBT as a model, though they had different views of the causes and treatment of depression.

ITP was thus not invented because clinicians had a theory about what would work, which they then tested to see if it was true. ITP was, rather, created *for the purpose of being studied in a clinical trial.* Only after that goal was set did its creators start to think about what would work.

Klerman was a psychopharmacologist and assumed depression had a biological basis. He did not, though, think that meant that only physical treatments like ECT or drugs could be effective. He thought, for example, that drugs could help restore normal sleep patterns, but that psychotherapy might help more with frayed relationships.

Though ITP was time-limited, and worked with the present more than early life, ITP's proponents were open about their debt to psychoanalysis. The psychoanalysts valued most in ITP were those who emphasized relationships, like Harry Stack Sullivan – one of the most famous doctors to work at Chestnut Lodge – and John Bowlby. ITP was also influenced by Meyer's interest in placing the patient in social context.[45]

Another new therapy had its roots in Martin Seligman's ideas. After shocking dogs led him to the theory of learned helplessness, Seligman became interested in exploring the brighter side of mental life. Instead of asking what makes people depressed, he started asking what makes them happy. In therapy, this shift in emphasis might mean, for example, giving less emphasis to problems than to promoting positive emotions such as hope and gratitude. But positive psychology has probably had more impact on "normal" psychology than as a treatment for illness. It is the cornerstone of what social critic William Davies has named the "happiness industry," a push for positivity, often monetized with commercial products, which Davies sees as a way of avoiding fraught social problems.[46]

In close kinship with the happiness industry is the gratitude industry. In recent years, for example, we have seen frequent encouragement to keep a gratitude journal, in order to promote our happiness. If you do not feel grateful because your life presents hardship, perhaps you can try to be grateful anyway – exercise it like a muscle. So argued Arthur Brooks in a *New York Times* column in 2015.[47] First, he said, express gratitude privately, then publicly, and finally learn to be grateful for trivial things – he gave the example of the spots on a trout. This sounds nice. And yes, we would all be happier with more appreciation of the wonder of everyday life. That may be more challenging, though, if you are struggling with poverty, for example. Brooks was the president of the American Enterprise Institute for nine years. The Institute is a right-wing think tank, generally opposed to government programs that help the poor. This seems relevant. Let them eat gratitude.

The Measure of Efficacy

Psychotherapy works; this is well documented.[48] In the middle of the twentieth century, some famously claimed that the number of people who get better from psychotherapy was no larger than the number whose symptoms disappear without any treatment. This claim, though, was based on a few studies that were not rigorously selected. With better methods of meta-analysis – the aggregation of multiple studies – psychotherapy received more support.[49] CBT and ITP are well-studied psychotherapies; both have efficacy rates at least as high as antidepressants in the acute stage.[50] The therapeutic effects of psychotherapy may last longer than that of drugs after treatment is stopped, and patients seem to be less likely to drop out of psychotherapy treatment than antidepressant treatment.[51] This is not surprising because although psychotherapy can be done poorly, you hear little about unwanted side effects from therapy. Psychotherapy and medication also work more powerfully together than either does alone.[52]

Whether any form of psychotherapy is more effective than the others is less clear. Some studies have found modest differences among different kinds, and other studies have not. CBT and IPT could be tested in the clinical trials. Having done so, they could say that they were, unlike psychoanalysis, evidence-based. Psychodynamic therapy is now being studied in trials, though, and seems as effective as others.[53] One recent meta-analysis even found that it did not matter if therapy was conducted face-to-face, on the phone, or over the internet. The case for the efficacy of psychotherapy for depression was so strong, the authors said, that denying people psychotherapy by using them as controls in trials was unethical.[54]

The similar efficacy of psychotherapies makes it hard to know exactly why they work – although the same can be said for antidepressants or ECT. Maybe just having a trained professional to listen to your problems, in a space where you can say anything you need to, is enough. The similar efficacy may also reflect a tendency of therapists to be eclectic in practice. Few psychodynamic practitioners are likely to ignore fallacious thoughts or interpersonal relationships. One guide to psychoanalytic therapy for depression, for example, suggests showing patients with guilty thoughts that thoughts show faulty reasoning.[55] Few cognitive therapists and interpersonal therapists are likely to avoid insight, and they may even make interpretations of unconscious conflict. Different psychotherapies may just work better for different patients, just as different antidepressants do.

Psychotherapy, like depression itself, is rife with intangibles. Like depression, an essence of it eludes easy definition, and there are lots of different types. The new therapies that came in the era of quantification added to the repertoire of clinicians, allowing a pluralism of approaches. Efforts at measuring and standardizing, though, would always face inherent limits. The measures to assess how a patient feels before and after are imperfect to begin with, and you generally cannot observe what goes on in therapy because privacy and confidentiality are foundations of its success.

Who Gets Depression?

One reason to measure depression in society is that it does not hit populations equally. Depression has a politics, a politics of inequality.

The jazz bassist Charles Mingus brimmed with vitality and creativity. But in addition to a notorious temper, he frequently thought of wanting to die. He even had episodes where he tried to *will* himself to die. While living in New York, he saw a psychotherapist named Edmund Pollock. In 1958, at a time of acute stress, he checked himself into the Bellevue Mental Hospital in New York City, hoping for a place of rest and respite. A doctor diagnosed him with paranoid schizophrenia, a label Mingus thought came from racist bias. He had good reason to; historian Jonathan Metzl has shown how disproportionately Black men got this diagnosis at that time, particularly if they voiced social grievances, which Mingus certainly did.[56] One doctor, Mingus reported, thought Black people *in general* were "paranoid" and proposed a lobotomy for Mingus, a fate fortunately avoided.[57] The jazz critic Nat Hentoff, who was a close of friend of Mingus's, thought instead that Mingus suffered from "classical clinical depression."[58]

After the hospitalization, Mingus asked Pollock to write the liner notes for his next album "The Black Saint and the Lady Sinner." Pollock wrote that the album "presents a brooding, moaning intensity about prejudice, hate and persecution . . . The suffering is terrible to hear."[59] Pollock said that the music is a call for revolution against any society that limits freedom and human rights.

Aside from any possible mood disorder, Mingus's talent, creativity, and fame were shadowed by a hard life. In his autobiography, he describes living in fear of bullying by racist gangs when he was young, for example. He told Pollock his fame was a phony prize in life: "They make us famous and give us names – the King of this, the Count of that, the Duke of *what!* We die broke anyhow – and sometimes I think I dig death more than I dig facing this white world."[60]

Neither Mingus nor Pollock, it seems, drew a line where persecution and injustice ends and sickness begins. Nor should we. The politics of Mingus's moods are relevant to illness, but cannot be reduced to them. Also, the reverse: illness is relevant to moods, but should not obscure politics.

Sylvia Plath also had a robust appetite for life. One of her many biographers says that she had a rare "capacity for exultation . . . a gift for rapture."[61] She was, though, also prone to dejection. Plath, like Mingus, was a voluntary depression patient, receiving two courses of ECT, one of which she found dreadful, and another which she found therapeutic.[62] Years later, finding herself lonely in a foreign country, in a disintegrating marriage with a man who had left her for another woman, she ultimately took her own life, in one of the most scrutinized suicides in history. After her death, she became iconic, not just for the searing precision of language in her writing, but also as a symbol of feminist protest. For good reason – Plath was not politically active, but her writing is filled with biting commentary on the obstacles women face, particularly ambitious women like herself.

Plath thought a lot about why she might have depression. Brain chemistry models were brewing in clinical science, but not yet among the wider public. Plath pointed, in loosely Freudian ways, to troubles in her childhood. Whatever her childhood or brain chemistry may have wrought, though, her writing makes clear that sexist society was a part of her unhappiness. Again, the politics and the sickness can be neither separated, nor reduced one to the other.

The stories of Mingus and Plath raise wider points about adversity, inequality, and depression. Counting depressions may be hard, but it is a necessary effort. As with any illness, we need to know who is at greatest risk for it, and why. This is one reason why the efforts to manualize depression matter, as fraught as they have been. Biological causes of depression are a shiny object in research. And inquiry into biological causes is important. But how much we know about social factors is often overlooked, and may be more certain than biological research right now. That adversity in life increases risk of depression is not controversial among experts.[63]

Gender has received a lot of attention controversy. More women are diagnosed with depression than men. [64] This is true cross-culturally. One study showed this by comparing rates across 15 countries, spanning every continent with permanent human settlements.[65]

The reasons for the gender difference are less clear. The range of explanations is dizzying.[66] One has been innate biology. Does anything in the physiology of sex differences, such as hormonal differences, make women more prone to depressive illness? Given the long and dismal history of medicine making a pathology out of having a female body, such accounts deserve skepticism. Caution, though, is not the same as treating all inquiry on the subject taboo, and research in this area continues.[67] Some life events that have been associated with depression can only happen with female anatomy, including childbirth and menopause. But if biology does have a role, it is not likely to be the only factor.

Sexist society may be more at fault. Disadvantages and adverse events women face may cause more depression. It's complicated because the stressors men and women face often differ. Men, for example, have more non-sexual assaults, injuries, car accidents, muggings, property crimes, and hospitalizing illnesses. Women experience more sexual assault and domestic violence, tend to have lower earnings, and less choice over when to do household tasks that have to be done repeatedly.[68] Divorce increases mental health problems for both sexes, but for different reasons. For men, divorce is often felt as a loss of social support, whereas for women it often means financial hardship.

Some question whether women really do get depressed more. Are clinicians simply more inclined to see depression in women than in men?[69] Or are different help-seeking patterns at work? Are women just more inclined to get help, because admitting to depressive affect is more acceptable for women? Or perhaps men's depression looks different – more apt to be combined with alcohol use, or more marked by irritability, for example. This would lead to an under-counting of male depression. This raises the same question the cross-cultural study of depression does – how much can the presentation of illness differ before you conclude you are seeing a different ailment?

Japan is one of the few countries where depressed men outnumber women. The difference is slight, but the illness is also regarded culturally as a male one. Similar puzzles appear – some Japanese psychiatrists think the difference is caused by men's higher level of social stress, while others believe women's lower status has led to an under-counting of female depression.[70]

Women outweigh in accounts of depression, and men in accounts of melancholia.[71] This reflects a change in cultural imagery, but may not reflect a real change in illness. In the eras of melancholia, women may also have been under-counted because their work was not valued enough for their sadness to warrant the sick role. The glamour of the melancholic male, the association with genius, has not been granted to the depressive woman.[72]

Biological explanations dominated psychiatry in the early twentieth century, when the profession was mostly men. Doctors sought the answer in hormones. The search for more social explanations followed the rise of second-wave feminism and focused on the hardships women face.

A definitive explanation for the gender ratio may not exist, at least now, and a search for a single one may be misguided. And social identities – such as class, sex, and race – are not in isolation from each other.[73] Let's look at some of the other social categories, and then return to gender.

Stressful events increase risk of depression, and disadvantaged groups are more prone to depression.[74] Numerous examples show both points. Abuse in childhood leads to likelihood of depression later in life.[75] Children of deployed soldiers experience more depression.[76] Following terrorist attacks, risks of major depression rise, and they rise higher among direct victims than in the general population of the area attacked.[77] Depression is a high risk for children who suffer disability and physical illness.[78] Political exiles, refugees, and civilian victims of war-time sexual violence all face increased risk for depression.[79] A history of depression in adolescence increases vulnerability to stressful events in early adulthood.[80]

A link between adversity and depression may seem intuitively obvious. But in the age of biological psychiatry, many have said depression was mainly a neurochemical process, or the result of genes. The biology matters, but excluding social forces is factually wrong.

Consider class.[81] Burton thought that lower social class caused depression in seventeenth-century England. He did not give evidence, but we have it now. Poverty and other adversity in lower social classes lead to higher rates of depression. This is true for several other mental illnesses, including schizophrenia. Again, this also might seem an intuitive point – why *wouldn't* economic hardship lead to depression? Oddly, though, it is also counter-intuitive. In a talk on depression, Andrew Solomon recalled telling his editor at the *New Yorker* about how much depression he had found among poor people. His editor was skeptical, because he had never heard this before, to which Solomon replied, yes, that is what makes it news.[82] I wonder if his editor's surprise showed more than lack of knowledge, though. The proportionality criterion disqualifies large numbers of people from being easily seen as clinically depressed. After all, poor people have reason for depressed mood; should this really be called illness? This is the trouble with the proportionality criterion. Not all people facing adversity, even extreme adversity, get clinical depression. The opposite is true. Only a small fraction of people in severe adversity do.[83] We know this logic of causation from other examples: smoking makes you more likely to get lung cancer, but does not guarantee that you will, nor does refraining from smoking guarantee that you will not. But the logic gets murky in depression because of the blurry border between illness state and normal human emotion. Lung cancer is not part of the universal range of human experience. You either have it or you do not. You do not get it for a few days before it passes on its own.

Solomon's editor may have been surprised, but the case for a link between lower social class and depression has been building at least since the 1970s. People have debated the direction of the causation – is the lower social class causing the depression, or is depression the reason for the social class? While both may contribute, a lot of evidence shows that lower social class is a factor in causing depression.[84] People of lower social class often have more severely stressful life events. They also have more vulnerabilities, such as social isolation, that worsen the impact of the stressful events.[85] The prognosis for people of lower social class with depression is also poorer.[86] Higher education level offers some protection against depression, and even every additional year of education lowers the risk.[87] Poorer people have less chance to extend their education.

Race and ethnicity also matter, though the research results vary. Early research on Black Americans found lower rates of depression than in White Americans.[88] But clinician bias has under-diagnosed depression and over-diagnosed schizophrenia in Black people,[89] who seem less likely to get a "quiet" diagnosis like depression. Recent work has found that depression rates may be higher for Black people.[90] Reasons included presence of life-threatening diseases, absence of health coverage, lifestyle (smoking and exercise), and higher rates of unemployment. The bias in diagnosis can lead to bias in treatment, too. Blacks are less likely to get antidepressants when the severity of depression is equal to that of White patients. Some have also found more depression in Latinos than in Black people. Immigrant Latinos have lower rates of depression than native born ones, but are less likely to seek treatment when they have it.[91] Latinos are also less likely, due to diagnostic discrimination, to get a diagnosis and treatment than White people.[92] Depression rates are also high in Native American communities.[93] Studies of Asian Americans have found varying rates, some studies finding lower rates than among White people, and some finding higher.[94] This may be another area where help-seeking behavior determines the numbers more than true prevalence. None of these are homogeneous groups, including White Americans, but research on variations in depressive illness within these groups are only starting.

LGBT people are at higher risk for depression than straight and cis-sexual (non-transgender) people. LGBT people are twice as likely to report suicidal ideation, and have higher rates of actual attempts.[95] Stressors include discrimination and persecution, higher levels of child abuse, unstable housing, internalized stigma, and the strain of concealing one's identity.[96] LGB people who faced rejecting behavior from their families had eight times higher risk of suicide attempts.[97] (I have omitted the "T" from LGBT when the research does not reference transgender people.) Bisexual people have especially high levels of anxiety and depressive symptoms.[98] LGBT people of color face more jeopardy from depression than White counterparts.[99] Victimization of LGBT people is greatest for young people, who have less choice over their social context and peers. Support provided by high schools can reduce symptoms of mental illness in sexual minorities.[100] Transgender people are also at high risk for depression and suicidality, though the literature on transgender people and depression is not as well-developed as that on LGB people.[101] Transgender people do face alarming risk of victimization, including employment discrimination and violence. The trauma of rejection by their own families is a cause of depression.[102] Peer victimization is high among transgender adolescents, across all ethnic groups, and often precedes suicidal ideation.[103] Transgender people also have to encounter the bigotry that says that their gender identity is not one among many variants, but is itself a mental illness.[104]

Depression is also linked with other chronic diseases, such as diabetes, cancer, and heart disease.[105] As early as 1684, physician Thomas Willis proposed that diabetes came from "sadness or long sorrow."[106] In all three of these cases, the connection appears bi-directional. A severe chronic illness is a major source of stress. Depression also leads to physical inactivity, smoking, failure to take medications, and other behaviors that cause or worsen other chronic illnesses. Depression may also lead to chronic illnesses in more direct ways – by an effect on particular hormones, for example – but this is less clear. In the case of diabetes, class is also a factor, with poverty making co-morbidity more likely.[107] The co-morbidity between depression and the other chronic diseases is high, but not total. Not everyone who has a heart attack, for example, is going to develop symptoms of depression.

To return to gender: many experts say that the reason for the gender ratio is not fully clear.[108] Yet the evidence that adversity is a major risk factor for depression is overwhelming. So is the evidence that women face greater adversity. People who face poverty, marginality, abuse, persecution, discrimination – because of their class, ethnicity or race, nationality, refugee status – are all more likely to suffer from depression. This is well documented and not controversial. Comparative gender studies also show that women are more likely to face poverty, marginality, abuse, persecution, and discrimination. Marriage offers protection against stress more for men than for women.[109] To say that adversity is a major cause of the gender ratio in depression hardly seems a stretch. Adversity also helps to make sense of the consistency of the gender imbalance cross-culturally.[110] The precise makeup of gender roles varies widely, but women's greater adversity is common, globally. The gap between men and women in depression rates seems to be lessening as some progress toward gender equality is achieved.[111] But depression in women has been studied more than in men, and underestimating male depression has its own risks.[112] Regarding depression as a "women's illness" can discourage men from seeking treatment.[113] Depression diagnoses in men are, in any event, rising.[114]

Depression is sometimes called an equal opportunity offender. It is not. No social status is an absolute protection against depression, and the socially privileged can get depression. Nor does social adversity automatically cause depression. The social sources of ill-health are rarely that simple for any sickness, but social position usually matters for ill-health. If you do an internet search on social origins of any sickness, you will likely find good research showing the role of social status. For many illnesses, being from an oppressed, marginalized, or persecuted group increases your chances of getting the illness. AIDS and tuberculosis thrive on poverty, though of course rich people can get them too. There are also diseases of affluence, such as gout. The idea that depression would be different, and have purely biological causes seems wrong, even bizarre.

The critic Ann Cvetkovich uses the phrase "political depression" to refer to feelings of despair caused by oppression and inequality, or the thwarting of efforts to end them. The concept of political depression highlights the limits of medical models of depression. Political depression is not identical with clinical depression, nor the sole cause of clinical depression, but it cannot be left out of any full reckoning with clinical depression. The power of the concept is in foregrounding the role of social inequalities and persecutions, which can be hidden in a biochemical approach.[115]

But the concept of political depression can complement a medical model, rather than oppose it. Purely medical models may not capture the social and political in depression – they do not for any illness. Seeing this does not banish depression from the medical domain. To return to the example of the current COVID-19 pandemic: the impact of the virus would unquestionably be blunted if we had less unequal societies, better social supports. But would we want to remove COVID-19 from the realm of medicine because it lays bare problems in our social systems? We do not have to choose between a political understanding and a medical understanding, any more than we have to choose between the physical and the psychological.

Looking at depression among Native Americans in Flathead, Montana, anthropologist Theresa DeLeane O'Nell also found a purely medical model wanting. O'Nell said that the DSM concept of depression could not capture the long-term effects of oppression, or local understandings of the roots of suffering.[116] The force of this argument raises a wider question though. How well does the DSM capture *anyone's* depression? When Andreasen said that psychiatrists themselves do not always agree, we may credit her for understatement.

Manualization and its Discontents: The DSM Wars

If new rating scales and new therapies were partly efforts to manualize depression, that effort reached full expression with revisions to
the DSM beginning in the 1970s. A growing sense that psychiatric
diagnosis was flawed haunted the mental health field. Some psychoanalysts avoided diagnoses, seeing them as rigid categories that miss the
individuality of the person in pain.[117] Outside of psychoanalysis, Meyer,
even as he promoted the term "depression," worried that *all* psychiatric
diagnoses risked narrowing clinical vision of the totality of the patient's
personality and environment.[118] But what is medical practice without
reliable diagnosis? And did psychiatry have any?

British and American psychiatrists gave different diagnoses when
seeing the same cases on tape.[119] Within America, psychiatrists agreed
on diagnosis of the same patient only about 30 percent of the time.[120]
Most infamously, psychologist David Rosenhan and his research team
pretended to be insane and easily got schizophrenia diagnoses and
mental hospital admissions.[121] Could psychiatrists not even tell the
difference between someone with psychosis and someone pretend-
ing? Rosenhan's study was methodologically weak, perhaps outright
fraudulent.[122] Fraud aside, all Rosenhan showed is that you can feign
illness.[123] Students with unfinished homework have always known this.
But Rosenhan struck at a time when psychiatry was already vulnerable.
An influential antipsychiatry movement, led by people like Thomas
Szasz, claimed that the whole field of psychiatry was a crock, and not
properly a part of medicine.

The crisis of diagnosis shadowed the creation of the third edition
of the DSM. The DSM has gone through several revisions, but the
change between DSM-II and DSM-III was the biggest and had a huge
impact on depression diagnosis. The key figure was Robert Spitzer,
a psychiatrist with psychoanalytic training. Spitzer grew disillusioned
with his own psychoanalyst, who was a follower of Wilhelm Reich.[124]
Reich had written insightful books about character formation and the
psychology of politics early in his career, but later had some flaky ideas,
and was a fringe figure in psychoanalysis by the time Spitzer was in
analysis. Spitzer would later seek to purge the DSM of psychoanalytic
assumptions. But more, he wanted a manual with no speculation about

the causes of mental disorders, one that stuck to symptoms everyone could observe.

The creation of the DSM-III has been widely criticized.[125] The authors hoped to find what psychiatrists could agree upon, or at least to avoid controversial moves that would alienate many. The meetings, though, were chaotic affairs where often the loudest voices won out, not necessarily the ones with the most scientific merit.[126] The chaos and politics of the process are unfortunate. A more orderly process might not have yielded a better manual, though, because available knowledge was not conclusive enough.

Psychoanalysts and Meyerians may have been less driven to fit each patient to a label, preferring attention to unique constellations of suffering. But insurance companies were less interested in unique constellations of suffering. The use of insurance to cover out-patient psychiatric treatment was growing in the 1970s.[127] To provide payment, the companies wanted a specific diagnosis. Spitzer was there to help. He hoped to make diagnosis uniform, by highlighting what clinicians agreed on.

In earlier work, Spitzer had already expanded the criteria for depression.[128] As he and his co-workers revised the DSM, they took the many types of depressive illness then in use, and put many of them in a single category. They wanted a category big enough to catch relapses, but did not want every slump in life to be called depression.[129] The result was Major Depressive Disorder. DSM-III also used the term "dysthymia" (more recently renamed "Persistent Depressive Disorder") for milder depression of long duration. According to DSM-III, if you had dysthymia, and then went through an acute episode of major depression, you had "double depression."

In 1987, DSM-III was updated to DSM-IIIR, with new changes for depression. In DSM-IIIR, for the first time, depressed mood was not a required symptom. A patient would need a number of symptoms, over a certain duration, but depressed mood was not a necessary one. If it were absent, "loss of interest" would have to be present.[130] This may seem like an odd move – what is "depression" without depressed mood? Whether the change was warranted or not, it had precedent in the old idea of masked depression.

DSM-III's architects hoped to purge the manual of "theory," which mostly meant omitting causal claims about illnesses when none were proven. Intended neutrality, though, often ends up favoring one side in practice. Psychiatrist Allen Frances, who supervised the revisions for DSM-IV and is no opponent of biological psychiatry, believes that DSM-III's emphasis on surface symptoms elevated the status of biological approaches.[131]

The manual was in for still more controversy with DSM-5, and it was not about the switch from Roman to Arabic numbers in the title. Published in 2013 after a decade of work, DSM-5 removed the "bereavement exclusion" from depression diagnosis. The bereavement exclusion meant that if you had recently lost a loved one, you would not get a depression diagnosis, even if you met the diagnostic criteria. In DSM-5, a grieving person would not be excluded from the diagnosis on the grounds that their reaction was normal. The "normal" mourning period given in DSM-IV was already just two months.[132]

Even before the DSM-5 came out, many worried about ending the bereavement exclusion.[133] Frances warned of medicalizing a normal part of life, uprooting "the sacred mourning rites that have survived for millenniums."[134] But others thought that the similarities between bereavement and other stressors were good reasons to get rid of the exclusion – depression was depression, even if a clear life event caused it.[135] The change in DSM-5, in any event, did not allow a depression diagnosis just because a person was grieving and sad. All other criteria for Major Depressive Disorder (MDD) had to be met.[136]

How much weight life events should have, and what makes a response to them normal or sick, is not a dilemma that springs from the DSM or even modern psychiatry. It has been an enduring question about depressive illness. When someone has suicidality, or severe lethargy and despair for years on end, it seems an easy call to say the person should get a diagnosis and a treatment, even if a clear event caused it. But an objective measure for how far short of these extremes disqualifies an illness label does not exist.[137] The length of proper mourning varies culturally and within cultures.[138] In earlier times, this might have been decided on an individual basis, in the encounter between physician and patient. Individual judgment, though, cannot be manualized.

Could depressions *without* a clear cause in life events be separately manualized? A diverse and impressive group of experts, including historians and psychiatrists – Spitzer among them – said yes, and wrote an article calling for its inclusion in DSM-5 as a separate disorder, by the name . . . melancholia.[139] They argued that this was a disease known since antiquity, branded by despondency, guilt, and not caused by a known life event. Melancholia, they said, also had known and measurable biological features, including reduced deep sleep and REM time; increased presence of cortisol, a stress hormone; and more responsiveness to ECT and tricyclics, and less responsiveness to placebos, SSRIs, and CBT. The hope was to make at least one form of depression in DSM-V a diagnosis with a biological basis. The effort was unsuccessful. In DSM-5, specifiers can be added to MDD, so you can diagnose, for example, depression with anxious distress, or depression with psychotic features. Depression with melancholic features is one of the specifiers. But melancholia is not listed as a distinct disorder.

The champions of including melancholia separately may well have identified a distinct illness. But their appeal to its long history treated "melancholia" as a stable category, unchanged over the centuries. It was not. Many older descriptions of melancholia featured delusion far more than the description they advocated. More importantly, melancholia had not been used at all times exclusively to refer either to severe or endogenous depression.

Some critiques of the DSM are antipsychiatric screeds by people who would prefer not to have any diagnostic labels at all – or, for that matter, any psychiatry. Others have a lot of merit. The DSM is fraught and imperfect. The problem, though, is not that the DSM comes from social processes. Scientific documents always have a social context, and scientific truth is always what is closest to a consensus among experts. DSM-III, though, did not represent a true consensus, but the leanings of a subset of the authors. Some good did come out of Spitzer's revolution. For example, he insisted that "subjective distress" should be required before calling anything an illness. This helped to remove gay sexuality from psychiatric diagnosis.[140]

Andreasen, who advocated for biological psychiatry, was an early, though not uncritical, proponent of DSM-III.[141] About a quarter of a century later, she lamented one result of it – lack of attention to the whole patient. Detailed portrayal of the whole clinical picture, she said, was replaced by labels, having a dehumanizing effect on psychiatry.[142] This result was exactly what Meyer, and many psycho-analysts, would have predicted. They were afraid that over-emphasis on diagnostic labels would hide the depth and complexity of the individual patient.

Surely psychiatry can find a middle ground between aversion to diagnosis and reducing patients to labels from symptom checklists.

Some look at the shifting criteria in the various editions of DSM and conclude that psychiatric diagnosis, including of depression, has no meaning. A cognitive therapist could point out the errors in this reasoning: all-or-nothing thinking, filtering out the positive, magnification. The DSM, and its process of creation, have been flawed. Mental health professionals work with imprecise knowledge. Psychiatric diagnoses often lack the precision doctors can produce for other areas of medicine. This does not mean that psychiatric diagnosis has no meaning or value at all.

So, Why So Much Depression?

Explaining rising diagnosis rates of depression, I have stressed, is a fraught project. I am going to hazard what I think is a plausible model anyway. It envisions an upward spiral, in which better detection and diagnostic drift reinforce one another, powered by wider political and cultural changes.

True prevalence is unlikely to be the main culprit, at least in a straightforward way. Some who argue for a rise in true prevalence point to depressing conditions in the world, rapid changes in social roles or expectations, or increased social isolation (due, say, to the internet), or even a worsening human diet.[143] It's important to draw attention to social factors contributing to ill-health, but these theories call to mind how much early twentieth-century social science also attributed apparent rising rates of mental illness to rapid social change and alienation. The illness labels used were neurasthenia, or hysteria, or simply "nerves."[144] While the world we live in is upsetting, it is not obviously more fertile for mental illness than the world of the first half of the twentieth century.

The upward spiral I envision works like this: over the course of the early twentieth century, the growth of out-patient psychiatry led to an increase in the number of people being treated for depressive illness. No longer was treatment reserved for the most severe depressive cases. The growing interest in depression led more people, both professional and lay, to learn to label problems as depression, which was a growing idiom of distress *before* the advent of antidepressants. That is part of the reason why some medications came to be called antidepressants at all. The medications, though, provided new incentives for multiple actors – pharmaceutical companies, doctors, patients, and patients' families – to identify cases of depression. The doctors, the patients, and their families had a new hope for effective and relatively safe treatment. People would not have to contemplate ECT, a treatment that scared many, both because of sensationalist media representations, but also because of realistic appraisals of its risks. Drug companies stood to make a lot of money, which they did.

A puzzle remains. The antidepressants came around the same time drugs for anxiety such as Miltown were becoming popular, more popular than antidepressants. Miltown and related drugs were also used for depression, but they primarily addressed anxiety. The earlier post-World War II society was *named* an age of anxiety.[145] Why first an age of anxiety, and why did it give way to an age of depression?

Sociologist Allan Horwitz cites growing concerns about the addictiveness of the tranquilizers by the 1970s.[146] Horwitz argues, though, that the increased demand for specific diagnoses was the main driver of the rise of depression, anxiety being more a state of being than a specific illness. But Major Depressive Disorder is not a highly specific diagnosis. As Horwitz points out, MDD captured so much stress-related affliction because it covered a large range of symptoms and experiences. A stronger explanation might draw not only on changes in psychiatry, or the pharmaceutical industry, but also on larger cultural shifts.

We need to ask two questions. First, how do the intimately-related emotions of anxiety and depression differ? Anxiety is an expectation of danger to come. Depression is a sense of loss already felt. The second question is, what was changing in the 1970s? The 1970s are often noted as a time marked by two large shifts. They bear names I use with reluctance. Both are too often used without precise definition, or used too casually. I think they may have usefulness here, however. They are neo-liberalism, and post-modernity.

Neo-liberalism is the end of the political and economic order of the post-World War II welfare state. The shifts include reduction of public services and social benefits in favor of government austerity, reduced taxes on the economic elite, and attacks on organized labor unions that weakened them. Neo-liberalism is hyper-individualistic, as expressed in Margaret Thatcher's slogan that society does not exist, only individuals and families. In practice, it has caused widening inequality, prosperity steadily shifting up to the already-wealthy. Geographer David Harvey points out that this upward shift in wealth distribution is widely documented, but that it is less often asked whether that was the purpose of the policies from the start.[147]

Post-modernity has meant a lot of things, across different domains. In knowledge production, it refers to weakened faith in scientific certainties, declining belief in the power of rationality to improve governance, a growing belief that knowledge claims reflect power and narrative structures more than objective truths, and attention to ways the instability of language undermines coherence.[148]

Progress was easier to believe in during the immediate postwar period. Wealth was distributed unevenly, but the growth of the middle class in industrialized countries, ambitious social welfare projects, and the Civil Rights movement held some promise for future shared prosperity. Much of the underdeveloped world was newly independent and holding great expectations for rapid development. Science and technology were in high regard, even idealized, and seemed to promise a better world. The state, with all its flaws, was seen as an agent of possible positive change, even to people of vastly different ideological views. Anxiety, though, was understandable. The Cold War and its weaponry threatened all of human life. Knowledge of the environmental costs of economic development was growing. And the contrast between the promise of prosperity for all and the reality of deep social divisions spawned serious and often violent conflict.

Neo-liberalism, post-modernity, and clinical depression share something: a lack of hope. While the worst fears of the age of anxiety were not realized, by the 1970s, faith in social progress had declined. Disillusionment with the state was growing. In the hyper-individualism of neo-liberalism, the only good was the economic good of the individual household – even as workers' wages entered a long period of stagnation. Nations in the developing world were pressured into Structural Adjustment Programs, where they had to shrink the public sector to receive foreign aid. This was guided by the ideology that a large public sector hindered economic growth. The result of these programs was reduced social services, such as health care. The promised economic growth was harder to find.

Projects for collective betterment came increasingly to draw collective sighs of resignation. The post-modern critique of "grand narratives" was inches from a skepticism toward grand social aspirations. As a historian of psychiatry, I have found Michel Foucault's explorations of the relations of power and knowledge insightful, even though many have found empirical flaws in his work. But I doubt Foucault, or any other thinker considered post-modern, has filled many with soaring hope for collective betterment. Meanwhile, neo-liberalism held out no collective good at all, only private. And depression is an illness of private despair and frayed social ties.

In neoliberal culture, according to one analysis, people don't see themselves as members of opposing classes – which, for exploited classes, at least has the virtue of fostering solidarity. Instead, everyone is an entrepreneur of the self, and for the self. Relentless internal pressure for self-improvement ensues, combined with constant calls to think positively, and root out negative thoughts. We attend "Countless self-management workshops, motivational retreats and seminars on personality or mental training [that] promise boundless self-optimization and heightened efficiency . . ."[149] Under this "auto-exploitation," rather than addressing their frustrations toward the social system, people "are turning their aggression *against themselves*."[150] Anger turned inward.

Whether these aspects of the wider social context directly cause mental illness is hard to show. Little evidence shows that the total amount of mental illness at any time in history is greater than at other times. But cultural trends and moods influence how people interpret the mental distress they feel. While we have seen many definitions of depression, one hallmark that recurs is the conviction that things are not only bad, but will not get better – and indeed, *cannot* get better. Post-modernism and neo-liberalism told us much the same.

Speculation about the moods of entire eras and their relation to individual emotional states is risky. Like many historians, I prefer claims that can be plainly documented. But perhaps this reluctance to make large claims is also part of our current malaise – to use Jimmy Carter's word.

Frances, who led the creation of DSM-IV, and many others, believe it is too easy to get a depression diagnosis now. Horwitz and Jerome Wakefield believe we are jeopardized by a "loss of sadness," that normal human sorrow has been transformed into a medical condition.[151] Frances concedes that as many as one third of the people with severe depression get no treatment at all, but worries that the DSM allows the depression label to be passed out like chewing gum to anyone who feels bad for two weeks after something bad has happened. For people with mild and passing symptoms, he says, SSRIs are expensive and possible harmful placebos.[152] Like Ifemelu in Adichie's *Americanah*, critics like this worry we are too quick to medicalize distress. They have a point.

But Adichie's scenario has power in part because her aunt Uju also has a point. Ifemelu was facing real adversity, and she did get better without doctors. She, or others, might not have. Plath was also facing real adversity. She might have fared better with more psychiatric treatment.

When we worry about the medicalization of sadness, we also have to remember that the full spectrum of emotions is felt by people who get successful treatment for depression, whether the treatment is psychotherapy, drugs, or ECT. The common and glib nickname for antidepressants as "happy pills" is inaccurate, and demeaning to those with depression. Treatments can free people from needless suffering, but by themselves they can't make anyone happy. If you have lost your job or someone you loved, you will still feel sad. If you are not also in clinical depression, the sadness may not be so desperate.

Most accounts of the rise of depression diagnosis are laments. The upside – more people getting treatment – deserves as much attention. Perhaps people who might earlier have identified their problems as "nerves," or "neurasthenia," or simply low spirits and lethargy, now call it depression. If they are now calling it depression and getting a treatment that helps, is that such a problem?

But this essay on depression's expansion has so far touched only lightly on a major factor. It concerns a certain pill.

The Drug That Named an Era

By the 1980s, the cultural power of biological psychiatry was ascending. The scientific advances were modest in comparison. Fluoxetine – Prozac – was rolled out with fanfare, but the older antidepressants, the MAOIs and tricyclics, had been around since the 1950s, and had not brought an "antidepressant era." The SSRIs were not more effective than earlier drugs. Many hoped the SSRIs would have fewer or milder adverse effects, but they certainly turned out to have bad effects of their own. The promotion of the SSRIs was well-timed, though. It followed decades of growing clinical attention to depression, somewhat fewer decades of other antidepressants, a flurry of research interest in depression in the 1970s, and the DSM-III's deletion of psychoanalytic influence.

People who take antidepressants, we began to hear, were no different from people with diabetes, who need to take insulin every day. The laudable goal was to show that depression was not a failure of will or a character flaw. At least since Timothy Bright in the Renaissance, people have thought that treating depressive illness as physical might lessen stigma. And in modernity, probably more than in the Renaissance, "physical" illness equated with "real" disease.

The SSRIs changed not just psychiatric treatment, but popular conceptions of illness, and even of the self and the nature of the body. These changes wrought by the SSRIs outstripped any claim they had to clinical advance. The cultural impact was deep, dramatic, and global.

Fluoxetine, and the serotonin it acts on, were unknown to Hippocrates, Rufus of Ephesus, Galen, Hildegard of Bingen, Marsilio Ficino, Martin Luther, Paracelsus, Robert Burton, Philippe Pinel, Emil Kraepelin, Karl Abraham, Sigmund Freud, Melanie Klein, Adolf Meyer, Abraham Myerson, and Edith Jacobson. Now millions of people swallow it worldwide, every day. An era of history received a commercial brand name: Prozac.

5

"Just Chemical"

"The very murkiness surrounding depression – involving as it does both a biological and a psychological component – has made it a . . . whipping boy of the ongoing nature/nurture debate . . . It has become a magnet for the worst projections of both our Puritan heritage and our pill-happy contemporary moment, with the unfortunate result being that it is both underdiagnosed and overmedicalized."

– Daphne Merkin[1]

"Nor do I deny that sometimes such afflictions are helped by the remedies of physicians or even cured. But those who attribute such mental afflictions to natural causes since they are cured by medicine, do not know the power of Satan and that God is more powerful than demons."

– Martin Luther[2]

Imbalance

Virginia Woolf famously wrote that "On or about December 1910, human character changed."[3] No doubt she was exaggerating for literary effect. Or maybe she just had the date wrong. Maybe human character changed on or about December 1987, when the United States Food and Drug Administration (FDA) allowed Eli Lilly to put Prozac on the

American market. In the decades since, millions of people, all over the planet, began taking drugs unimaginable 80 years ago.

Suddenly, the phrase "chemical imbalance" flooded talk about depression. Drug companies were allowed direct-to-consumer advertising in the United States in 1985, two years before Prozac hit the market. The drug company Pfizer soon promoted Zoloft as correcting a "chemical imbalance."[4] Companies liked this approach, as a way to cast depression as a "real" illness – meaning, one requiring medicine. Doctors sometimes found it a handy way to convince their patients to take a medicine. Patients adopted it as well – it became an "idiom of distress."[5] "Chemical imbalance" was not a phrase that appeared in psychopharmacology textbooks, and it was not a phrase used by most people closely involved with the scientific research. Like Prozac, though, it became a widely swallowed capsule (see figure 7).

When Prozac became a cultural sensation, some started saying that depression was *only* a physical thing. Some doctors told patients: you have a disease, no different from diabetes, you can take a medicine to fix it. The diabetes analogy is a nice one for the drug companies, because it makes the drugs less like antibiotics or aspirin, taken as needed, but something you will need every day, for life. Patients adopted the trope, saying, "I have depression, but it is just chemical," as if to say, do not trouble yourself about my childhood, or get the idea that I have a lot of other problems. Writer Andrew Solomon interviewed many patients with depression, and many of them said their depression was "just chemical." As Solomon countered, though, "Everything about a person is just chemical if one wants to think in those terms."[6] Pointing out the physical is useful when it is not readily seen. For example, psychotherapy is not called a physical treatment, but it definitely changes the brain.[7] (Why wouldn't it?) Describing depression as "chemical" now conceals as much as it reveals. It conceals how limited our knowledge of the chemistry of depression is, and it conceals how much we know about what is not strictly chemical.

Sometimes an inexact comparison helps. Imagine you are a college student in a literature course, asked to do an analysis of Woolf's masterpiece, *To the Lighthouse*. You take a week or so and report that the book, composed of ink and paper, is therefore made up of carbon, mixed

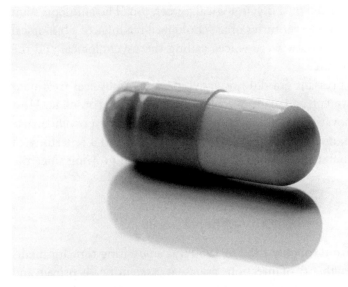

Figure 7 *Prozac: a medicine that named an era. Actress Carrie Fisher, who wrote with wit and courage about mental illness, was buried in an urn fashioned after one of these pills*
Source: Christian Hopewell/Alamy

with some organic and inorganic compounds. You would be technically right. Something would be missing.

Many professionals questioned the "chemical imbalance" trope. They raised concerns about psychological and social factors left out, about how strong the evidence for "imbalance" was, and about the dangers of over-reliance on drugs. And despite the popularity of the trope, patients held to other explanations of depression. Many continue to favor social and psychological explanations, in populations as diverse as Mexican-Americans in the United States and White Britons in London.[8]

The appeal is easy to see, though. Parents would not be blamed. The sick would be released from stigma. People with depression would get the chance at a real illness, because many people think real illnesses need a physical basis. Doctors who had been on the side of biological psychiatry all along were having their moment of cultural triumph.

Melancholia was inherently physical, though few humoralists thought it was *purely* physical, without psychological or social aspects. Psychoanalysts believed in inborn tendencies toward depression, though they insisted on a psychological aspect, too. The antidepressant era was not an end to centuries of psychological readings of a biological process. What *was* new were voices calling the psychological and the social unimportant.

The antidepressant era did not arrive because a physical treatment suddenly showed up and made psychological approaches obsolete. Most of the key innovation in biological psychiatry came when psychoanalysis dominated, not after.[9] Prozac was a late addition to a repertoire of physical treatments for mental illness that had been growing since the 1920s.

Before Antidepressants

The century from roughly 1850 to 1950 was an exciting time for medicine. The germ theory of infectious disease was scientifically proven and popularly accepted. Dramatic improvements in public health, disease prevention, and disease cure followed. Psychiatrists hoped for similar gains, grounded in knowledge of the brain. A flurry of experimentation with physical methods to treat mental illnesses started in the early twentieth century. Growth in knowledge of the brain contributed little to these new treatments. Some were discovered through accident, some were based on faulty premises, and most had serious adverse effects. They were also tested on small samples of patients, without informed consent, in a research culture far removed from ours. But they had the combined effect of raising confidence that mental illnesses could be treated with physical means.[10]

Largely forgotten by the lay public, Malaria Fever Therapy to treat neurosyphilis was pivotal in raising this confidence. In the 1880s, Austrian doctor Julius Wagner-Jauregg had a mentally ill patient who developed a high fever from an infectious disease. When the fever lifted, the symptoms of her mental illness seemed to lift, too. Wagner-Jauregg began to use infectious agents to cause fevers, hoping to find a cure for mental illnesses. In 1917, he succeeded with "general paralysis of the insane," now known to be neurosyphilis. The treatment worked in a significant number of patients. Many who were stuck in asylums could now be cured and released, in an early wave of deinstitutionalization. Wagner-Jauregg was the first psychiatrist to win a Nobel Prize.[11]

More vivid in public memory, though not used much now, was lobotomy.[12] In 1927, Egas Moniz, a Portuguese neurologist, attended a scientific session about monkeys who became subdued after parts of the frontal lobe of their brains had been removed. Moniz wondered if surgery could be used in a similar way to treat symptoms such as agitation in mental illness. Moniz also won a Nobel, but the figure who did the most to promote lobotomy was American neurologist Walter Freeman. Lobotomy was widely used in the mid-twentieth century on thousands of patients. Its abysmal public image is partly deserved. It did serious long-term damage to cognitive abilities. Doctors, as well as patients and their families, often valued it though, because it did relieve symptoms, often in patients who had been struggling with them for years. The damage lobotomy did to cognition was not fully apparent at first. Adverse effects of many psychiatric treatments were often not seen or conceded by the profession when the treatments were new.

One antidepressant drug came well before the modern antidepressant era. Amphetamine was developed by a chemist looking for an allergy medication, in an august tradition of psychiatric treatments created by people who were looking for something else. The stimulant effects of amphetamine were known by the early twentieth century. Myerson, the psychiatrist who wrote about anhedonia, tried amphetamine himself, and found lecturing more enjoyable. During the 1930s he started giving it to depressed patients and thought it worked. Wider clinical opinion held that amphetamine was not useful for severe depression and psychoses, but might help for mild depression. Attention to the adverse effects of amphetamine also took longer to emerge.[13]

A number of new treatments for psychosis were invented in the 1920s and 1930s. Swiss psychiatrist Jacob Klaesi developed prolonged sleep therapy. Drugs would keep patients asleep for days at a time, and they would have some remission of symptoms when finally awake. Shortly after, several treatments grouped as "shock therapies" were also developed for psychosis, though why they all were grouped together, and why they were all "shock" treatments, was a little fuzzy. One was Insulin Coma Therapy, perhaps best known now because of its depiction in the film *A Beautiful Mind*, as a treatment for the schizophrenia of mathematician John Nash. The treatment was the invention of Manfred Sakel, a Viennese psychiatrist. Sakel used insulin to cause comas in psychotic patients, and found their symptoms dispelled on their revival. Whether Insulin Coma Therapy was effective, and if so how, have both been controversial, but it did became widely used. Around the same time, some thought that schizophrenia and epilepsy were antagonistic – if you had one, you would be unlikely to have the other. Hungarian psychiatrist Ladislas Meduna wondered, then, if inducing seizures could reverse schizophrenia. This was the idea behind convulsive therapy. In its early years, the seizures were caused by a chemical the patient would drink. Schizophrenia and epilepsy are no longer considered antagonistic, but remarkably, the treatment worked anyway. Perhaps as strange, convulsive therapy came not to be used mainly for psychosis at all, but for mood disorders. Chemical Convulsive Therapy also became widely used. Doctors treating chronic mental patients were eager to try new treatments that seemed to work, especially as mental hospitals became ever more over-crowded. Insulin Coma Therapy and Chemical Convulsive Therapy both had serious drawbacks, though. Chemical Convulsive Therapy was detested by patients, who often felt extreme dread in the time between taking the dose and the onset of the seizure. Electroconvulsive therapy, ECT, came as an alternative. This much-feared therapy, one of the most dreaded in medicine, came from the search for a less frightening way to cause convulsions.[14]

ECT is the main physical treatment for mental illness from the first half of the twentieth century that is still widely used. Many psychiatrists think it is not only the most powerful treatment for depression, but the most effective treatment in all of psychiatry. It causes convulsions in the patient by running electricity through the brain. Why the convulsions work on mood disorders remains mysterious. In the early years, doctors gave a form of ECT (now called "unmodified"), without anesthesia for the pain of the electricity, or muscle relaxants, which keep the body from going into a full convulsion. Unmodified ECT was horrible. The modifications were added soon after ECT was invented, but took time to become the standard of care, as they are now.

The meaning of the history of ECT is hotly contested because the treatment itself is. Critics of ECT often refer darkly to its origins in fascist Italy, and how one of its creators, Lucio Bini, got the idea for it while watching pigs being stunned with electricity in a slaughterhouse. ECT's history has grim aspects, and reasonable concerns about its adverse effects continue, but these arguments about its origins are misleading. The Italian psychiatrists who invented ECT, Ugo Cerletti and Bini, were not fascists. Lothar Kalinowsky, the member of their team who did the most to promote ECT's spread to other countries, was a Jew who fled fascism. The slaughterhouse is a sensational image, but the use of electricity was motivated not by the desire to slaughter anyone, but to find a more tolerable way to cause the seizures.

Nearly every aspect of ECT's history has had vastly different readings. When Cerletti and his team tried it on the first patient, a vagrant person with psychosis who was brought to them by the police in Rome, he cried out something like "Not another one! It's murder!" after the first jolt of electricity. Some ECT advocates have considered Cerletti's decision to go ahead with another jolt a sign of his bravery, while ECT critics have seen it as a cruel example of doctors not listening to patients. The aftermath was also ambiguous. The patient's symptoms cleared up after the treatment, but he relapsed soon after. This is not surprising from our current perspective. ECT rarely brings a permanent cure of any mental illness, and a short course of it is less effective in reducing symptoms than one that goes on for several weeks.

ECT use followed a curve of rise, decline, and rise again. It spread rapidly in the industrialized world during the 1940s and 1950s, and into parts of the non-industrialized world. Because the reason it works was unknown, it was tried on many mental illnesses. It was also used on at least one thing we no longer consider an illness, homosexuality. Not surprisingly, from our current perspective, it did not change anyone's sexuality, and gay people subjected to it were traumatized, contributing to ECT's poor public image. ECT was also used in many mental hospitals to discipline patients – a stereotype of ECT that has origins in reality.

ECT use declined in the 1960s and 1970s. The first antipsychotics and antidepressants provided alternatives. Distrust of psychiatry was growing, partly because of terrible conditions in mental hospitals. The distrust reached its strongest form in the antipsychiatry movement, which saw the whole profession as oppressive. ECT's abuses became the movement's prime exhibit. The fear of ECT as a tool of social control was made vivid in the novel and film *One Flew Over the Cuckoo's*

Nest. A lively, non-conformist individual ends up in a mental hospital, seeking to avoid prison. ECT is used to discipline the inmates, including him. He gets unmodified ECT; the audience sees him strapped unwillingly to a table, screaming and writhing. At the end of the story he gets a punitive lobotomy. Perhaps no other fictional story in history has such a powerful association with a medical treatment. I teach a history unit for psychiatry residents at University Hospitals of Cleveland. Each year, I ask if their patients react with panicked associations to *Cuckoo's Nest* when ECT is offered to them. Every year, most of the residents say yes, even their younger patients, though the film was released 45 years ago. ECT *was* widely used to discipline patients in mental hospitals. Even when used for more purely therapeutic purposes, in its early decades, many hospitals gave unmodified ECT. The depiction in the film was not pure fantasy for the time it is set, in the early 1960s. The grim aspects of ECT's history should not be whitewashed.

By the late 1970s, psychiatrists saw that many people, especially with severe depression, might not be helped by antidepressants and psychotherapy. By this time, ECT was mostly used for mood disorders, and it got another look. Its use has grown since the early 1980s, though it is still mainly used for a minority, when other treatments have failed.

Early psychoanalytic response to ECT was mixed. Few analysts doubted its efficacy. The clinical results were too dramatic. Some worried about brain damage, and some even thought ECT use showed an unconscious sadism toward the patient. But a number of analysts used ECT, and some valued it as a way to get the patient well enough for dynamic therapy to be viable. Analysts tried to find a psychological reason why it worked. Many thought the mentally ill suffered because of unconscious attacks from a punitive conscience – anger turned inward – and that the punishment of the ECT served as a substitute. This theory filtered down to some patients. Sylvia Plath, one of the most famous ECT patients, wrote in her journals after an ECT treatment, "Why, after the 'amazingly short' three or so shock treatments did I rocket uphill? Why did I feel I needed to be punished, to punish myself."[15] In her novel *The Bell Jar*, the narrator, Esther Greenwood comments after an ECT treatment: "I wondered what terrible thing it was that I had done."[16] In the late 1950s, researchers showed the current had to be strong enough to cause convulsions for ECT to work. This probably undercut the theory that the therapy worked because it was punitive because it was hard to see why shocks would not seem punitive if they did not cause convulsions.

Clinicians and patients have both seen ECT's powerful therapeutic efficacy throughout its 60-year history. Most of the treatment's many critics concede it. In recent decades a growing number of people – both clinicians and patients – have written about its therapeutic and even life-saving power. Controversy remains, however, about adverse effects, especially memory loss. ECT usually causes some short-term loss of memories of events near the treatment, which are often recovered. Some patients, though, have long-term and permanent memory loss, which can be traumatic. Memoirs of ECT by patients, even many who valued the treatment, are filled with mourning of memory loss. The scientific literature on ECT and memory loss is mountainous, but inconclusive. The extent of the risk of permanent memory loss remains unsettled. It would be good to know this if you were considering having this treatment. ECT's proponents complain about the treatment being unfairly demonized. Many critics have indeed made unfair arguments, and have refused to concede the therapeutic benefits. But, many proponents have also idealized ECT, downplaying both sordid aspects of its history and the chance of serious side effects.

The physical treatments for mental illness from the 1920s and 1930s formed a precedent, but most of them did not last. More durable treatments came in the decades that followed. In 1949, Australian doctor John Cade showed the efficacy of lithium to treat bipolar disorder, though it did not become widely used until the 1970s. In the 1950s, the first of the drugs now called antipsychotics and antidepressants were invented. Antidepressant medication's origins lie partly in the antipsychotic drugs. But the antipsychotic drugs themselves came from a quest to treat other medical problems.

Henri Laborit, a French surgeon, wanted to reduce postsurgical shock. He thought the shock resembled symptoms of allergic reactions and hoped allergy drugs could help. The company Rhône-Poulenc had been developing a group of antihistamines and gave some to Laborit. The drugs made the patients less anxious about the surgery. This led to the creation of chlorpromazine, the first drug called an antipsychotic, though non-Western medical traditions had long made use of plants with similar chemical makeup to treat mental distress. Nathan Kline thought chlorpromazine worked by reducing "psychic energy" and reduced need for "defense against unacceptable urges and impulses."[17]

The minor tranquilizers, which were cultural sensations the way Prozac would be decades later, came about in a similar way. No one was looking for one. A physician named Frank Berger wanted a muscle relaxant, and developed meprobomate, and found it was more calming than sedating. It was sold as Miltown.[18]

These treatments, and their histories, have several things in common that were repeated with the antidepressants developed since the 1950s. They rarely *cured* any mental illness, though they relieved symptoms.[19] The psychiatric profession greeted them with excitement, because of the hope to treat terrible chronic illnesses, but it was often excessive. In several cases, the treatments were valued at first because they seemed safer than earlier treatments. In most cases, serious adverse effects became known only after years passed. Chlorpromazine, for example, causes a permanent movement disorder called Tardive Dyskinesia, an effect psychiatry was slow to concede.[20]

Adverse effects are common in medicine. Deciding whether the effects are worth it requires complex weighing of risks and benefits. The severity of the adverse effects, their likelihood, the severity of the illness, and the likely efficacy of the treatment all come in to play. The severity of an illness or an adverse effect in an individual can sometimes be hard to judge. Likelihood of an adverse effect and likelihood of improvement from the treatment are matters for the study of populations, and the data are often less conclusive than we would like.

Enter the Antidepressants

A new model of depression emerged starting in the 1950s. Depression was related to the available supply of certain neurotransmitters – chemicals that convey messages between neurons, including neurons in the brain. The summary of this story is as follows: New drugs, meant originally for other problems, seemed to influence mood. People groping for treatments for other illnesses found what they called anti-depressants in their hands instead. These chance observations of mood changes, from a tuberculosis medication and one for schizophrenia, set much of the direction of research on depression for decades. The new drugs seemed to increase the availability of particular neurotransmitters in the brain. Perhaps, the new theory held, the cause of the depression was a low supply of the neurotransmitters.[21] Some of the neurotransmitters belong to a group called catecholamines, and these got a lot of attention in the early science – in a "catecholamine hypothesis" of depression. The sequence matters – observations that the drugs influenced mood came before a grasp of what they did in the body.[22]

The most relevant neurotransmitters in the treatment of depression are norepinephrine, dopamine, and serotonin, all part of a group called monoamines. (Histamine and melatonin are also monoamines.) Monoamines, and other neurotransmitters, are released from the sending neuron into a space called the synaptic cleft. There, they send their signal by interacting with receptors on the receiving neuron. Once the signaling is done, the neurotransmitters are removed from the synaptic cleft (see figure 8). One way they are removed is through *reuptake*, in which neurotransmitters are re-absorbed into the receiving neuron. The more reuptake, the less neurotransmitter is left on the synaptic cleft. Once monoamines are re-absorbed, they can be used again, or they can be *broken down* by an enzyme called monoamine oxidase, the second way they can be removed. The action of monoamine oxidase and the reuptake both influence the level of the neurotransmitters.

The action of the enzyme to break down the neurotransmitters, and the reuptake of them, are both normal, natural processes in healthy brains. But, the emerging theory held, if those processes could be inhibited in people with depression, perhaps the depression would lift. Monoamine oxidase inhibitors (MAOIs) deter the enzyme. Most other antidepressants, including the tricyclics and the selective serotonin reuptake inhibitors (SSRIs), inhibit reuptake.

The MAOIs grew out of tuberculosis treatment. TB patients on iproniazid, a medication from the company Hoffmann-LaRoche, felt upbeat, even euphoric. Some were dancing in the wards, and the drug did not even work all that well for TB. Iproniazid was the first MAOI. Hoffmann-LaRoche was not looking for a mood drug and did not pay much attention.[23] A number of psychiatric researchers did, though.

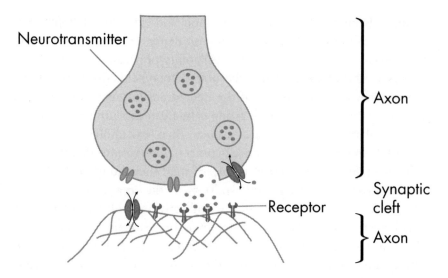

Figure 8   *This schematic gives an idea of how neurotransmitters convey messages
between the brain's neurons*
Source: Adapted from "Schematic of a Synapse" by Thomas Splettstoesser:
https://commons.wikimedia.org/wiki/File:SynapseSchematic_en.svg

Nathan Kline, who went on to treat Rafael Osheroff, Mark Rothko, and
many other patients, was one of them.[24]

Kline was sympathetic to both psychoanalytic and physical
approaches, and was working with a psychoanalyst to find a "psychic
energizer." Kline took iproniazid himself and was excited to see that
he needed only three hours of sleep per night. Kline took the idea
of "psychic energy" from the psychodynamic tradition of Freud and
Jung, so this innovation in drug treatment was partly the offspring of
depth psychology.[25] Some credit may be due to Abraham Myerson, too.
Amphetamine is an MAOI, though a weak one.[26]

The MAOIs were and are effective. They were also risky, which
is why they are not used much. Effects include constipation, dizziness, problems urinating, jaundice, and most scary, fatal reactions from
cheese and chocolate.[27] They are not as risky to use now, but it was
natural to look for alternatives then.[28]

The tricyclics came from observation of patients with psychoses.
The antipsychotics were becoming lucrative, and mental hospitals were

over-filled with chronic patients. The Swiss company Geigy hoped one of its compounds might work for schizophrenia. A student of Klaesi's, Ronald Kuhn, was working in Switzerland in the early 1950s, looking for a new drug to induce prolonged sleep therapy.[29] His hospital could not afford enough chlorpromazine. He had worked with Geigy on certain antihistamines, and thought they had psychiatric promise.

Eventually, Kuhn tried one called imipramine, the first tricyclic. It did not help all patients with psychoses. Patients with psychoses *and* depressed mood, however, had improved mood. He then gave tricyclics to patients who only had depression, and the results were good.[30] Kuhn treated hundreds of patients and found that they had more vitality, renewed interest in formerly enjoyed activities, and were more socially engaged.[31] An early clinical trial of imipramine was conducted by Hilda Abraham, Karl's granddaughter, herself a psychoanalyst.[32] A number of other tricyclics followed, and some were better tolerated by patients than imipramine.[33] Tricyclics also had safety risks. Above all, they can be lethal in overdose, so it is unwise to give large amounts to suicidal patients.[34]

Next came the task of figuring out why the MAOIs and tricyclics worked. Knowledge of the brain might flow from the action of the drugs, and in turn might lead to better drugs.

A major advance came from rabbits on reserpine, a drug used to treat high blood pressure and schizophrenia. The rabbits had a period of excitement, followed by a period of inactivity, hunched posture, and immobility. The second period looked like depression. Reserpine caused monoamine transmitters to leak into synapses, causing the excitement in the rabbits in the first phase. Monoamine oxidase broke down the neurotransmitters, causing the "depression" of the second phase. The second phase was absent, though, when the rabbits were given iproniazid before the reserpine – presumably because the break-down of the monoamines was hampered. A theory of depression was born: reduced level of the neurotransmitters caused the depression.[35]

Tricyclics, however, do not inhibit monoamine oxidase, which meant the level of the neurotransmitters could be raised in other ways. In the early 1960s, American biochemist Julius Axelrod discovered that tricyclics blocked the reuptake of neurotransmitters into nerve cell bodies. This seemed to confirm that low levels of neurotransmitters might be causing the depression. Norepinephrine became the leading contender for the most important neurotransmitter involved, though the tricyclics also inhibit reuptake of serotonin.[36] The MAOIs increase levels of norepinephrine, serotonin, and also dopamine.[37]

The emerging theory got the pithy name, the "catecholamine hypothesis."

Dopamine and norepinephrine (but not serotonin) are catecholamines. Psychiatrist Joseph Schildkraut published a famous paper on this in 1965.[38] Schildkraut trained in psychiatry at Harvard, hoping to become a psychoanalyst. When he started his residency, though, he was captivated by the therapeutic power of the MAOIs and tricyclics. Working with Gerald Klerman, he looked at the effects of an MAOI on norepinephrine. Klerman and Schildkraut examined the patients' urine. The urine showed that the MAOIs and tricyclics both increased levels of catecholamines.[39] Schildkraut concluded that some depressions, and *maybe* all, were associated with lowered catecholamines. He hoped that these tentative ideas about cause would produce ideas for new drugs.

Schildkraut stressed the role of norepinephrine. Swedish pharmacologist Arvid Carlsson found, though, that tricyclics blocked reuptake of serotonin more effectively than they did norepinephrine.[40] Might lowered serotonin be the cause of depression? Researchers began to pursue drugs that only blocked serotonin uptake. A drug with more specific action might avoid the unwanted effects of other drugs.

Unlike many physical treatments for depression that were based on chance observations of mood, the SSRIs came from a prior theory of the cause of depression. Carlsson patented zimelidine, the first SSRI, but it caused a possibly-fatal neurological condition.[41] Eli Lilly pursued serotonin research, and developed fluoxetine – Prozac – as early as 1972. Approved for sale a full fifteen years later, it quickly overtook the tricyclic nortriptyline (Pamelor), as the most prescribed antidepressant. A few years later, another SSRI, Zoloft, began to outsell Prozac. Related drugs followed – serotonin antagonist and reuptake inhibitors (SARIs) and serotonin–norepinephrine reuptake inhibitor (SNRIs). Bupropion (Wellbutrin), which inhibits dopamine and norepinephrine reuptake but not serotonin, was invented in 1969, but not approved for sale until 1985. Wellbutrin came into wider use because it does not have the sexual side effects often caused by SSRIs.

Chemical theories of depression were not wild guesses. They were smart ones, based on what was known, and they sparked excitement for good reasons. There was, though, a major irony. The catecholamine hypothesis was the defining scientific theory of the antidepressant era. The culturally-defining drugs of that era, like Prozac and Zoloft, work on serotonin. But serotonin is *not* a catecholamine.

No chemical theory had to imply that depression was *just* chemical. When Prozac became a cultural marvel in the 1990s, many claimed that Freud, literally dead since 1939, was now *really* dead. After all, the reasoning went, if we could fix depression with a pill, how important could unconscious conflict be? This was never good reasoning. Whatever you think about the psychoanalysis of depression, or of drugs, the dearth of neurotransmitters could logically be caused by inner conflict, and remedied with a pill. Little was known about what might be causing lowered levels of catecholamines anyway. Reduced levels of certain neurotransmitters could be what anger turned inward, or object loss, looks like at the chemical level. After all, they would have to look like something. Any mental event is an event in the brain. If you get pleasure from reading *To the Lighthouse*, it can only be because the pattern of ink on the page, after taken in by the eye, sends a message to the brain. As John Bowlby pointed out in his classic work on loss, chemical changes in the brain in depression do not have to mean the chemical changes are the cause of the depression.

Freud knew and welcomed the power of substances to change mood. If effective physical treatments were logically opposed to his ideas, he could have been discredited in the 1930s with the use of amphetamines, in the 1940s by convulsive therapy, in the 1950s by the first antidepressants, or in the 1960s and 1970s by the growing use of minor tranquilizers. The either/or reasoning that caused Freud's belated public funeral was a sign of a cultural shift, not a scientific find. We also know now that childhood trauma and neglect can cause changes in the brain that make stress in adulthood more likely to lead to depression.[42] This is exactly what the theories of Karl Abraham and his followers, who did not have the brain research available to them, would have predicted.

The psychoanalytic ancestry of Kline's idea that antidepressants recharge "psychic energy" seemed like a vestigial organ stuck to the body of psychiatry after the field evolved to where it was no longer needed. It could as logically have been seen as the link between dynamic and biological psychiatry that Kline thought it was. But the catecholamine theory became central just before DSM-III de-emphasized psychological causes, and just before a decline in the prestige of psychoanalysis.

Chemical theories also flourished when genetic inquiry was confirming what many had long suspected – heritability of depression. The degree of heritability for unipolar depression is lower than that for schizophrenia or bipolar disorder, but significant.[43] Twin studies of depression showed that the greater the genetic similarity, the more likely depression was to occur in both siblings. The co-occurrence of depression is far from total even in identical twins, though, so while some degree of heritability could be inferred, other causes were also likely. Knowledge about the specifics of the genetics remained limited.[44]

Specific links between genetic makeups and neurochemical pictures were hard to find. Still, depression seemed ever more bodily in nature. A lot of hope sprang from this change. Sometimes the hope spilled over into hype.

Books of the Times

Two books by psychiatrists written for lay audiences show the mood of the late twentieth-century boom in biopsychiatry. Nancy Andreasen's *The Broken Brain: The Biological Revolution in Psychiatry* came out in 1984, sandwiched between the arrivals of DSM-III (1980) and Prozac (1987). Peter Kramer's *Listening to Prozac* came out in 1993, as SSRIs were becoming widespread. Both, in different ways, promoted enthusiasm for biopsychiatry. Both expressed reasonable concerns and cautions.

Andreasen became linked to the slogan "a disease like any other." Mental illnesses were physical illnesses, she said, with the brain the afflicted organ. She hoped that mental illnesses would no longer be separate from the rest of disease in medical and public imagination. Stigma might be reduced, because people would not be blamed for their illness. Depression would shed the taint of poor character. Psychiatry would no longer be a disfavored stepchild in medicine, lacking the prestige of the favored siblings who successfully treated real diseases. Biology would be psychiatry's fairy godmother, and medications the glass slipper that proved the fit.

What does it mean, though, to say a depression (or other mental illness) is a "disease like any other"? Does it mean that depression is "just chemical"? Only if other diseases are just chemical, with no psychological or social causes, no cultural setting. This is not the case. Does it mean we can banish inquiry into psychological meaning? This is also not true of all diseases, and certainly not of depression. Does it mean free from moral stigma? Kline hoped that depression stigma would be reduced, because once you have a medication for something, he thought, people will think it is a real disease.[45] Biological models may have decreased some stigma for depression, more so than for schizophrenia.[46] Biological models of mental illness have seeped into popular understanding, and they have also probably helped get people into medical treatments. But stigma is a dogged and shape-shifting beast, not easily slayed by biological fact. As for getting depression the status of real disease, the border separating those who need medication from those who do not remains disputed. Efforts to end moral judgments about people with diseases are worthy, but making the diseases biological is not the way. Ask anyone who has felt blamed – because of their "lifestyle" for example – for chronic illnesses such as cancer and heart disease.

This digression on the meaning of "a disease like any other," though, is not meant as a criticism of Andreasen. A growing cultural mood of the time may have inclined toward "just chemical," but Andreasen was cautious. She said the antidepressants were useful, but granted that they were slow to act. She also did not think mental states could be reduced to the inborn brain. The brain was not a static organ, but one that changed in response to experience over a lifetime. Patients would still need psychotherapy for insight into their minds and lives. While seeing mental illness as brain disease could make psychiatry more like other specialties, she hoped its continuing attention to the patient's wider world would continue to humanize the rest of medicine, which could be too narrowly biological. Psychiatry's special window into personal and social experience would endure, partly because people drawn to the specialty would care about those things.

Andreasen outlined the catecholamine hypothesis, which was, still in

1984, only a hypothesis. It never achieved the status of settled scientific knowledge. But it was not the only physical explanation around. The catecholamine hypothesis, she said, had been joined by another: the "serotonin hypothesis."

About a decade later, the serotonin hypothesis was hotcakes. So was Kramer's *Listening to Prozac*. Kramer himself said that the hype for brain explanations of human affairs (including mental illnesses, but other things too) was a cultural spectacle out of proportion to advances in scientific knowledge.[47]

Listening to Prozac has been blamed both for causing an over-hyping of antidepressants, and for a later backlash.[48] Kramer described patients with dramatic recoveries. Some said they finally felt like their true selves, which must have made a deep impact on readers – many of whom likely bought the book wondering if this newly-famous drug might help them. Kramer was not the only person, patient or doctor, who was observing these effects. The book likely did increase demand for antidepressants. But it is an ambivalent book.

Later critique of SSRIs would focus on the calculus of benefit versus harm. Kramer did not focus much on adverse effects – not many of them had yet been observed widely. Kramer's doubts revolved around the meaning of the self. What even *was* the self if it could be so altered by a chemical? Many patients wondered the same thing.

Listening to Prozac promoted a controversial term: "cosmetic pharmacology." Like cosmetic surgery, it was not medically necessary, but could make your life better. A key phrase was "better than well." Was Prozac giving people an edge in the workplace, beyond its effects on illness? Was it making people more charismatic and outgoing? If so, *should* Prozac be used as an enhancement for people who were not really sick, or really only a little depressed? Ethicists and journalists gave a lot of attention to these questions when Prozac was new. The debate took the shape of all debates over enhancements – on the one hand, if it makes people's lives better, then why not? On the other hand, does it give some people an unfair advantage – those who have more money for the drugs, for example? And what are the costs?

Listening to Prozac reached a large audience, as did *The Anatomy of Melancholy* centuries earlier, and as did Freud and Jung's books in the decades before. It may have had a similar effect on demand for the treatment that psychoanalytic writing did. People often sought out depth psychology as a means to work through common life problems, more than a cure for actual disease. People may have also heard about cosmetic psychopharmacology and sought Prozac. Who would not want to be better than well, if possible? Psychoanalysis required a long and painful encounter with thoughts and impulses people would rather ignore. Prozac was easily washed down with orange juice at breakfast.

The debate over cosmetic psychopharmacology evaporated more than it was resolved. No one worries much anymore about whether Prozac or any other antidepressant is an enhancement. Kramer himself has turned to writing defenses of depression as an illness category, and antidepressants as a way to treat it. The cosmetic pharmacology debate died partly because Prozac's costs became clearer. The debate makes sense only if the costs of the drug are modest. But now most agree that antidepressants can have effects worth avoiding, if possible. And taking an antidepressant will not elevate the mood of a healthy person.[49]

Some critics of Prozac feared that it was sapping emotional strength. SSRIs were part of a decline of character, a loss of resolve against life's inevitable arrows and slings.[50] One ethicist, while granting the need for treatment of the severely depressed, saw Prozac as part of a childish culture where people wear sneakers and casual clothes to work, instead of formal suits.[51] (Not caring so much what people wear to work may be a better gauge of maturity than wearing a suit, though.) According to this line of criticism of antidepressants, we now run crying to the psychiatrist for every emotional skinned knee, unlike our stoic ancestors. Like many claims about the sinister cultural effects of antidepressants, this is more often asserted than shown.

Prozac and the other SSRIs caused a lot of bewilderment about the nature of the self. Who, or what, am I if my mood and orientation to the world can be altered with a pill? Yet other physical treatments for affective illness did not cause so much philosophical reflection, including the older antidepressants. That could be because they were not so widely used. I have not seen memoirs with titles like "Me and My Marsilid" or "Pamelor Nation." Nor have I seen any memoirs about the life-changing effects of CBT. The only treatment for depression that has inspired as much memoir writing as the SSRIs is ECT.

In this era where Freud was being declared dead because drugs work, no one said CBT was dead. The same reasoning could have applied – why fix illogical thoughts if the disease is chemical? Why bother with therapy at all when you can take a pill? CBT and Prozac were of a piece, however. They fit the changing culture because they require no deep self-examination, they are readily reimbursable, and they are well-suited to clinical trials. The trials, we would learn, had problems of their own.

Backlash: Clinical Trials and Other Tribulations

The appeal of biopsychiatry of depression was not just scientific, but also psychological. Many people *like* thinking depression is purely physical. The shine is off a bit now, though. The adverse effects of drugs are better known. The drugs sometimes have a "poop-out" effect, in which the efficacy wanes after a while. They can be hard to stop taking. Scathing exposés of the pharmaceutical industry have led to justified mistrust. Brain science has not advanced at the rate many had hoped. Drugs are not making people "better than well." The large numbers of people on the drugs may itself also be causing disillusionment – if the drugs are so great, and so many people are taking them, why do we have so much depression, not to mention ordinary sadness? We should not, though, have contempt for the hopefulness of biopsychiatry in the late twentieth century. Real advances in both knowledge and treatment led to some incautious claims. Some authors who were credited with incautious claims were more cautious than many readers realized.

Scientific and political critiques have made telling points. The critiques have looked at continued mysteries about the biological bases of depression, concerns about adverse effects, and challenges to the results and integrity of the clinical trials in support of drug treatment.

Describing activity in the brain and knowing what the activity means for mood are different things.[52] Precise links between chemical changes and mood have not been easy to find. Many depressed people do not show high monoamine oxidase levels, for example, and many non-depressed people do. Many patients might have welcomed the idea of "chemical imbalance" but later found it one-dimensional, missing important aspects of their experience.[53]

Scorn is now sometimes cast on the phrase "chemical imbalance."

Scorn is rarely a good historical attitude, though. In the history of science, scorn is justified mostly for instances of pseudo-science, in which results are deliberately faked, not for reasonable ideas that do not hold up well over time. "Chemical imbalance," was, in any event – like the earlier catchphrase "anger turned inward" – a shorthand for complex ideas.

The phrase "chemical imbalance" was attractive to *critics* of drug treatment in psychiatry. For people hostile to biological psychiatry, the debunking of "chemical imbalance" was a windfall. If "chemical imbalance" as the cause of depression was based on weak science, doesn't the whole rationale for drug treatment of depression collapse?

Not really. This is why the sequence of the science matters. Doctors began using antidepressants because of their observed effects on mood, not because of a well-understood physical process. Observations about the brain chemistry came after. If a treatment for an illness works, it makes sense to reason back from its action to the cause of the illness. If that effort fails, the treatment does not stop working. Scientific progress comes in unplanned ways, and fails to unravel all mysteries. Expecting otherwise is a warm invitation to disillusionment.

If antidepressants do not work, millions of people are spending a lot of money on drugs that are not doing good. Critics have examined the clinical trials and found serious problems. Many of them pertain most to the results of SSRI trials.

One problem in antidepressant trials is publication bias toward positive results.[54] Worse, the pharmaceutical industry has suppressed negative results.[55] FDA rules permit hiding negative results of trials, provided they produce two positive ones.[56] Studies have to show that the drug does better than placebo, in which the anticipation of remedy creates the improvement, not something inherent in the treatment. A majority of *published* trials show antidepressants perform better than placebo, but not by a lot, in some cases not at all, and in some the drugs did worse.[57] Non-therapeutic actions of the drugs – side effects – can allow patients in trials to know whether they are on a placebo or not. The trial is not really blind, then. The placebo effect will not work if you know you are on placebo, so people on the real drug may have an "amplified placebo effect."[58]

The placebo effect for antidepressants (and for other psychiatric drugs) in trials has also been rising in recent years. No one is certain why. Maybe as antidepressants have become well known, the expectation that they will work is greater. The attention patients get in trials is greater than they might get if taking a medicine outside of a trial, so they may be getting benefits and support that come with a therapeutic relationship.[59] The length of the studies has also increased, and the placebo effect is greater in longer studies.[60] Daniel Pine, a major figure in antidepressant trial research, believes poorer studies are being done, and that placebo response is greater in poorly-designed studies.[61]

Taking a drug always has costs – physiological and financial. Why incur them if you are only getting a placebo effect, or its equivalent? If the trials cannot show that the drugs are meaningfully better, in what sense can we say that the drugs work?[62]

Remember, though, that the mood effects of MAOIs and tricyclics were first seen by people who were not looking for mood drugs at all, and taken by patients who were not expecting mood changes, so the effects were not likely due to placebo. Also, psychiatrists cannot easily predict who will respond to which antidepressant. They try to match the treatment plan to the patient, but some guesswork is involved. A given patient will respond well to some antidepressants and not others. This is called the tailoring effect. The placebo effect does not explain it well. If the expectation that drugs work is what makes them work, why would some work better than others in the same patient? The tailoring effect may help explain the gap between the weakness of the data from trials and the experience of doctors and patients that medicines work.[63]

Millions of people are taking antidepressants and finding them helpful. All over the world, clinicians prescribe them and see improvements in their patients. This is another measure of efficacy. We have clinical trials because the everyday experience of clinicians and patients is subjective, and could be caused by placebo. The problem is acute for an illness like depression, for which the causes are not definitively known, and the ways the treatments work are unclear. Using trials as the only way to measure a treatment also has risks, though. Might the drugs work better than the data from trials suggest? The centers doing the studies need a supportive atmosphere, or they lose subjects. This support may improve outcomes in the placebo group. Recovery is often measured by the Hamilton scale or similar instrument. On these scales, some symptoms can add more points to a score than others, which may drag down recovery rates. Many patients in recent trials may also be people who failed to respond to one antidepressant already, so they may be the more treatment-resistant patients. The average scores in the studies may also obscure the extent of benefit for patients who do benefit. The flaws in antidepressant trials may not all run in one direction.[64]

Much of medical practice is not backed up by dramatic positive clinical trials. Clinical experience matters too.[65] No serious student of the subject thinks the data from antidepressant trials are impressive. Concluding that antidepressants are worthless, when so many doctors and patients say they work, proposes a rather grand illusion.

Another critique of antidepressant culture is that reliance on pills, even if they do work, is a poor substitute for making the social changes we need to prevent depression in the first place. A less unequal, less isolating, less precarious, less ruthless social system might well reduce the incidence. But people with depression should not have to suffer while waiting for social progress.

It can be true that big pharma pushed profit more than health, and that we have over-medicated societies, and also true that medications help suffering people. You do not have to like big pharma to vaccinate your kids. The cases are different, because the data supporting vaccination are so strong, and because most vaccines are for diseases with a clear definition and known physical basis. Still, the profits the companies make do not automatically show the product is bad.

Critique of antidepressants is also too often close to pill-shaming of depressed people, who have enough problems. Many critics of antidepressants are careful and sensitive. Many are not. In a few minutes on the internet, it is easy to find people with big platforms (such as a large Twitter following) who say antidepressants are a "crutch," or even a poison. This is often tied to an implied judgment that depression is not an illness. We do not tell people who use antibiotics for an ear infection to suck it up and bear their pain, or that they are poisoning themselves. People take antibiotics for infections to reduce suffering. Call me old-fashioned, but I think reducing suffering is good. Antibiotic use is bad for you in some ways, and its overuse is also a real problem. You should not take antibiotics when you are healthy, or even when you're sick with something other than a bacterial infection. We should similarly guard against overuse of antidepressants. They have known drawbacks, and for many people psychotherapy may be a better option. But different things work for different people.

One of Kramer's patients said of being without antidepressants: "It's like being forced to move to a country with no electricity. It's not that humans never lived like that, but in our world, it's deprivation . . ."[66] That world increasingly means literally the whole world.

Antidepressants Go Global

"Psychiatric language in Latvia has been invaded by the diagnosis of depression."

– Vieda Skultans[67]

The hype about antidepressants may be more restrained now, but their use continues to rise. And whether or not depression is an illness of great antiquity all over the world, antidepressant use is becoming as global as cigarettes, Coca-Cola, and Oprah. Antidepressants are commodities that cross cultural frontiers. You can sell them with a body concept ("depression is a chemical imbalance in the brain") or fit the antidepressants into a local body concept – or some combination of the two. Medical anthropologists have shown how antidepressant use has been made to fit, sometimes awkwardly, into new cultural spaces. A quarter of a century ago, it was possible to say that the antidepressant era was "confined to the Western world."[68] Not anymore.

Latvia is a Baltic state, a part of the former Union of Soviet Socialist Republics (USSR). The Baltic states were among those most eager for the fall of the USSR and for separation from it. The downfall of the USSR, though, has led to worsening conditions for many, especially the vulnerable, such as the elderly, single women with children, and the disabled and chronically ill. The Soviet system, like some other communist systems, encouraged a somatic view of distress. Neurasthenia was a common diagnosis.[69] Soviet medicine had, though, also been holistic, looking at affect, bodily experience, and behavior.

Recent medical policy has held that Latvians were over-doctored under the Soviet regime. The number of specialists has been reduced, especially psychiatrists and neurologists. Medicine increasingly addresses the individual, not the social system. Doctors are aware of the hard lives of their patients, but cannot do much about them. Conferences organized by pharmaceutical companies promote not only drugs themselves, but the diagnoses, such as depression, that warrant their use. Western psychiatry has high social status. Somatic distress is increasingly seen as somatization, or masked depression. Patients adopt pharmaceutical language, but antidepressants remain a luxury item, likened to opera.[70] In Latvia's antidepressant era, the dominant view of distress is individualistic and drug reliant, but the drugs are hard to get.

Depression diagnoses and antidepressant use have also been surging in Iran since the 1980s. In Iranian collective memory, the surge is linked to the harrowing effects of the Iran–Iraq war that began with Iraq's invasion in 1980, and ended with a ceasefire in 1988.

Prior to the Iranian Revolution in 1979, Iranians discussed psychological distress in poetic or spiritual terms. Some degree of melancholy showed character and spiritual achievement. Freudian psychoanalysis was used, but it was not part of medicine. Iranian psychiatry emphasized the brain. After the revolution, Freudian thought was further marginalized, because the state considered it a Westernization.

The war legitimized psychiatric views of suffering, as wars often do. The educated and younger were quickest to absorb psychiatric language, but gradually psychiatric discourse seeped deeply into public media. Depression became more than an illness, but a national character trait. The use of "Prozak" (used to refer to all antidepressant drugs) became common and an important part of national discussion. Iranians see the cause of depression as social, pointing to the long-term traumatic effects of war, but also responsive to physical treatment. The efficacy of drugs never implied that the illness was "just chemical." If anything, Iran's age of Prozac looked more to social explanations for depression than earlier psychiatric culture in the country.[71]

Japan is also a place where depression has become a signature national illness.[72] Ironically, it was once one of the candidates for a place with no depression at all, at least not until big pharma drummed up depression for consumption. The history is more complex.

Japanese scholars who picked up on Ruth Benedict's contrast with America argued that Japan lacked depression. Some saw in Benedict an implication of Western superiority. For these scholars, the more socially-embedded Japanese self was a cultural achievement, protective against depression.

A medical language of depression as sickness, including medical words for it, dates back at least to the sixteenth century in Japan, however. The discourse was based on the concept of *ki*, similar to the Chinese *chi*, a life force flowing through the body. *Ki* could, because of changes in things like climate, diet, or lifestyle, become blocked or stagnant. A gloomy state followed, driving people to such deep sorrow they became ill or died. In the first Japanese textbook of internal medicine, a translation from a Dutch one, melancholia appeared, explained with *ki*. But Japanese psychiatry began to phase out melancholia in favor of depression around the time Western psychiatry did, and became more brain-based, less based on *ki*. Most of the major Western physical treatments for mental illness, such as ICT and Convulsive Therapy, came to Japan within months of their appearance in Europe.[73] Anxiety medications also made inroads.[74] Depression was seen as a hereditary brain disease – and then became so deeply stigmatized that no one in Japan wanted to admit having it. Grounding an illness in the body is no guarantee against stigma.

This picture began to change with the influence of the antipsychiatry movement in Japan. Antipsychiatry's influence was brief, but it dislodged the dominance of biology. The search for alternatives led to the creation of community mental health centers. As in Western contexts, the reach of psychiatry outside of large institutions increased treatment of depression. Yet stigma remained. In order to get patients to take antidepressants, doctors stressed that depression was a disease, with a biology. A lot of patients started taking antidepressants. But it seems that when this happens, disillusionment follows. Doctors were disappointed by patients who did not recover. Patients became frustrated by the limits of the biological frame, which ignored so much of what they were going through. Japan had little tradition of psychotherapy – Freud had been rejected as non-scientific. The psychiatric profession lacked an approach adaptable for more holistic treatment.

Treatments developed in the West, such as the shock treatments, were also introduced into India during the twentieth century, as was psychoanalysis.[75] The antidepressants were subject to some translation. In Calcutta, psychiatrists describe antidepressants to patients as food for the mind. In Bengali medical concepts, the belly is the center of good health. Illness and health are thought to most deeply involve the digestive system. Direct-to-consumer advertising is not legal, but drug companies distribute leaflets with depression symptom checklists and run awareness campaigns, warning that depression is under-diagnosed. These campaigns have been effective with doctors, but patients are more resistant. Doctors think that patients are "bowel obsessed," tending to view health in terms of the digestive system. Many problems, including hair loss, headaches, impotence, skin disease, and fatigue, are explained by digestive imbalance. Bengali psychiatrists also perceive a lot of masked depression. If a patient complains of GI problems, they look for depression. If they are found, an antidepressant might be warranted – and if the GI problems go away, this might prove that the problem was depression all along.

Cultural differences are important, but can also be exaggerated. Kramer reports that a lot of his patients also come in with puzzling GI complaints. They are "employed in unrewarding service jobs, came with stories of disrupted childhoods, conflict-ridden marriages, workplace abuse, and money troubles. They experienced their problems as physical." These patients, he finds, often do well on tricyclics.[76] Still, Kramer probably did not have to compare Prozac to food to convince his patients to try it. In Calcutta, doctors only bring up brain chemistry to compare it with food metabolism. Diabetes has also been on the rise in India, and the diabetes/depression comparison is popular with doctors to encourage taking drugs.[77]

Western psychiatric language and methods can influence other idioms and traditions without displacing them. In Kerala, far on the other side of India, depression and tension are increasingly used as a way to describe distress, though older ideas such as possession retain power. The idea of depression as a neurochemical imbalance, though, is considered compatible with older Ayurvedic ideas of imbalances and blockages of channels. The Ayurvedic texts also held that there were inborn predispositions to mental illness. The study of classic Ayurvedic texts, reread in biopsychiatric terms, is a part of the training of Ayurvedic psychiatric doctors. They do not consider the texts outdated by biopsychiatry, but rather as anticipating it. The validity of the texts is demonstrated by their compatibility.[78]

Introduction of antidepressants into new cultural settings produces varied results, just as their use in individuals does. Some commonalities emerge, though. One is the pressure to use Western psychiatric language.[79] Western psychiatry is associated with progress and science in many areas – perhaps more than in the West itself. Prevailing local body concepts, though, often prove to be resilient. But, whether because they are able to fit the drugs to their existing concepts, or simply because they feel better, many take the medicines anyway.

Diagnosis and drug use are in a reciprocal relationship. If the drugs are antidepressants, and the drugs are prescribed, the diagnosis of depression needs to be used. Antidepressants did not create depression, but the rise of the diagnosis is tied to the world the drugs helped create. We should not lose sight of how much that upward spiral may relieve suffering. It's possible, as critics argue, that many people may be taking medicines they do not really need, and might be better without, though people who have unwanted effects that outweigh benefits can stop taking the drugs, as many do. Many others, though, may be freed from misery they had been enduring for years.

After Prozac: New Biopsychiatry of Depression

The biological science of depression continues to make uneven progress. Current biological psychiatry combines hopeful new developments, disappointment, and caution. The hope comes from new causal theories and new exploratory treatments. The disappointment comes from knowing the unfulfilled promise of the late twentieth-century research, which did not yield the level of discovery that was hoped for: not in genetics, not in brain science, and not in drug development. The caution comes from knowing that hopes were over-hyped. Critics of psychiatry sometimes see the present uncertainty and say that all the biological research and pharmacology has gotten us nowhere. I disagree. The observations stimulated in the beginning by the effects of MAOIs and tricyclics led to a lot of new knowledge. The new knowledge led to some simplifications. The simplification probably led to an unfortunate devaluing of psychotherapy. That was a cost, but does not mean the new knowledge was worthless.

The disillusionment itself is a kind of progress. It reminds us that depression is complex.

Claims that a single cause will explain depression are rare in current research. Psychiatry now has no unified theory of depression with the prestige the psychoanalytic view once held, or the catecholamine hypothesis afterwards. This is healthy. Research articles on the neurobiology of depression do not claim that life events and social factors are unimportant. And the reverse: little research on the sociology or psychology of depression dismisses biology. The challenge remains to see how everything interacts. That challenge will never be met if any of these domains are dismissed as irrelevant.

Some newer biological theories on depression link it to inflammation; disruptions in neuroendocrine mechanisms beginning in fetal development; and problems in the gut microbiome.[80] New physical treatments for depression include transcranial magnetic stimulation (TMS), which seeks to mimic the effects of ECT with fewer adverse effects.[81] Psychedelic drugs are also getting renewed attention as treatments for depression and other mental illnesses.

Some non-Western medical traditions have long used psychedelic substances therapeutically, just as many have used plants that do similar work to the antipsychotics.[82] After it was first synthesized in a laboratory, LSD was developed as a psychiatric drug, before it became the recreational drug of the 1960s counter-culture. LSD stimulates a serotonin receptor in the brain.[83] In its early days, it was hoped to enhance self-awareness and recollection, making psychotherapy easier. By 1965, over a thousand studies reported therapeutic promise from LSD.[84] Ketamine, which is also used recreationally, is a psychedelic that is receiving a lot of attention for depression treatment.[85] Ketamine seems to work quickly, in a matter of hours or days instead of the weeks most antidepressants usually take to have effect, and may also be effective in patients for whom other treatments have failed. A derivative, esketamine, was approved for use in 2019 by the FDA, and sold by Janssen Pharmaceuticals as Spavato – a nasal spray.

How good Spavato is remains to be seen. The history of somatic treatments for mental illness counsels caution. If we rush to hail a treatment as a miracle cure, we have learned nothing from history. Efficacy is often overstated when a treatment is new, and adverse effects are not always apparent right away. Only one of Janssen's three clinical trials for Spavato showed an advantage over placebo, and the difference was small.[86] And as with previous antidepressants, it does not cure depression; relapse after discontinuation is common.[87] Some critics say that the FDA approval was rushed.[88]

Same as it ever was. Despite progress in psychological and biological knowledge – in classical antiquity, in the Middle Ages, in early modernity, in modernity, in the heyday of psychoanalysis, to the antidepressant era – depression has presented a multi-faceted problem. Inborn characteristics, lifestyle, and life events all have a role in the genesis of illness, and all may be relevant to treatment. The era of reductionisms, physical *or* psychological, may be coming to an end. One can hope.

A summary of the antidepressant era might say: a new treatment for depression was developed, in the form of antidepressant drugs. The treatment had some variations, but the variations were based on shared premises. The treatment was widely perceived to be effective, by both doctors and patients. A theory was offered about what causes depression, but it had only modest empirical support. The excitement over the treatment led to some inflated claims, both about causes and treatment. Some clinicians began to use the treatment to the exclusion of all others. After some of the inflated claims failed to match reality, backlash followed. While some felt disillusionment with treatment they thought was good, critics came to see the treatment as worthless at best, or a positive evil.[89] If the treatment was indeed worthless, the money being spent on it was an enormous waste.

The arc of this story may sound familiar. It is the same arc as we saw in chapter 3, which also showed how a new treatment for depression was developed, psychoanalytic psychotherapy. It too had some variations, though based on shared premises. Doctors and patients thought the treatment was effective. Psychoanalysis also offered theories about what causes depression, but those theories also had modest empirical support. Enthusiasm led to inflated claims. And, as would happen again with the rise of antidepressants, some clinicians used psychoanalytic therapy to the exclusion of all others. Backlash followed when the more inflated claims for psychoanalysis fell short of reality. Some felt only disillusionment with psychoanalytic therapy, but critics came to see the treatment as worthless at best – or a positive evil. If the treatment was indeed worthless, the money being spent on it, too, was an enormous waste.

One theory about how psychotherapy works is that patients are locked into repeatedly telling the same story about themselves – about their loneliness, or their victimization, for example. The therapy helps patients see that they do not have to repeat the same story. They can tell new stories of their lives. History can have a similar role. When new treatments are developed, we can be more realistic about their empirical basis. We do not have to over-hype them, or discard older knowledge about what helps. We can be wary of claims that the treatment is harmless. We do not have to live the same story, time after time.

From Brain to Person

Virginia Woolf struggled for years with a mood disorder before taking her life by drowning in 1941. Two years after her essay marking the date human nature changed, Woolf wrote an essay, "On Being Ill," in which she observed that illness was seldom a subject of writing. Illness had an embarrassing quality that made it hard to render in a public forum. Perhaps in the 1920s. Not in the age of Prozac. A flood of published depression memoirs has appeared in the last 30 years or so.

Depression is not the only illness people have been writing about. Illness memoirs of all kinds have been coming out in large numbers. The interest in these narratives is a reaction to several strands of modern medical history: advanced medical technology that heightens distance between clinicians and patient; a research culture that sees illness in numbers more than individuals; a profit-driven medical system that hinders long office visits. Technology and statistical research can bring a lot of benefits. They do not hear the complex stories sick people have about their bodies and lives. Neither does a doctor under pressure to see as many patients in a day as possible. Insurance companies certainly do not. You are lucky if you can get someone on the phone to fix a billing error.

I doubt, though, that we have seen as many memoirs for any ailment as we have for depression. In part, this reflects the nature of the ailment. Terminal ailments yield few memoirs, for obvious reasons. Depression can be fatal, but it usually is not. Certain ailments, like schizophrenia and Alzheimer's disease, make writing hard (though we do have memoirs even of these). Mild or short-lived illnesses are not typically thought worthy of autobiography. They are also not usually a part of one's sense of self, as depression often is. And the age of Prozac is also an age when depression is a cultural preoccupation.

The memoirs ask the questions this book has asked and give them an autobiographical cast: Do I have an ancient and universal ailment, or is my diagnosis a cultural fad? What makes my illness real, what does it even mean for an illness to be real? Does my suffering come from psychic traumas I suffered, or my chemistry? If chemistry, does talk therapy have a role in my recovery? If trauma, do medications have a role in my recovery? Who or what am I, if a pill can change how I feel about life itself? What are the financial, social, and personal costs of these medications? The memoirs show that having depression means not only to suffer from an ailment. It is to live these questions on a daily basis.

6

Darkness Legible

"Professor Higashi often emphasizes that depression lies at the 'limit of language'... [and] creates a fundamental disruption in the sense of self."
— Junko Kitanaka, *Depression in Japan*[1]

"You feel the thinness of your identity."
— Bruce Springsteen, *Born To Run*[2]

Mood and Metaphor

"Bell jar. noun: a bell-shaped usually glass vessel designed to cover objects or to contain gases or a vacuum."[3]

In *The Bell Jar*, Plath chose an odd image. Metaphors often make something strange more accessible, by comparing it to something more familiar. "This is your brain on drugs" – we have all seen an egg frying, and we know that it will change, harden. Once in its new form, it cannot be changed back. The campaign was a gut-level appeal, to make vivid the risks of recreational drug use. You cannot see your brain on drugs, so their dangerous effects may seem remote. Depression is also hard to understand. Certainly, many who have had it feel that others just don't get it. Yet when Sylvia Plath tried to render it, she compared it to being under an obscure scientific instrument, something few will encounter.

Plath's image, a vessel designed to contain a vacuum, has a certain power, though. It expresses a sense of suffocation, as well as the "portability" of depression – you are stuck with it wherever you go. As the protagonist Esther Greenwood says, "on the deck of a ship or at a street café in Paris or Bangkok – I would be sitting under the same glass bell jar, stewing in my own sour air."[4]

But while it is a powerful image, it is still an obscure one. Maybe that is the point. A familiar image might be too tame for this beastly illness. An image from everyday life would risk exactly what people with depression want to avoid – the impression that the monster they fight is like everyone else's bad mood. And while metaphors can help to convey the unfamiliar, they can themselves become overly familiar – does Churchill's image of a "black dog" help anyone understand depression? Plath was expert at pushing language to the rawness of life, as in the stark and musical *Ariel* poems, written shortly before her suicide. In the novel, she uses metaphor to explain metaphor, heaping images one on another:

> To the person in the bell jar, blank and stopped as a dead baby, the world itself is the bad dream.[5]

Any questions?

The Depression Memoir as Genre and Source

I began with a scene from Chimamanda Ngozi Adichie's novel, *Americanah*. The debate between Ifemelu and her physician aunt Uju dramatizes complex issues swirling around depression: is it a real illness? How much do depression diagnoses medicalize distress, and how much do they helpfully name medical problems? The depression memoirs of recent years wrestle with the same questions. A major theme has been: *do not confuse my illness with your bad mood: I have a real illness.* The urgency of the message may explain the explosion of depression memoirs. And yet, many of the authors confess that it is not just those around them who fail to see their illness and its reality. Often, they have trouble recognizing it themselves.

Styron's *Darkness Visible* came out in 1990.[6] By that time, medical interest in depression had been growing for four decades and Prozac was newly-approved. A memoir of the illness by an already-famous author was bound to get a lot of attention, and it did. After Styron, deluge. These books command interest as documents of an era marked by the rise of depression and antidepressants.

What kind of stories do they tell? Arthur Frank argues that illness narratives can be divided into three types. The first is the restitution narrative: the sick person's self and well-being are restored by successful treatment or remission. The second is the quest narrative: the illness provides the sufferer with a new sense of purpose. The third is chaos – no clear path – the illness is not conquered, and provides no redemptive meaning.[7] Depression memoirs contain elements of all three of these. The majority contain elements of restitution. Most of the writers found a treatment that gave relief and convey a sense of hope. Many of them also found purpose, writing in the hopes of educating the non-depressed about what it is like, conveying to others with depression that they are not alone, that they are seen and understood, and showing solutions. Yet the majority of them also contain a lot of what Frank calls chaos. Most lack a clear sense of resolution. The chaos stems from two problems. First, depression has no reliable cure. Some people get a treatment, feel better, and that is the end of it, but they are not typical. Treatments often provide relief, often immense, but depression usually lingers or recurs. Second, the treatments become problems themselves. They have adverse effects, some can be hard to quit, and in some cases, they disrupt the patient's sense of self as much as the illness. Some of the memoirs are even ambivalent towards recovery.

Norman Endler's *Holiday of Darkness* (1982), is an exception. Written before depression memoirs became common, it is a "clean" restitution narrative. Endler, a psychologist then in his forties, had some setbacks – failure to get a grant he wanted, a rejection from a woman from whom he wanted greater intimacy. His symptoms seemed out of proportion to these losses, though. He lost motivation and hope, and often went to the bathroom to cry, until he sought treatment. When other therapies failed, he tried ECT, which was, for him, a miracle cure. Endler's story also has elements of the quest narrative, as he finds purpose in telling of his recovery through a feared treatment. A type of narrative Frank does not consider is also visible: conversion. Endler had not only shared the common fear of ECT, but had a professional distaste for it, having seen it used on howling patients without anesthesia during his training. He overcame his fear, however, and was blessed by recovery.[8] He became an ECT evangelist – not the first or last patient in ECT history to do so. Many accounts of ECT, including those that express appreciation for its therapeutic power, also express sorrow at memory losses. Endler, though, gives an account of robust cure, with minimal side effects.[9] Few depression memoirs have such a spotless happy ending.

While hope is not the whole story of depression in these memoirs, it is usually a part of it. The memoirs document steep challenge, often to the point of despair, but also paths out, even for some of the most afflicted.

The memoirs have limitations as historical sources. Their authors may not be typical depression patients, at least not in all respects. Severe depression is incapacitating. How many severely depressed people lack the will to make it to the keyboard anyway? What about those who simply don't have the skills or resources to write? Bias toward stories of at least partial recovery is likely. People who have gotten better may have both more motivation and more capacity to write. Publishers also might prefer stories of redemption and hope. The memoirs are also written mostly by middle-class White people, many of them mental health professionals. This is a serious limitation, since poverty and other forms of adversity increase the risk of depression. The authors are also mostly middle-aged. We hear little from children or the elderly in depression memoirs.

All historical sources, though, have limitations. Archives only contain the record people thought worthy of preserving. Newspapers only document what editors thought was news. Oral history is limited by who is available and willing to talk to you. The depression memoir may not provide a complete record of the experience of depression in our era, but it provides a valuable one. Historians would treasure a cache of first-person narratives like this for most any illness, at any time in history.

These memoirists want us to know what it was like for them. Their urgent agenda is to have their illness *seen*. Despite the torrent of attention to depression over the past 100 years, and even more over the last

40, many sufferers find their anguish invisible, misread, or dismissed. And if the memoirists have one message they all wish to convey it is this: those who have not had it just don't understand.

And *what* they don't understand, above all, is that depression is an illness.

You Don't Get It

Styron's openness about his illness in *Darkness Visible* is honored for helping to decrease depression stigma. Many have said how splendidly it conveys the experience of depression. Yet it has an odd vagueness. Even as Styron tries to describe depression, he keeps saying it is impossible to do so. Early in the book, Styron says the illness is "very close to being beyond description,"[10] and repeatedly says we will not understand if we have not had it. For him, he said, it was "most closely connected to drowning or suffocation – but even those images are off the mark."[11] A renowned wordsmith, Styron is saying that words fail him. We know Styron felt awful. We learn little about what he was thinking and doing through the anguish. Styron's title refers to vision, but he himself is somewhat invisible.

Psychoanalyst Darian Leader says that historical case reports and clinical practice both often reveal that depressives need to express their state, but find language inadequate.[12] In *Prozac Diary* (1998), Lauren Slater says: "How do you describe emptiness?"[13]

The resistance to description is not only about the poverty of language for certain inner states. It is an argument of its own, an argument for the realness and seriousness of depression. In one passage, Styron laments that the word depression is a "wimp" of a word for such a beastly experience.[14] The weakness of the word is partly in its ambiguity, referring to illness and mood. As Tracy Thompson says in *The Beast* (1996), "a person who says they're 'depressed' could mean they had a fender bender on the way to work, or that they might get a gun and shoot their self."[15]

The word "cancer" is scary because we know that people who get cancer are often sick indeed, and it is not something everyone gets. No one has a few blue days of having a passing cancer because their pet died. This is one of the most urgent messages in depression memoirs:

I have an illness, not a bad mood. If you got over your bad mood by "taking charge of your life," or ramping up your exercise regime, or getting out more, I am here to tell you that your recovery by those measures shows that you did not have the illness. You had a bad mood with the same name.

We can blame Adolf Meyer. Styron did.[16]

Getting Real

"I found myself looking for a real ailment."

– Elizabeth Wurtzel[17]

I assigned Daphne Merkin's depression memoir, *This Close to Happy* (2017) to my class on depression.[18] It came late in the course, after the students had looked at all the problems I have posed in this book: challenges posed by cross-cultural study of depression, melancholia in earlier eras, psychoanalytic theories, the rise of psychopharmacology. The class was versed in critiques of depression as an illness category – and the students largely rejected them. Several were open about their own depression and treatment for it. I advise students to be cautious about self-disclosure, but in class I often learn things such as what medications they are on, which ones those are replacing, and how long they have been in treatment. To my surprise, many of them found Merkin's book, which I found brisk and engaging, to be off-putting. Merkin grew up in an affluent Manhattan family, and from a material point of view had every advantage. Several students were annoyed to see a privileged person suffering so much. What does she have to complain about? This went on for a few minutes, until one student asked, would we be resenting her wealth so much if this were a cancer memoir? Would we be saying, what business does she have, getting cancer in the midst of affluence?[19]

The story shows how fraught depression remains as an illness category even now, decades into the antidepressant era, with the World Health Organization naming it a serious global public health problem. Wurtzel's *Prozac Nation* (1994) addressed this problem at length. *Prozac Nation* is partly a response to Styron, whose book she found restrained and lacking candor.[20] Wurtzel's narrative is powerful in its lack of inhibition. She knows that not everything she reveals about her thoughts or her choices are attractive, and this candor makes her story vivid. Yet she shares with Styron an urgent need to express the reality of illness, its discontinuity from normal life experience:

> That's the thing I want to make clear about depression: It's got nothing to do with life. In the course of life there is sadness and pain and sorrow, all of which, in their right time and season, are normal – unpleasant, but normal. Depression is in an altogether different zone because it involves a complete absence: absence of affect, absence of feeling, absence of response, absence of interest. The pain you feel in the course of a major clinical depression is an attempt on nature's part (nature, after all, abhors a vacuum) to fill up the empty space.[21]

The rest of the book tells a different story, though. Her depression had a lot to do with her life: her harried and sometimes unavailable mother, her distant father, and the pain of being in the middle during their divorce. In her depressions, she also felt plenty of affect. Sadness, despair, sometimes rage – not all blankness.

So why does Wurtzel insist that depression is not about life? She wants to make clear that depression belongs to the realm of sickness. Wurtzel uses the word "clinical" to modify "depression." If the status as illness were secure, you would not need to. No one speaks of "clinical tuberculosis" or "clinical cancer."

The skepticism that depressed people have to endure about the reality of illness is acute when they do not seem outwardly depressed, or when their lives do not seem to warrant it. Think of how much trouble people had trying to reconcile Robin Williams's suicide with his public persona. In *Running Uphill* (2007), Lora Inman says someone told her that she could not be depressed, since she was attractive and smart, and had a great husband and home.[22] Merkin adds that depression does not "look" crazy.[23]

The memoirists say repeatedly, no, I can't just "cheer up," go for a run, clean my room, or simply will it away, in order to "snap out of it." Merkin suggests that when people say you should get a massage or take a yoga class, they are really expressing their own boredom and impatience: "*Just don't go on and on about it*, is what they don't say."[24]

Merkin thinks they may also be defending themselves against "catching" the despair. Some of these measures, such as exercising, may help, but saying that they are all that is necessary misreads the illness. People who say exercise more, or have a more positive attitude, or go into the woods and get in touch with nature, may be expressing their own solutions to bad moods well. They have not, though, been in a chasm so deep these measures could not pull them out. What makes them so sure their advice works for everyone? What makes them so sure that what was a bad mood for them is not an illness requiring treatment for others?[25]

Some sufferers of depression have their own doubts about realness. The widely-held belief that illness always has a clear physical sign may be internalized.[26] So might the suspicion that what is really going on is a failure of will and character. Tracy Thompson's depression was bad enough for hospitalization, but once admitted, she looked at her fellow patients and wondered: "Were these people really ill, the same way that having diabetes or a brain tumor made you ill?"[27] In *Skating to Antarctica* (1997), Jenny Diski saw her depression as illness, requiring medical attention, but also struggled to see where it departed from the not-illness in her life. Where did her dour personality end and sickness begin?[28] Gillian Marchenko (*Still Life*, 2016), was bed-ridden for months at a time, lost interest in everything she had cared about, withdrew from her social life, and had suicidal ideation. Marchenko had been through post-partum depression three times, and two of her children have serious disabilities. "It's a lot, right? So, is it a depression or a challenging life?"[29] Where did her adversity end and her illness begin? Sally Brampton, whose *Shoot the Damn Dog* (2008) is a record of a severe, treatment-resistant depression, had to reassure herself that she was sick: "I still had a place to live, money from a redundancy payout, a child I adored, friends I loved, work if I wanted it. What right did I have to be depressed?"[30]

Imagine feeling you have no right to the pain you are in.

Several textual tactics show realness, to push back against people who tell them to "get their act together." The tactics of realness include analogy to other ailments (no one expects someone with a serious physical illness to "pull themselves together"), reference to physical process (if it is biochemical, exerting will may not be an option), and appeal to antiquity (people have been calling this an illness for millennia, so it is not just the normal blue moods of life). Marchenko found validation simply in the name "Major Depressive Disorder," which sounded more like a real biomedical problem than "depression."

Styron used medical analogy, stressing that depression can be as serious as diabetes or cancer.[31] Meri Nana-Ama Danquah faced a doubled stigma as a Black woman. Some told her that having depression was inconsistent with the strength Black women are supposed to have. In *Willow, Weep for Me: A Black Woman's Journey Through Depression* (1998) she tells of acquaintances who said things like, "What do you have to be depressed about? If our people could make it through slavery, we can make it through anything."[32] She responded that "depression, in its most basic, clinical form, is biochemical. It is an illness."[33] Or as Inman puts it, "Many people still seem to believe you can just 'pull yourself together.' They don't understand that it is a *chemical imbalance* . . . it is a *physical disorder*."[34] Thompson appealed to the biochemical too, but also to history. She liked reading Stanley Jackson's history of depression, because it drew a continuous line from the melancholia of antiquity to the depression of the age of Prozac.[35] If it is so old, it must be real.

These appeals to analogy, biochemistry, and history serve a pressing purpose. We should imagine, though, what it would be like if they were not necessary. Depression may be like other illnesses, it may be a biochemical process, it may have great antiquity. What if not, though? Would it then be OK to dismiss the suffering? What if we could imagine that depression as real even if it were *not* like other illnesses, *not* a biochemical process, and *not* of great antiquity?

The biological revolution in psychiatry was supposed to change everything. Mental illness was supposed to become a disease like any other, as Nancy Andreasen put it. Nathan Kline hoped simply having medicines would help people think of depression as illness. For Wurtzel, though, if depression is now everywhere, it is nowhere: "I can't escape the icky feeling I get every time I'm sitting in a full car and everyone but the driver is on Prozac."[36]

Brampton insisted, though, that we must continue to underline the realness of illness. If we do not, stigma and secrecy will continue to shroud it. Brampton had fears about disclosure – how it would affect her career, for example.[37] In most cases, we tell our co-workers when we are sick. This is, after all, a key aspect of the sick role as sociologist Talcott Parsons conceived it: when we assume the social role of a sick person, we get benefits, such as the right to miss work and other obligations. We also assume new obligations, such as those to follow doctor's orders and to try to get better. Taking the sick role gets messy when you worry that people will see it as a character flaw instead of a real illness, or go too far the other way, and think you are "crazy," whatever that means. People with depression can lead a double life, masquerading as healthy people day to day. People who disclose their depression risk stigma, and once you disclose, you lose the option of secrecy forever. But lack of disclosures reinforces stigma.

Loneliness lives in these dilemmas. Several of the memoirists published summaries in the popular press, and each received numerous letters from strangers who felt seen in a new way, relieved to know they were not alone. Many of those who wrote to Thompson said they had never before seen their pain described as illness, rather than character flaw.[38]

How Did I Get Here?

"Causes are more like vapours than facts."

– Tim Lott[39]

For Esther Greenwood, ECT was a scary experience. For Plath herself, the story was more complicated. It was scary, but one of her ECT treatments was deeply and rapidly therapeutic. ECT might seem a most physical of treatments, but Plath interpreted her illness, and the therapy's success, in psychoanalytic terms. She assumed her illness was due to unconscious guilt, which the ECT relieved because it was itself a punishment.[40]

Patients' explanations for their illnesses and recoveries can draw on prevailing medical models and also challenge them. Plath used psychoanalytic ideas dominant in her time. Many ECT memoirs have appeared more recently, and while several complain about the procedure, they do not usually describe it as punitive. Few of the recent depression memoirs invoke unconscious guilt or aggression turned inward as the source of their illness. Not surprisingly, many of them use the language of chemical imbalance – but many also push back against it.

In a hybrid history of modern depression/depression memoir, psychologist Gary Greenberg reports that during his time as a subject in an antidepressant clinical trial, the idea of his illness as biochemical grew on him.[41] Slater echoes: "I slowly came to see Prozac's point of view, which posits God as a matter of molecules and witchcraft as a neural mishap."[42] But something counter-intuitive lingers. Inman: "I don't understand why my mood is black because of some chemicals floating around – or not floating around correctly – in my brain."[43]

While the meaning of molecular mishap may be elusive, it helps to make sense of other enigmas. Psychiatrist Linda Gask (*The Other Side of Silence*, 2015) struggles with a past that strikes her as not traumatic enough to warrant her illness.[44] She felt that maybe she was born with a low threshold for stress. Marchenko thought the worst "trauma" she had as a child was a couple of broken bones which, she confesses, brought her a lot of desired attention – though she was prone to asking existential questions about why she was alive to begin with at an age that seemed, in retrospect, a little early.[45] Wurtzel looked at herself at times and had the same question my students had about Merkin: how dare affluent Manhattan me have depression? Wurtzel had a strong attraction to Bruce Springsteen, longing for an identification, because his working-class roots would justify her depression.[46] (As we will see, Wurtzel had more in common with Springsteen than she realized.) Wurtzel also perversely valued a miscarriage she had, because it gave her a good excuse to feel so bad.[47] Many carry an intuition that to feel this bad, something really bad has to happen. Chemistry fills the gap.

But while serving this purpose, and cementing depression as illness, most of the memoirists find chemistry lacking, by itself. No matter how much they may value physical treatments for symptom relief, they often bristle if those treatments are unaccompanied by exploration of their inner, and outer, lives. In *My Fight for Sanity* (1959), Judith Kruger expressed a deep ambivalence with a course of ECT. The treatment did relieve her symptoms, but also caused physical pain and mental disorientation, and perhaps worst of all, left her feeling unseen. She only felt a robust sense of recovery after work with an attentive psychoanalyst – work which uncovered suppressed feelings of hostility and envy toward her younger brother.[48] Wurtzel was quicker to try medication than therapy, but says she went "from a thorough certainty that [depression's] origins are in bad biology to a more flexible belief that after an accumulation of life events made my head such an ugly thing to be stuck in, my brain's chemicals started to agree."[49]

The past, the deep and personal past, matters to these writers. And the past that matters the most is the past with their parents. Or perhaps better put, the past *without* their parents. Karl Abraham would have found these cases sadly familiar.

Seen and Not Seen

Abraham, and later André Green and Alice Miller, found that many depressed patients had parents who, because of their own traumas or insecurities, were emotionally absent even if they were physically present. Physically or emotionally absent parents come up a lot in the memoirs.

The restrained Styron does not tell us much about his childhood. He puts it abstractly. The causes of depression remain incompletely known, he says, but loss and especially childhood loss, "has been established beyond reasonable doubt" as a cause of depression.[50] Styron's father suffered from depression himself, and his mother died of cancer when he was 14. Neither of these losses are mentioned in *Darkness Visible*.

Often, even if a parent is physically with the child, the child does not feel attended to. Wurtzel's parents divorced. "I don't think it matters how many parents you've got, so long as the ones who are around make their presence felt in a positive way. But I got two parents who were constantly at odds with each other, and all they gave me was an empty foundation that split down the middle of my empty, anguished self."[51] Her father was completely unavailable. When she did get time with him, he would sleep. Thompson describes her father as "jovial" but remote, and says her mother, a devout Christian, couldn't see her for who she was, being too invested in her image of what a Christian girl should be like. Diski's mother, herself depressed, sent Diski to skating lessons. Diski felt this was not so much for the daughter's benefit, but for the mother's wish for an accomplished child to display. Danquah, who insists depression is biochemical, considered her parents' divorce pivotal.[52] Brampton describes loving parents, but her father, who she thinks was on the autism spectrum though undiagnosed, was not emotionally giving. She had to deal with her parents' deep discontent with each other, which left her emotional needs unmet.[53] They sent her to boarding school which she hated, and left her feeling abandoned. (One of Brampton's therapists said that 80 percent of her patients went to boarding school.[54]) Inman says she never really knew her father. Slater describes her mother as "distant."[55]

Bruce Springsteen's autobiography *Born to Run* is both a celebration of the joys of rock and roll and a meditation on the origins of Springsteen's depression. Like Plath, Mingus, and Robin Williams, Springsteen is a depressive with vibrant creativity and a voracious appetite for life. The contrast between the dynamo reveling on stage and the morose depressive in bed is poignant, but both are real. The bleak lives and towns that fill his songs are not the product of some uncanny empathic imagination, but portraits of places and people he knew, including his father and himself. His father, he is sure, had undiagnosed depression. The depression, in Springsteen's account, left his father emotionally hobbled and compromised any ability to engage with his talented child. In later life, the elder Springsteen developed paranoid schizophrenia. Springsteen's father was well-meaning, but he was not fully present when he and Bruce were together.

Plath and her mother were close, but her mother was also preoccupied by ailments suffered by Sylvia's brother Warren. Plath's father died when she was eight. Read her poem "Daddy" some time. It gently suggests this may have had some effect on her.[56]

The theme of absent parents in the memoirs may support some of the psychological theories of depression. But aside from cause, this theme in the memoirs shows how psychological meaning always matters, whatever the biochemistry. Life presents all of us with adversity, inner conflict, and loss. These will matter in the most "endogenous" depressions, whether they are the cause of the depression or not.

In addition to absent parents, many of the writers had palpably traumatic events in childhood. Thompson was hit by a car in a near fatal accident, disfiguring her face when she was on the cusp of puberty.[57] Inman was sexually molested in early puberty.[58] Diski was once sent to sleep with her naked father and was also sexually abused by her mother.[59] In a dramatic example of feeling unseen, Diski once found her mother in a psychotic state, and her mother literally did not know who Diski was.[60] Merkin was beaten by an aloof nanny her mother had hired, leaving Merkin to wonder why her mother would entrust her to such a person.[61] Slater's mother was full of anxious intensity, sometimes slapping Slater hard across the cheeks, sometimes rubbing her hands in apparent disapproval across her developing breasts in early puberty.[62] One time she forced Slater to swallow detergent.[63]

In research literature, stuff like this has the strangely dead name "life events."

The Body and Biology

Purely biological explanations feel flat. Work by Frank and others in recent decades has shown how vital it is for people with serious illness to create a narrative about it. Biology is limited, but not simply because it leaves out the psychological and social aspects. The biology itself remains so unclear. Cancer sufferers may or may not have a clear story about an exposure to a carcinogen. But they do have a story about cell growth to tell, one that has a lot of scientific support, and is widely accepted. A depression illness narrative will always have some chaos to it, because any reflection on the causes will leave the sick person stuck in the swamps of the unsettled science.

Biology clearly matters for depression, though, and not only for clinical reasons. While biological explanations alone are limited, they help to make sense of the intensity of bodily experience in depression.

The embodied quality of depression is not only intense. For some it is unexpected. This is a loss we bear when we call it a "mood disorder." Brampton: "Why do they call it a 'mental' illness? The pain isn't just in my head; it's everywhere, but mainly at my throat and in my heart." She was surprised at the physicality, which at another point she found mostly in stiff arms and legs.[64] David Karp, a sociologist who collected people's reports of their depressions and placed them alongside his own in *Speaking of Sadness* (1996) found the physicality bracing, as it seemed to shift from one part of the body to another: a "grief knot" in his throat, chest pains, heavy eyes, pressure in the head, "sadness in the cheeks," shaky hands and legs.[65] Though most physical descriptions

range from a dull woodenness to searing agony, Danquah's description
of the sensual quality seems ambivalent:

> Depression offers layers, textures, noises. At times depression is as
> flimsy as a feather, barely penetrating the surface of my life, hovering
> like a slight halo of pessimism. Other times it comes on gradually
> like a common cold or a storm, each day presenting new signals and
> symptoms until finally I am drowning in it. Most times, in its most
> superficial and seductive sense, it is rich and enticing. A field of velvet
> waiting to embrace me. It is loud and dizzying, inviting the tenors and
> screeching sopranos of thoughts, unrelenting sadness, and the sense of
> impending doom.[66]

Gender

The biological era in depression may affect men and women differently. The memoirs have surprisingly little explicit discussion of
gender. Perhaps the writers feel that they can only speak to their own
experience, and not to social generalizations. Thompson's guess is that
men and women become depressed at equal rates, but that women
appear in the statistics more because they are more inclined to seek
treatment. Sharon O'Brien, in *The Family Silver* (2004), suspects that
the problem for women is that they are expected to be nice.[67] If you're
socialized to be nice, what happens when you feel mean, as everyone
will? Presumably, it gets turned inward. Merkin thinks that although
women get depression more, the men write about it more. I am not
sure this is true. Observations she makes about the content of depression memoirs may be more convincing: the men are more inclined to
biological explanations of their own sickness, and less revealing about
their lives. "Men, that is, have cannily figured out how to sidestep the
implications of moral failing that attaches to mental illness – as well
as the specific criticism of self-indulgence that is attributed to more
introspective accounts of this condition – by insisting on a force outside
themselves."[68]

In Bed

Depression causes immobility. In *Where the Roots Reach for Water: A Personal and Natural History of Melancholia* (1999), Jeffrey Smith says that it "seems your vital fluid has seeped out some invisible rent in your flesh" and that "The melancholic's limbs feel weighted, blood and bone and muscle alike gone viscid with some invisible burden."[69] This paralysis is often keenly felt in bed. Wurtzel had dreams about paralysis, and then had the waking experience of literally being unable to move while in bed. Marchenko wrote of her "cinder-block legs" while trying to get out of bed.[70]

The memoirs depict a lot of time in bed, sleeping too much, too little, or not at all. The being and staying in bed have multiple meanings and motivations. Physical fatigue, a relentless lethargy, is one part. So is low motivation, hopelessness, futility. Brampton tells of "duvet diving," hiding in bed, not answering the phone, turning down invitations, the social withdrawal observed in melancholics since antiquity.[71] For O'Brien, the prospect of bedtime and sleeping pills offered respite from the agony of waking life.[72] Springsteen, legendary for his explosive energy on stage, had a bout of depression where, buried in unwanted thoughts and relentless anxiety, he could not get out of bed:

> I was uncomfortable doing anything. Standing . . . walking . . . sitting down . . . everything brought waves of an agitated anxiety . . . Demise and foreboding were all that awaited and sleep was the only respite. If I can't work, how will I provide for my family? Will I be bedridden? Who the fuck am I? You feel the thinness of your identity.[73]

The confinement to bed may feel overwhelming to the point of being involuntary. Yet the depressed person still has to wonder about the border between their sickness and the normal challenges of living. If active suicidality is a fair measure of severity, Inman was sick indeed, as she made more than one attempt. Yet when she had trouble getting out of bed, Inman asked herself, doesn't everyone?[74]

Getting out of bed is easier if you are interested in things. Loss of interest is one of depression's keenest losses. Diski, on a ship with others spotting a whale: "I like a whale as much as the next person."[75]

As if to say, not at all. Diski – the author of 19 books – is eloquent on her capacity for inaction:

> Indolence has always been my most essential quality ... the single quality I am convinced I possess ... and also in the sense that I feel most essentially myself when I am exercising it. I cannot recall a time when the idea of going for a walk was not a torment to me ... As to the freshness of the air, I'm not so eager for it. Though it is invigorating I admit, I very rarely have the desire to be invigorated.[76]

Taunted by the Beautiful and the Good

Things that are supposed to give pleasure offer a special torment. Psychologist Martha Manning, vacationing in Montana, during the depths of depression: "I know it's beautiful and everything, but to be perfectly honest, I hate nature."[77] On a visit to Disneyland, Karp was pierced by the contrast between how he felt and how he was supposed to feel at the happiest place on earth.[78] A girlfriend tried to cheer Smith with some upbeat music, but its cheer and vibrancy felt like an assault.[79] "Nice" weather mocks the depressed person. Brampton: "I hate the sun. When the sun is shining, I should be happy."[80] On a nice day, a friend asked Brampton how she can be depressed on a day like that. Brampton asked if she would have the same question if it were flu.[81] Merkin says that the surest test of depression is a dismal loitering of your wintry state on the first beautiful day of Spring when for most people hope and enthusiasm renew.[82]

Christian writers may feel that their faith itself requires them to be cheerful.[83] Like the medieval monks with acedia, they have the added burden of seeing their sickness as sin. Martin Luther thought Christians should be cheerful, so having melancholia was reason for guilt. As Marchenko writes, a central premise of Christianity is hope, and depression is above all loss of hope. Throughout Marchenko's writing runs underlying guilt for having the illness in the first place, implying that God's love isn't enough, and also because her loss of interest in things extends even to Jesus. In this too, though, she wonders what is illness and what is not. Faith, she says, comes hard to her.

But, she remembers, doesn't it come hard to everyone, just as getting up in the morning does?[84]

Oblivion

If someone like Diski does not long for vigor, what did she long for? The answer is often *oblivion*. The word appears regularly in depression memoirs – not as how the depressed people feel, but as what they *want*. Brampton: "I don't want sleep. I want oblivion."[85] On an upswing from the worst of depression, Marchenko said "one of my biggest struggles still is whether to cease to exist."[86] The longing for oblivion often leads to drugs. Brampton sought oblivion in combining Valium or Xanax with heavy alcohol use. Diski took an overdose of her mother's Nembutal, not so much seeking death, but wanting everything to stop.[87] This can look like suicidality, which is of course a real risk in people with depression, but several of the writers are clear that the longing for oblivion is not the same as a wish for death. It is a wish for release from pain. Matt Haig writes "I wanted to be dead. No, that's not quite right. I didn't want to be dead. I just didn't want to be alive."[88]

Suicidality has gradations, ranging from a vague feeling that it would be better to be dead, to more active fantasy about how that could be achieved, to concrete planning and steps.[89] Brampton wrote that these gradations are known to all depressives. She ultimately did take her own life.

Treatments, Recoveries, Damages, and Regrets

Most of the writers have found some treatment that has helped and give vivid descriptions of medicine's restorative powers. Many of these dramatic and unexpected transformations make a placebo explanation feel hard to sustain.[90] Tim Lott was sure medicines would not help him, decided to take them anyway, and thought the symptom relief was unmistakable. After a short time on Prozac, Slater felt healthy for the first time. Obsessive symptoms cleared, and she started to feel at home in her body in a new way. She felt that she was becoming the person she was meant to be.[91] She finally moved out of a dank basement apartment she had been living in, and had a new ability to find pleasure:

I bit into an apple, and I enjoyed the gesture. I enjoyed the white chair on which, over many weeks, I snoozed and rocked, my defenses dwindling down. I started to take more baths, some, even, with petals and scent. Prozac brought me to pumpkin muffins, yellowfin tuna, and plum sauce.[92]

Most ECT memoirs stress that ECT works. Many memoirs of depression are written to make the illness understood; ECT memoirs are often written to make the treatment understood. Endler's story of complete success is not typical but also not unique. Celebrities such as Kitty Dukakis and Carrie Fisher wrote about how vital ECT was to their recovery from depression.[93] Manning's own first thoughts upon the recommendation of ECT were of *Cuckoo's Nest*. She feared that if she needed such an extreme treatment, she must be really sick. But after several treatments, she had improved sleep and appetite, and decreased agitation: "The weight of the depression has definitely eased."[94] Many writers on ECT struggled to explain to their friends why they were willing to have the treatment. At a party, someone said to Manning, "How could you let them do that to you?"

> I bristle and answer, "I didn't let them do it to me. I asked them to do it." "But why would you ever do that?" she insists. "Because I was trying to save my life," I answer, hoping to end the conversation. Emboldened by a couple of bourbons, she challenges. "Aren't you being just a bit dramatic? Depression is hardly a life-and-death condition."[95]

But the writers of the ECT memoirs frequently feel that the treatment is also misunderstood by the doctors who provide it. The writers may want to erase *Cuckoo's Nest* images from the mind of the lay public, but they also resent doctors who say the treatment is harmless. Kruger recounted how ECT helped bring her back from an episode of what looks like psychotic depression. After treatment she slept normally for the first time in weeks and had a sense of calm relief. But relief did not translate into love of the treatment, which she continued to dread. She also resented how impersonal her doctor was, that he had no interest in her story, and only wanted to provide the ECT. After emerging from acute depression, she found a psychoanalyst whom she found rigid at first, but who finally helped her, she said, to uncover some suppressed hostility toward her family.[96]

Complaints about ECT in the memoirs are primarily about memory loss and the dismissal of memory loss by some clinicians. ECT handbooks and textbooks sometimes portray the treatment as painless and harmless. Doctors often say that any memory loss will concern short-term memories of events near the treatment, and that memory losses are usually temporary. This may or may not be true for the majority of patients. I do not think the science is conclusive. ECT memoirs, though, are loaded with complaints about memory loss. Anne Donohue published an account in 2000 which contrasted the mild warning she received with the severity of loss that she experienced. She felt like she was being "mocked by science."[97] In his autobiography, physician Sherwin Nuland credits the memory loss with his recovery, thinking ECT must have blotted out some trauma.[98] Most accounts, though, see the memory losses as a grim sacrifice. The complaints about memory loss are compelling because they do not come only from patients who consider ECT worthless, though some do. Many come from patients, including Manning, Dukakis, and Fisher, who all wrote to convey how much ECT helped them, who said they would do it again even if they knew they would lose the memories, and who went back for voluntary treatments.[99]

The picture is similar in some ways for how drugs are written about – a minority of writers present them as unambiguous goods, but more express ambivalence. Springsteen is emphatic that both medicines and psychotherapy helped him. On one occasion, a bout of relentless weeping halted within days of starting an antidepressant.[100] Gask – a psychiatrist – was shocked at the speed of her recovery, and she related no adverse effects. But in most of these books, unwanted effects of the drugs must be reckoned with. In most, these do not occasion the massive sense of loss that comes from the memory gaps from ECT. They are not minor, though. The SSRIs were launched with hopes that they would have milder side effects than MAOIs or tricyclics, but sexual side effects are common. Sex is important to most people. Slater: "I know of no theorist, from Stack Sullivan and Freud to Horney and Lifton, who would claim it's OK to be, shall we say, dysphoric in the genitals."[101]

Sometimes people taking antidepressants fear that the drugs *must* be bad for you. Wurtzel describes at one point being on both lithium and Prozac. Side effects were unwelcome but tolerable, and outweighed by the relief the medicines provided. But she was sure that the drugs must be bad for you, a price must be paid, even if she did not know what the price was. The worry may seem superstitious, and it may indeed have elements of magical thinking, but drugs usually *do* have costs, and often these costs are not all known, particularly when the drugs are new. Slater: "Taking a pill, especially a recently developed psychotropic pill about which researchers have more questions than answers, is always an exercise in the existential, because whatever happens, happens to your body alone. Each time you swallow a pill you are swallowing not only a chemical compound but yourself unmoored."[102]

The very word "drug" raises specters. The antidepressant era was born and raised with a twin: the war on drugs. As if in a psychological study, they were raised in contrasting environments. The antidepressants were a fair-haired child, brought up told how promising they were. They were medicine, a gifted child, the gift of healing. Recreational drugs were the bad seed who would never amount to anything, destined for prison or early death, sometimes evil incarnate, society's greatest menace. To be clear, I am not saying that the line drawn between prescription and recreational drugs is completely arbitrary. But it is also not completely objective or scientific. Some substances, like amphetamine, migrate from the medical realm, where they were used for depression, to the recreational realm, and sometimes back again, as they are now used to treat attention deficit.[103] LSD has followed a similar trajectory.[104] Cultural associations bear heavily, and remain a barrier to medical marijuana and to LSD's medicinal use.

Slater worried that she became an addict on Prozac. Wurtzel began referring to her psychiatrist's office as "the crack house."[105] A recent column about trying to get off antidepressants was entitled "Hi, I'm David. I'm a Drug Addict."[106]

These anxieties about drugs are close to the doubt about the realness of depression as illness. Merkin writes:

> Although I have been on antidepressants for three and a half decades, I continue to feel defensive about them . . . Even as I faithfully took my pills I couldn't help wondering: Was I medicating a bad childhood or a

chemical irregularity? And did it matter what the cause was if the drugs helped keep me going, steered me away from the thoughts of suicide that had haunted me ever since I was a young girl?[107]

One can say, and on one level believe, that depression is an illness like diabetes, requiring regular doses of medicine. Whatever distaste people with diabetes might have toward taking insulin, though, it does not cause them to worry that they have become a drug addict, with all the grave associations cast on that identity.

Doubts about treatments are heightened by adverse effects, which are common. Few things frustrate these writers more than dismissal from their doctors when they complain about adverse effects. For decades, patients have been saying they have permanent memory losses from ECT. ECT providers often say the complaints are rare (though the rarity is not proven) or perhaps the result of the depression itself.[108] Brampton told one doctor of weight gain she thought was from her medication, but which he was sure had another cause. An adverse effect from a treatment may be rare, yet still occur for that particular patient. When an adverse effect is felt only when on the drug, and never when on another drug or no drugs at all, it is hard for a patient to hear that they should or could not be getting the effect from the drug. When a treatment is new, an adverse effect may not yet have registered in the clinical science, and it takes complaining patients to bring it to light. When she was on another medication, one of Brampton's doctors dismissed her complaints about side effects – which included physical aches, poor vision, shaking, troubled sleep, and nausea – on the grounds that the drug (Venlafaxine, or Effexor) is ordinarily tolerated. He did not relent even after she showed him articles she had found about people having the same side effect (these are all now known side effects of Effexor).[109] Patients can, of course, also be wrong about a drug causing their problem, but they are understandably dismayed when a clinician assumes them to be, as with the doctor who told Jeffrey Smith "I've never heard of any such thing. I don't see how the pills could be causing that. The PDR [*Physician's Desk Reference*] doesn't mention it."[110]

Medication's drawbacks are often used to support talk therapies, but therapy can arouse complaints too. Inman regretted seeing a therapist who told her the best thing she could do was sit and let herself feel the pain.[111] Brampton complained about the rigidity of a psychodynamic therapist who made her stand in the rain when she was early for an appointment. Such rigidity is not as common among psychoanalysts as is often thought, but it does occur.[112] Brampton found some help in CBT, but found it too cognitive, and too behavioral. Brampton disapproved precisely of one of its selling points, time-limitedness, which she thought fails to see depression's complexity, and how hard it is to work through. CBT "might teach me how to function more happily and effectively but it does not teach me what the point of functioning well (or badly) is in the first place."[113]

Ambivalence toward depression treatments is likely, in part because they do not usually provide permanent cure. Manning felt recovered after ECT, but in the midst of mourning memory losses, she also bore some recurrence of depression, though milder than before the ECT. Wurtzel wrote that "The secret I sometimes think that only I know is that Prozac really isn't that great. Of course, I can say this and still believe that Prozac was the miracle that saved my life."[114]

Weirdly, even recovery can cause ambivalence. Wurtzel:

In a strange way, I had fallen in love with my depression . . . I loved it because I thought it was all I had. I thought depression was the part of my character that made me worthwhile. I thought so little of myself, felt that I had such scant offerings to give to the world, that the one thing that justified my existence at all was my agony . . . I was so scared to give up depression, fearing that somehow the worst part of me was actually all of me.[115]

Similarly, Thompson: "To eliminate the disease would eliminate everything I thought of as me."[116] After recovery on medications, Gask confessed she did not want to think the solution could be so simple.[117]

Some writers rejected medications altogether. Simple dislike of side effects, by itself, seems not to be the reason. Ann Cvetkovich did so for partly political reasons. She sees the causes of depression in capitalism – the inequalities and alienation it produces, and how its relentless demands on our time crowd out the opportunities for creativity. The symptoms of depression, in this view, are political signs that demand attention, and covering them up with drugs is hiding the problem, not solving it.[118] Smith, who adopted a humoral way of thinking about his depression and prefers to call it melancholia, came to think (as Jung did) that depression was telling you something important about yourself and that you should listen.[119] Cvetkovich and Smith are both saying that depression tells us something important, whether personal or political, and that medications silence the messenger. They both came to this view honestly, because both got some symptom relief from the medications they gave up. They made a brave choice, though as Cvetkovich acknowledges, it is not right for everyone.

Memoir as Manifesto

In *Americanah*, the tension between Ifemelu and her aunt about whether depression is an illness is not resolved. In non-fictional reflection on her own experience, though, Adichie takes a stand: depression is an illness, and needs to be understood and de-stigmatized.[120] The memoirs have points to make: depression is an illness, though one that is hard to describe. Not being treated as a sick person is one of the hardest things about it – even if the writers sometimes have trouble seeing themselves as sick. As people with sickness, they want and benefit from medical treatment. They also feel that their life stories and present psychology matter. The memoirs support, from a subjective point of view, the view that drugs and psychotherapy are most effective combined. Whether or not the biology is well-described as a "chemical imbalance," people with depression feel they have lives out of balance. They welcome what helps them to feel better, whether it is physical or psychological.

Put another way, the memoirs are manifestos against biological reductionism. They anticipate the state of the science, which says depression has a biology, many specifics of the biology remain unclear, and the biological treatments are incomplete. Memoirs said this during the boom years of the biological model.

The memoirs have an attraction-repulsion response to "chemical imbalance" theories of depression, welcoming them for affirming the realness of illness, while rejecting them for failing to see how many-faceted depression is. They are often ahead of the science in finding adverse effects.

Medical anthropologists have shown that DSM labeling and giving antidepressants can hide the complexity of the suffering person, their life history, and their social world.[121] The ethnographers often tell us that the people being studied, who are distant from the culture of Western psychiatry, have, and also demand, more complex explanatory models. They have a particular life trajectory and social context, and they want more than a pill. They want *to be seen*, not merely labeled.

The depression memoirs, though, say that you do not have to be far away from Western psychiatry to feel the same. From the beginnings of ECT through the rise of the SSRIs, patients have been saying that they want more than relief from their symptoms. Psychoanalysis got this right, with its immersion into the inner life and history of the patient.

Meyer also got this right. The patient, he insisted, is a biological organism, *and* an individual with distinct needs, *and* embedded in a set of social relations. Meyer was once considered the most influential psychiatrist in America. He trained many psychiatrists, many of whom went on to chair psychiatry departments.[122] Yet his vision has often been disregarded. It's worth thinking about why. Meyer was not a great writer, and he had no bestselling book. But a deeper reason his influence waned may ironically lie in the virtue of his approach: its complexity. It was hard to put into slogans, and hard to practice.

It is not easy for doctors to hold in view the biological, the psychological, and the social, even if they are supported in the effort. That effort is not supported by a medical culture deeply driven by profit, where profit is driven by speed. The whole person is hard to grasp in short office visits that are limited in number by a third-party payer. Treating a whole person takes time. The whole person is not captured in a randomized, double-blind, clinical trial. The complexity of depression is hard to manualize.

Epilogue:
Depression's Past and Future

"The last word about melancholy will probably never be written."
                                                                    – Judith Shklar[1]

"The treatment of mental health is an inexact science. But, as I am slowly coming to understand, depression is an inexact illness."
                                                                    – Sally Brampton[2]

Sorrow Is Everywhere You Turn

As the COVID-19 pandemic progresses, many are experiencing new hardships and griefs. Everything we know suggests this will be accompanied and followed by increased rates of depression and mental illnesses. Many people already at risk for depression will not only face more adversity, but will have to do so in isolating circumstances – the worst possible scenario for a depressive person. Disruptions in supply chains may make antidepressants less available – a scary prospect for many, whatever you think of the data from clinical trials.

Meanwhile, human action has rendered the earth's climate dangerous for human survival, and efforts to slow or reverse the change are met with massive counterattacks by the people making money from the causes of the change. In industrialized countries, wealth inequality has been rising since the 1970s. Elites have so much money they are planning personal space travel, while their employees need public assistance to buy basic necessities. The elites remain unsatisfied, and say they are still over-taxed. Much of the world is enduring terrible violent conflicts.

And apart from the specifics of our historical moment, one enduring lesson has been passed down in virtually every religious and philosophical tradition, all over the world: life is hard.

Babies and children confront, on an hourly basis, lack of autonomy and power, their dependence on the bigger and stronger, and the frustration dependence causes. Older children remain hemmed in by rules grown-ups impose. Most people will know the sting of unreturned love, or the wasteland of lost love. Middle age can be a slog; most people have heavy responsibilities, and many are stuck in dull, alienating jobs. Some people find they have made a mistake in marriage, and have to decide between the pain of leaving or the pain of staying. The easiest and most loving of children will stretch one's endurance and patience. Those who have known the best health and most prosperity will still know mourning, aging, and physical pain. And at every age, the question: what is it all for?

And yet, not everyone gets depression, the illness. Many people in terrible life situations do not. Many people in the best of circumstances do.

Despite our inability to help all who get ill with depression, we have a wide array of treatments, some old and some just being tested; that they can help many people is reason for celebration. Those who worry about unrealistic expectation of happiness have a point. People with depression – "clinical" depression – do not, however, expect unbridled joy. They want to have a massive extra burden lifted, so they can live with rewarding interests, better connections with others, enough energy to do normal tasks, release from constant sorrow, and the ability to go to sleep when tired and wake up feeling restored.

We cannot change some of the problems that make life hard. Depression, however, is a problem that can be relieved. We will mostly likely not eradicate it, and we have no reliable permanent cure. But we have effective treatments, and we also know of preventive measures, such as education and lifestyle advice that could reduce the burden of the illness.[3] We also know of social factors that increase the risk of depression and worsen its course. These social factors can be changed. We could, for example, treat mental health care, and all health care, as a human right and provide universal access. Instead, many of our political leaders, at least in the United States, pretend to care about mental health only when they want to distract us from the real causes of gun violence.

How well we manage the future of depression depends in part on how well we understand its past.

History Against Compulsive Repetition

History does not simply enrich us, or humanize us in some vague or abstract sense. It is worth knowing, because as psychoanalysis tells us, our past sets us in patterns of thought. If we do not examine them, they will control us without our realizing it.

With regard to depression, we learn that:

We do not have to keep having the same arguments. Rigid proponents of psychological approaches and their counterparts in the biological camp have spent the last 100 years like an unhappy married couple, having the same fights over and over. Wise voices have, like a good marriage counselor, urged each to try to remember what is lovable in their spouse. The least productive idea is that only one approach has merit. Reductionism in the treatment of depression has led to dead ends.

Counting depressions is a vexed project. Epidemics may be more apparent than real. Whether in the Renaissance or now, claims of depression reaching epidemic levels should not be dismissed. They should, however, be evaluated with care, since definitions and treatment patterns vary. The case for over-diagnosis, though, should get as much critical scrutiny as the case for rising prevalence. Overly broad definitions of illness have costs, but so do restrictive ones.

Don't Scorn the Past. Current science, no matter how valuable, is always a product of a historical moment, and the reigning assumptions of that moment. Past views that do not conform to those assumptions may have insights we struggle to see if we idealize current views. Many earlier students of depression – from Rufus and Burton, to Abraham and Melanie Klein, through to biological psychiatrists of a scant generation ago – may have had insights worth preserving. They may, even some of the recent ones, have expressed the insights in language that seems quaint now. But as my professor said in my college course on English literature from Beowulf to Milton, "If we know more than they do, it is only because we know them."

Don't believe the hype. New treatments will be coming. Some of them may build on existing ideas, and some may come from entirely new, now-unimagined paradigms. Either way, if the treatments are good, people will be tempted to declare past approaches to depression obsolete. Given the flaws in our current treatment repertoire, better ones would be welcome. But when new ones come, we should be wary of claims that they lack downsides, or that the final truths about depression are close at hand.

Listen to patients. You don't have to take my word about reductionism (though I think I have made a good case). Patients say they don't like it. Yes, some may like a certain somatic intervention. Yes, some prefer psychotherapy. Much evidence agrees, though, that patients want their individual biology, psychology, and social setting considered. The product they want resembles the one Meyer was selling, though it is hard to find in the current market. Patients are also attuned to adverse effects of treatments, sometimes before those effects are acknowledged in clinical science.

The Way Forward

What to do, faced with the explosive growth in depression diagnoses, combined with troubles such as poor efficacy data from clinical trials for antidepressants, and the realization that the drugs have adverse effects? One response might be that psychiatry needs to get back to basics, treat the severely ill – those with a "real medical problem."

Making judgments about severity is crucial for making treatment plans and is obviously important. The history of depression shows, though, that the line between really sick and healthy is not easily drawn. Instead of treating the blurry border as a damning flaw of diagnosis, we could use it as inherited wisdom. Instead of insisting that the line must be drawn more sharply, we could admit the need for some flexibility and even uncertainty. Depression is not monolithic, but a group of illness states with enough in common to bear the same name. It is more like a family name than a given name.

A wide definition of clinical depression does have costs. Concern for those costs needs to weighed against benefits, however. There is much to be said for the ability to bear suffering. There is also much to be said for not suffering needlessly.[4]

Note on the Historiography

I tried (though at times failed) not to get overly involved in debates with other scholars in the main body of the text. I want to explain some of my choices further here.

The trend in recent years has been for historians to stress the newness of the current conceptions of depression. As I mentioned in chapter 2, the recent focus by historians on the newness of depression is itself new, and largely a post-Prozac trend. Before the 1990s, many psychiatrists used melancholia and depression interchangeably. Some historians did too, though few historians had written much about depression before Prozac came out. In his 1986 book, Stanley Jackson stressed continuities between modern depressive illnesses and precursor syndromes, mainly melancholia. Janet Oppenheim's work assumed that melancholia and depression are the same thing.[1] More recently, other scholars have focused more on the dramatic increase in the use of the term depression starting in the second half of the twentieth century, and seen it as discontinuous with earlier uses. Clark Lawlor's 2012 book is more similar to Jackson's in its approach than much of the other recent work.

Flux in conceptions and categories has been a constant, however, and was so before DSM-III and before Prozac. I have not wanted to revive the emphasis on continuity in Jackson. For all the virtues in his book, one big flaw in it is that it traces continuities in descriptions without grappling adequately with the tendency of many writers to copy from each other. Still less have I wanted to assume identity between melancholia and depression, as Oppenheim did. I do think, though, that reasonable concerns about the dangers of retrospective diagnosis can spill over into a rigid taboo that forecloses meaningful comparisons across time and space. No one can reasonably argue for perfect continuity over time and place in the meaning of depressive illness – and few have. Treating the DSM-III or DSM-5 definitions of Major Depressive Disorder as utterly and entirely discontinuous with either twentieth-century antecedents or earlier ones, seems to me an over-emphasis in the other direction.

Historians use a lot of categories that have varying and contested meanings over time, including some of the most foundational – male, female, class, labor, race, sex – without concluding that we cannot compare their meanings and functions across time and space. I wonder if our nervousness about making these comparisons about mental illnesses reflects an implicit suspicion that they are too "socially constructed" to be really real. But which of the categories in this paragraph has not been shown to be a social construction in important ways?

I tried to make this project as global as possible. I tried especially to look beyond North America and Western Europe, where most histories of depression have been confined. I would have liked to have done still better. We are limited by the state of the research, though. Most of the writing on depression in non-Western contexts is by medical anthropologists and mental health professionals, not historians, although some of it has been historically informed. I have used work in other disciplines in writing this. Still, I hope future synthetic histories of depression will be able to draw on a richer source pool of research in diverse contexts. If depression is as widespread as the WHO says it is, a focus on the West is too limited, and if it is not that widespread, then we need to explain how the WHO came to its conclusion. We will also have a better understanding of depression in the West once we have a better comparative frame. I hope I will have spurred further discussion of this knotty problem. There is, though, also some justification for looking closely at Europe and the United States, where the labels now used, and the ideas underpinning them, were forged.

I also have looked more closely at two twentieth-century treatments for depression that preceded the antidepressant era – psychoanalysis and ECT – than most general histories of depression have. I often feel, reading histories of depression, that the authors were not interested in psychoanalysis, and gave it a section out of a sense of duty. While its influence has waned in recent decades, it remains a vital source of thinking about depression. A lot of psychoanalytic thinking on depression is simply omitted in most histories of depression. Psychoanalysis has less prestige in recent decades, but was dominant for much of modernity. To pay it less attention in historical writing now because it no longer has the prestige it once had is presentist. Psychoanalysis is also important beyond the era of its heyday. It birthed much of what came afterwards, sometimes in expected ways (such as reaction against it), but also in some surprising continuities.

As for ECT, it has mostly been looked at in work devoted specifically to ECT, and skipped over even more lightly than psychoanalysis in general histories of depression. For historical writing on any illness to touch so lightly on what so many clinicians consider the most effective treatment is more than a little strange. I am, of course, aware that ECT is controversial. That's what my book on ECT is about. The controversies make ECT more important to grasp historically, not less.

My account is as interdisciplinary as I could make it. Interdisciplinarity is often idealized in academia, depicted as a magic wand that will end all barriers to knowledge. Worse, it can be used – often by administrators who want to avoid the costs of building up disciplines – to undermine any disciplinarity at all. I use disciplines besides history for concrete practical reasons. You cannot get a good look at depression outside of the countries in the North Atlantic Treaty Organization if you don't use anthropology. The story of depression is also a story of inequalities. You can't make a serious engagement with social disparities, such as of class, race, and gender, without looking at the sociology and epidemiology. The role of social inequality in depression is considerably under-studied by historians.

I also am not shy about commenting on efficacy of treatments. Too many historians of psychiatry, in my opinion, decline to say whether treatments work, calling that a clinical, and not a historical, question. Historians often say they intend to explore what the treatment *means*, rather than whether it works. For people with an illness, though, the meaning of a treatment cannot be separated from the question of whether it works. No one would write about the history of antibiotics or chemotherapy and decline to say whether they work. Sometimes the evidence may be inconclusive, and when it is, we can say so. That is different from saying the question of efficacy is not the historian's business at all. Sometimes historians do assess efficacy, in a harshly critical way, focusing on treatments they do not approve of. Or, we offer critique of treatments for their negative effects, or social control utility. If it is our job to make those kinds of assessments – and it is – we have to take the responsibility of making judgments about the positives. This is not just a matter of being fair to psychiatry. It is also an ethical responsibility to people who are ill, because we can give the impression that they should not seek treatment. Any historian who truly believes there is no utility in psychiatry at all – and some seem to write as though that is the case – is of course free to argue and document that claim. I disagree with it. I think evidence shows that effective treatments for depression (and for other mental illnesses) exist – not all equally effective, sometimes differing in the way they are effective, and often having costs. In any event, for someone to say they have no opinion about whether a treatment works, after spending years studying it, is an abdication of responsibility.

We should not, I think, be afraid to assert any progress in clinical science. History of medicine, as a field, has worked hard over roughly the last half century to overcome an earlier tendency to tell naïve stories of inevitable, but nonetheless heroic, progress. The earlier "progress narratives" left out too much – about, for example, coercive and abusive practices, blind alleys in research, excessive medicalization, or those left out of the progress because they received no treatment at all. Historical narratives that allow no possibility of progress at all are also incomplete, however. The impulse of medical historians to be skeptical of progress may have been over-learned, to the point where simply calling a work of history a progress narrative is supposed to be a critique by itself. I think this is a problem in history of psychiatry above all. Reading much work in the field, one might often feel that nothing has been accomplished in psychiatry at all. We do not have to idealize any treatments to acknowledge that some offer benefit. For those who can obtain treatment – and there are too many who cannot – more hope is available for people with mental illness than there was in 1850.

Notes

Preface

1 Virginia Heffernan, "A Delicious Placebo," in Nell Casey, *Unholy Ghost: Writers on Depression* (New York: HarperCollins, 2001).

2 John Scott Price, "If I Had . . . Chronic Depressive Illness," *British Medical Journal* 1 (1978) 1200–1. Thanks to Alex Riley for the reference.

3 I have tried to write as though this could be the only book on depression or mental illness, the only work of medical history, or even the only work of history – the reader has ever picked up. I ask for patience from experts in the field when they see things they already know. The book contains some original research, and I certainly hope original interpretation and ideas. But it is also a work of synthesis. My debts to other scholars in the field are clear in the footnotes and bibliography.

4 Stephen M. Stahl, *Stahl's Essential Psychopharmacology: Neuroscientific Basis and Practical Applications* (4th edn, Cambridge: Cambridge University Press, 2013), 245.

5 Medical anthropology sometimes distinguishes between "disease," defined as a state diagnosed by a clinician, and "illness," defined as the subjective state of feeling ill. This distinction is useful for some

purposes, but because the use of the term illness is so widespread in the clinical science and diagnosis of depression, it would bring more confusion than clarity to my discussion. A classic text on the distinction is Arthur Kleinman, *The Illness Narratives* (New York: Basic Books, 1989).

6 I have elsewhere argued that the division between "physical" and "psychological treatments" is fundamentally flawed. But because it has been so widely believed in, it is hard to write the history without using it. See Jonathan Sadowsky, "Somatic Treatments," in Greg Eghigian, *The Routledge History of Madness and Mental Health* (New York: Routledge, 2017).

7 Sadowsky, "Somatic Treatments."

8 This paragraph was inspired by an exchange I had with Sloan Mahone at the conference "Global Histories of Psychiatry," in Groningen, the Netherlands, in November 2018.

9 Susan Sontag, *Illness as Metaphor and AIDS and Its Metaphors* (New York: Picador, 2001).

10 These are words of a depression patient quoted in Janis Hunter Jenkins and Norma Cofresi, "The Sociomatic Course of Depression and Trauma: A Cultural Analysis of Suffering and Resilience in the Life of a Puerto Rican Woman," *Psychosomatic Medicine* 60 (1998) 439–47.

Chapter 1: Depression is a Thing

1 http://bookslive.co.za/blog/2015/03/13/i-felt-violated-chimaman da-ngozi-adichie-reveals-her-anger-at-the-guardian-over-article-on -depression/, accessed October 25, 2019.

2 Chimamanda Ngozi Adichie, *Americanah* (London: HarperCollins, 2014). See especially pages 150–8.

3 http://www.who.int/mediacentre/news/releases/2017/world-health-day/en/, accessed July 7, 2017. See also Alice Walton, "The Strategies that Science Actually Shows are Effective for Depression," *Forbes*, June 15, 2017, https://www.forbes.com/sites/alicegwalton/2017/06/15/the-strategies-that-science-actually-shows-are-effective-for-depression/#547748b75117, accessed July 8, 2017.

4 https://psychnews.psychiatryonline.org/doi/10.1176/appi.pn.20 17.pp9b2, accessed August 20, 2019.

5 See, for example, Dan G. Blazer, *The Age of Melancholy: Major Depression and Its Social Origins* (New York: Routledge, 2005).

6 Christopher M. Callahan and German E. Berrios, *Reinventing Depression: A History of the Treatment of Depression in Primary Care, 1940–2004* (Oxford: Oxford University Press, 2005), 116–17.

7 Terri Airov, "Is the Definition of Depression Deficient? Examining the Validity of a Common Diagnosis," *Psych Congress Network*, Fall/ Winter 2017, 28–9.

8 Douglas F. Levinson and Walter E. Nichols, "Genetics of Depression," in Dennis S. Charney, Joseph D. Buxbaum, Pamela Sklar, and Eric J. Nestler, *Charney and Nestler's Neurobiology of Mental Illness* (5th edn, New York: Oxford University Press, 2018), 301.

9 Ibid.

10 Scott Monroe and Richard A. Depue, "Life Stress and Depression," in Joseph Becker and Arthur Kleinman, eds., *Psychosocial Aspects of Depression* (New York: Routledge, 1991), 102.

11 Quoted in Tim Lott, *The Scent of Dried Roses* (London: Penguin, 1996), 70. My emphasis.

12 Silvano Arieti and Jules Bemporad, *Severe and Mild Depression: The Psychotherapeutic Approach* (New York: Basic Books, 1978), 3.

13 The examples in this paragraph are detailed and documented in later chapters: classical antiquity in chapter 2, Freud in chapter 3, and the bereavement exclusion in chapter 4.

14 Jonathan Sadowsky, *Electroconvulsive Therapy in America* (New York: Routledge, 2006), 83–6.

15 Nancy C. Andreasen, *The Broken Brain: The Biological Revolution in Psychiatry* (New York: Harper and Row, 1984), 34.

16 The concept of the sick role was classically expressed in Talcott Parsons, "Social Structure and Dynamic Process: The Case of Modern Medical Practice," in *The Social System* (Glencoe: The Free Press, 1951), 428–79. It has lost some status in sociology, but I still find it useful; see John C. Burnham, "Why Sociologists Abandoned the Sick Role Concept," *History of the Human Sciences* 27, 1 (2014) 70–87. I thank Disha Bhargava for helpful comments on a previous draft of this paragraph.

17 On the process of transforming conditions into illnesses, see
    Peter Conrad, *The Medicalization of Society: On the Transformation
    of Human Conditions into Treatable Diseases* (Baltimore: The Johns
    Hopkins University Press, 2007).
18 Randall M. Packard, *White Plague, Black Labor: Tuberculosis and the
    Political Economy of Health and Disease in South Africa* (Berkeley:
    University of California Press, 1989); Georgina D. Feldberg,
    *Disease and Class: Tuberculosis and the Shaping of North American
    Society* (New Brunswick: Rutgers University Press, 1995).
19 Sontag's *Illness as Metaphor* gives a classic account of this.
20 On the pros and cons of psychiatric diagnosis, see also Felicity
    Callard, "Psychiatric Diagnosis: The Indispensability of
    Ambivalence," *Journal of Medical Ethics* 40 (2014) 526–30; and
    George Szmukler, "When Psychiatric Diagnosis Becomes an
    Overworked Tool," *Journal of Medical Ethics* 40, 8 (August 2014),
    517–20.
21 I obviously cannot prove that there are literally no psychiatrists
    who do not recognize limitations of the DSM. I read and meet a
    lot of psychiatrists, though. I know of none who do not recognize
    that the manual has flaws.
22 Gary Greenberg, *The Book of Woe: The DSM and the Unmaking
    of Psychiatry* (New York: Plume, 2013) is one of the scathing cri-
    tiques of the DSM books, and uses the "bible" comparison. But
    Greenberg himself recognizes throughout that psychiatrists see
    the DSM as, at best, a rough guide with modest claims to scien-
    tific rigor. Historian Anne Harrington notes that unease about the
    DSM has been growing since the 1990s. This is likely true, but as
    we will see in chapter 4, there has been a substantial amount of
    unease with the DSM at least since the 1970s. Anne Harrington,
    *Mind Fixers: Psychiatry's Troubled Search for the Biology of Mental
    Illness* (New York: W. W. Norton and Sons, 2019), 267.
23 Wendy Gonaver has recently argued that the diagnosis was even
    more ideological than it is usually taken to be, since no one seems
    to have actually used it in medical practice. Wendy Gonaver, *The
    Peculiar Institution and the Making of Modern Psychiatry, 1840–1880*
    (Chapel Hill: University of North Carolina Press, 2018), 6–7.
24 Chiara Thumiger offers a smart set of four premises for thinking

confined to the brain, but involve other parts of the body, (3) the mind is acculturated, and (4) there is further an irreducible individual quality, a private-ness to every person. Chiara Thumiger, *A History of the Mind and Mental Health in Classical Greek Medical Thought* (Cambridge: Cambridge University Press, 2017), 27–9. I only question the implied notion here that brain and biology are universal, and mind cultural. Mind can only be subject to culture if brain is, and since we know mind is, we also know brain is. This does not mean that the brain is infinitely plastic to culture.

25 In my work on the history of mental illness in colonial Nigeria, I found that in relatively early contacts between Europeans and West Africans, "madness" was a category that was recognized across cultural divides. Jonathan Sadowsky, *Imperial Bedlam: Institutions of Madness and Colonialism in Southwest Nigeria* (Berkeley: University of California Press, 1999), ch. 1.

26 Sushrut Jadhav, "The Cultural Construction of Western Depression," in Vieda Skultans and John Cox, eds., *Anthropological Approaches to Psychological Medicine* (Philadelphia: Jessica Kingsley Publishers, 2000).

27 See, for example, Christopher Dorwick, "Depression as a Culture-Bound Syndrome: Implications for Primary Care," *British Journal of General Practice* 63, 610 (2013) 229–30. Matthew Bell, *Melancholia, The Western Malady* (Cambridge: Cambridge University Press, 2014) argues at length that depression is uniquely Western, but the argument is not strong because it is not deeply-steeped in the cross-cultural literature.

28 The term "Culture-Bound Syndrome" was coined in the 1960s by psychiatrist P. M. Yap. See P. M. Yap, "Koro: A Culture-bound Depersonalization Syndrome," *British Journal of Psychiatry* 111 (1965) 43–50. There have been many subsequent discussions. See, for example, Peter Guarnaccia and L. H. Rogler, "Research on Culture-Bound Syndromes," *American Journal of Psychiatry* 156 (1999), 1322–7.

29 Raymond Prince, "The Changing Picture of Depressive Syndromes in Africa: Is It Fact or Diagnostic Fashion?" *Canadian Journal of African Studies* 1, 2 (November 1967) 177–92; John Orley and John K. Wing, "Psychiatric Disorders in Two African Villages,"

Archives of General Psychiatry 36 (May 1979) 513–20; Melanie A. Abas and Jeremy C. Broadhead, "Depression and Anxiety among Women in an Urban Setting in Zimbabwe," *Psychological Medicine* 27 (1997) 59–71.

30 Leonard Smith, *Insanity, Race, and Colonialism: Managing Mental Disorder in The Post-Emancipation Caribbean, 1838–1914* (London: Palgrave Macmillan, 2014), 2, 34.

31 Sowande' M. Mustakeem, *Slavery at Sea: Terror, Sex, and Sickness in the Middle Passage* (Urbana: University of Illinois Press, 2016), 115–17.

32 See T. Duncan Greenlees, "Insanity among the Natives of South Africa," *Journal of Mental Science* 41 (1895) 71–82; C. G. F. Smartt, "Mental Maladjustment in the East African," *Journal of Mental Science* 428 (July 1956) 441–66.

33 Keith Wailoo, *How Cancer Crossed the Color Line* (Oxford: Oxford University Press, 2011).

34 Quoted in Herb Kutchins and Stuart A. Kirk, *Making Us Crazy: DSM: The Psychiatric Bible and the Creation of Mental Disorders* (New York: The Free Press, 1997), 219.

35 Arthur J. Prange and M. M. Vitols, "Cultural Aspects of The Relatively Low Incidence of Depression in Southern Negroes," *International Journal of Social Psychiatry* 8, 2 (February 1962) 104–12. The circular logic of this article is an example of what Barbara Fields and Karen Fields have called "Racecraft," the way racist thinking can so deeply inflect baseline assumptions that it can defy evidence and logic. Barbara Fields and Karen Fields, *Racecraft: The Soul of Inequality on American Life* (London: Verso, 2014).

36 T. Adeoye Lambo, "Neuropsychiatric Observations in the Western Region of Nigeria," *British Medical Journal* (December 15, 1956), 1388–94. Alexander H. Leighton, T. Adeoye Lambo, Charles C. Hughes, Dorothea C. Leighton, Jane M. Murphy, and David B. Macklin, *Psychiatric Disorder Among the Yoruba* (Ithaca: Cornell University Press, 1963).

37 David G. Schuster, *Neurasthenic Nation: America's Search for Health, Happiness, and Comfort, 1869–1920* (New Brunswick: Rutgers University Press, 2011), 11.

38 Ibid., 145.

39 Similarly, no Navajo word translates exactly as depression, but many depressive symptoms are considered as signs of illness, warranting treatment. Michael Storck, Thomas J. Csordas, and Milton Strauss, "Depressive Illness and Navajo Healing," *Medical Anthropology Quarterly* 14, 4 (2000) 571–97.

40 Leighton et al., *Psychiatric Disorder Among the Yoruba*, 112. See also M. O. Olatuwara, "The Problem of Diagnosing Depression in Nigeria," *Psychopathologie Africaine* 9 (1973) 389–403.

41 See, for example, Chude Jideonwo, "Nigeria Is Finally Paying Attention to Depression, And Not A Moment Too Soon," https://www.thriveglobal.com/stories/35629-nigeria-is-finally-paying-attention-to-depression, accessed October 19, 2018; "There's a Culture of Silence around the Mental Health of Young Nigerian Men," *Pulse.ng*, https://www.pulse.ng/gist/pop-culture/depression-theres-a-culture-of-silence-around-the-mental-health-of-young-nigerian-men-id7822498.html, accessed October 25, 2018.

42 As Megan Vaughan has put it, writing about the history of suicide in Africa, "The history of suicide is in part a history of subjectivity, and no history of that sort is ever going to be straightforward." Megan Vaughan, "Suicide in Late Colonial Africa: The Evidence of Inquests from Nyasaland," *The American Historical Review* 115, 2 (April 2010) 385–404.

43 Anthony J. Marsella, "Depressive Experience and Disorder across Cultures," in H. Triandis and J. Draguns, eds., *Handbook of Cross-Cultural Psychiatry* (Boston: Allyn and Bacon, 1980).

44 https://www.sde.co.ke/article/2000131772/how-depression-has-never-been-an-african-disease, accessed October 31, 2019. Thanks to Njambe Kimani for this reference.

45 A classic statement of this is Gananath Obeyesekere, "Depression, Buddhism and the Work of Culture in Sri Lanka," in Arthur Kleinman and Byron Good, eds., *Culture and Depression: Studies in the Anthropology and Cross-Cultural Psychiatry of Affect and Disorder* (Berkeley: University of California Press, 1985). For an important commentary on Obeyesekere, see Alain Bottéro, "Consumption by Semen Loss in India and Elsewhere," *Culture,*

Medicine, and Psychiatry 15 (1991), 303–20. See also Catherine Lutz, "Depression and the Translation of Emotional Worlds," in Kleinman and Good, *Culture and Depression*.

46 See Junko Kitanaka, *Depression in Japan: Psychiatric Cures for a Society in Distress* (Princeton: Princeton University Press, 2012), 15–36. I look at this case more in chapter 5. In a 1930s colonial-era glossary translating Vietnamese medical terms into French, one Vietnamese term translated literally as "no interest in anything." The French called this a form of *mélancolie* that carried risk of suicide. See Claire E. Edgington, *Beyond the Asylum: Mental Illness in French Colonial Vietnam* (Ithaca: Cornell University Press, 2019), 160–2.

47 Byron J. Good, Mary-Jo DelVecchio Good, and Robert Moradi, "The Interpretation of Iranian Depressive Illness and Dysphoric Affect," in Kleinman and Good, *Culture and Depression*.

48 The concept has been fertile for cross-cultural study, especially since medical anthropologist Arthur Kleinman introduced a thoughtful treatment in a 1986 book about distress in China. Arthur Kleinman, *Social Origins of Distress and Disease: Depression, Neurasthenia, and Pain in Modern China* (New Haven: Yale University Press, 1986).

49 Prince, "The Changing Picture of Depressive Syndromes in Africa." Prince says the concept of masked depression in Western psychiatry can be traced back to 1912. According to Wikipedia, prominent German psychiatrist Kurt Schneider used the concept in the 1920s, calling it "depression without depression," https:// en.wikipedia.org/wiki/Masked_depression, accessed October 10, 2018.

50 See, for example, B. B. Sethi, S. S. Nathawat, and S. C. Gupta, "Depression in India," *The Journal of Social Psychology* 91 (1973) 3–13; John Racy, "Somatization in Saudi Women: A Therapeutic Challenge," *British Journal of Psychiatry* 137 (1980) 212–16; Fanny M. Cheung, "Psychological Symptoms among Chinese in Urban Hong Kong," *Social Science and Medicine* 16 (1982) 1339–44.

51 Kleinman, *Social Origins*, 52.

52 Daniel R. Wilson, Reuben B. Widmer, Remi J. Cadoret, and Kenneth Judiesch, "Somatic Symptoms: A Major Feature of

Depression in a Family Practice," *Journal of Affective Disorders* 5 (1983) 199–207.

53 Dividing the world into somatizing and non-somatizing cultures risks stereotyping both. This is argued, for example, in Brandon A. Kohrt, Emily Mendenhall, and Peter J. Brown, "Historical Background: Medical Anthropology and Global Mental Health," in Brandon A. Kohrt and Emily Mendenhall, eds., *Global Mental Health: Anthropological Perspectives* (New York: Routledge, 2016).

54 Philosopher of psychiatry Jennifer Radden reaches this conclusion. Jennifer Radden, "Is This Dame Melancholy? Equating Today's Depression and Past Melancholia," *Philosophy, Psychiatry, and Psychology* 10, 1 (2003) 37–52.

55 J. J. López Ibor, "Masked Depressions," *British Journal of Psychiatry* 120 (1972) 245–58.

56 V. A. Kral, "Masked Depression in Middle Aged Men," *Canadian Medical Association Journal* 79, 1 (July 1, 1958) 1–5.

57 These concerns are explored, for example, in Ethan Watters, *Crazy Like Us: The Globalization of the American Psyche* (New York: The Free Press, 2010). For an even more critical view, see China Mills, *Decolonizing Global Mental Health: The Psychiatrization of the Majority World* (London: Routledge, 2014). For another discussion, see Doerte Bemme, "Global Health and its Discontents," *Somatosphere*, July 23, 2012.

58 See, for example, Mark Nichter, "Idioms of Distress: Alternatives in the Expression of Psychosocial Distress: A Case Study from South India," *Culture, Medicine, and Psychiatry* 5 (1981) 379–408. In this article "idioms of distress" refers to what might seem at first to be symptoms of illness but might instead be healthy adaptations to stress. In many usages, though, "idioms of distress" is used more to refer to ways of feeling bad. See also Bonnie N. Kaiser and Lesley Jo Weaver, "Culture-Bound Syndromes, Idioms of Distress, and Cultural Concepts of Distress: New Directions in Psychological Anthropology," *Transcultural Psychiatry* 56, 2 (2019) 589–98.

59 Inga-Britt Krause, "Sinking Heart: A Punjabi Communication of Distress," *Social Science and Medicine* 29, 4 (1989) 563–75. Krause, I should stress, is not insisting on exclusive focus on emic categories,

and on the contrary argues for the inadequacy of a rigid opposition of universalist and relativist approaches.

60 Ibid., 566.

61 Ibid., 571.

62 Bonnie N. Kaiser, Emily E. Haroz, Brandon A. Kohrt, Paul Bolton, Judith K. Bass, and Devon E. Hinton, "'Thinking Too Much': A Systematic Review of a Common Idiom of Distress," *Social Science and Medicine* 147 (2015) 170–83; Inga-Britt Krause, "Sinking Heart: A Punjabi Communication of Distress"; Kristin Elizabeth Yarris, "The Pain of 'Thinking Too Much': *Dolor de Cerebro* and the Embodiment of Social Hardship among Nicaraguan Women," *Ethos* 39, 2 (2011) 226–48; Kristen Elizabeth Yarris, "'*Pensando Mucho*' ('Thinking Too Much'): Embodied Distress Among Grandmothers in Nicaraguan Transnational Families," *Culture, Medicine, and Psychiatry* 38 (2014) 473–98; V. Patel, E. Simyunu, and F. Gwanzura, "*Kufungisisa* (Thinking Too Much): A Shona Idiom for Non-Psychotic Mental Illness," *Central African Journal of Medicine* 41, 7 (1995) 209–15; Bonnie N. Kaiser, Kristen E. McLean, Brandon A. Kohrt, Ashley K. Hagaman, Bradley H. Wagenaar, Nayla M. Khoury, and Hunter M. Keys, "*Reflechi twòp* – Thinking Too Much: Description of a Cultural Syndrome in Haiti's Central Plateau," *Culture, Medicine, and Psychiatry* 38 (2014) 448–72, quote on 448–9. See also Devon E. Hinton, Ria Reis, and Joop de Jong, "The 'Thinking a Lot' Idiom of Distress and PTSD: An Examination of Their Relationship among Traumatized Cambodian Refugees Using the 'Thinking a Lot' Questionnaire," *Medical Anthropology Quarterly* 29, 3 (2015), 357–80; T. N. den Hertog, M. de Jong, A. J. van der Ham, D. Hinton, and R. Reis, "'Thinking a Lot Among the Khwe of South Africa: A Key Idiom of Personal and Interpersonal Distress," *Culture, Medicine, and Psychiatry* 40 (2016) 383–403; Emily Mendenhall, Rebecca Rinehart, Christine Musyimi, Edne Bosire, David Ndetei, and Victorio Mutiso, "An Ethnopsychology of Idioms of Distress in Urban Kenya," *Transcultural Psychiatry* 56, 4 (2019) 620–42.

63 See, for example, Atwood D. Gaines and Paul E. Farmer, "Visible Saints: Social Cynosures and Dysphoria in the Mediterranean Tradition," *Culture, Medicine, and Psychiatry* 10, 4 (December

1986) 295–330; Vieda Skultans, "From Damaged Nerves to Masked Depression: Inevitability and Hope in Latvian Psychiatric Narratives," *Social Science and Medicine* 56 (2003) 2421–31.

64 Colin McClarty and Jay Kaufman, separately, helped me articulate this point, in conversations many years ago.

65 The precise relationship between anxiety and depression has an unsettled status in psychiatry. See Lee Anna Clark and David Watson, "Theoretical and Empirical Issues in Differentiating Depression from Anxiety," in Kleinman and Becker, *Psychosocial Aspects of Depression.*

66 Lutz, "Depression and the Translation of Emotional Worlds," 90. Lutz is drawing here on the work of Julian Leff, another important figure in the cross-cultural study of mental illness.

67 Ibid.: "the greater the geographical or sociohistorical distance from London, the more deficient people are in the ability to tell depression from anxiety."

68 Radden dates it to Emil Kraepelin in the early twentieth century. Jennifer Radden, *Moody Minds Distempered: Essays in Melancholy and Depression* (Oxford: Oxford University Press, 2009), 7.

69 Arthur Kleinman also points out that psychiatry privileges biology by seeing it as the underlying substrate of mental illness, relegating culture to a force that shapes the presumably less essential "content," such as the subject of delusions, for example. Arthur Kleinman, *Rethinking Psychiatry: From Cultural Category to Personal Experience* (New York: The Free Press, 1991), 24–6.

70 Moudhy Al-Rahid, "How My Journey with Depression Goes Back Thousands of Years," *Papyrus Stories,* https://papyrus-sto ries.com/2018/10/10/i-am-dying-of-a-broken-heart, accessed February 25, 2019.

71 Andreasen, *The Broken Brain,* 36.

72 Callahan and Berrios, *Reinventing Depression: A History of the Treatment of Depression in Primary Care, 1940–2004* (Oxford: Oxford University Press, 2005), viii.

73 Joshua Shenk, *Lincoln's Melancholy: How Depression Challenged a President and Fueled His Greatness* (New York: Houghton Mifflin Harcourt, 2005).

74 On this point, see Elizabeth Wurtzel, *Prozac Nation: Young and Depressed in America* (New York: Riverhead Books, 1994), 295.

75 Shelley Taylor and Jonathan Brown, "Illusion and Well Being: A Social Psychological Perspective on Mental Health," *Psychological Bulletin* 103 (1988) 193–210.

76 Susanna Kaysen, "One Cheer for Melancholy," in Nell Casey, *Unholy Ghost: Writers on Depression* (New York: HarperCollins, 2001), 39.

77 See chapter 4.

78 Kay Redfield Jamison, *An Unquiet Mind: A Memoir of Moods and Madness* (New York: Vintage Books, 2011, originally published 1995); Elyn R. Saks, *The Center Cannot Hold: My Journey Through Madness* (New York: Hachette Books, 2007).

Chapter 2: Too Dry and too Cold

1 A. C. Bradley, *Shakespearean Tragedy* (Greenwich: Fawcett Publications, 1904), 104–9, 134. Bradley calls Hamlet's illness alternately melancholy or melancholia, while warning readers against reducing analysis of the play to medical diagnosis.

2 Duncan Salkeld, *Madness and Drama in the Age of Shakespeare* (Manchester, Manchester University Press, 1993), 94–6.

3 Elizabeth Wurtzel, *Prozac Nation: Young and Depressed in America* (New York: Riverhead Books, 1994), 341.

4 Angus Gowland, *The Worlds of Renaissance Melancholy: Robert Burton in Context* (Cambridge: Cambridge University Press, 2006), 1; Bell, *Melancholia*, 100–6.

5 Angus Gowland, "The Problem of Early Modern Melancholy," *Past and Present* 191 (May 2006) 79.

6 Ibid., 80.

7 On Renaissance explanations for a supposed increase in melancholy, see Gowland, *The Worlds of Renaissance Melancholy*, 1–2, 18.

8 Noga Arikha, *Passions and Tempers: A History of the Humours* (New York: Harper Perennial, 2007).

9 Ibid., 121.

10 In 1986, a year before Prozac was approved by the US Food and Drug Administration (FDA), Stanley Jackson published the first important history of depression. Jackson stressed continuity

between melancholia and depression, showing core symptoms described over the centuries and common to both diagnoses. Stanley W. Jackson, *Melancholia and Depression: From Hippocratic Times to Modern Times* (New Haven: Yale University Press, 1986). Jean Starobinski, *History of the Treatment of Melancholy from the Earliest Times to 1900* (Geneva: J. R. Geigy, 1962) is a similar but less thorough account. Arguments for continuity between melancholia and depression also include Peter Toohey, *Melancholy, Love, and Time: Boundaries of the Self in Ancient Literature* (Ann Arbor: University of Michigan Press, 2004). An argument for discontinuity is in German E. Berrios, *The History of Mental Symptoms: Descriptive Psychopathology Since the Nineteenth Century* (Cambridge: Cambridge University Press, 1996). Berrios notes that for melancholia, sadness of spirit was sometimes counted as a symptom, but not a necessary or sufficient one (p. 291). But DSM-5 diagnosis of Major Depressive Disorder is not that different: depressed mood is one of nine symptoms, of which there must be five to make the diagnosis, though it is one of two necessary ones. Jennifer Radden debates the issue with others in a series of articles in *Philosophy, Psychiatry, and Psychology*: Jennifer Radden, "Is This Dame Melancholy? Equating Today's Depression and Past Melancholia," *Philosophy, Psychiatry, and Psychology* 10, 1 (2003) 37–52; David H. Brendel, "A Pragmatic Consideration of the Relation Between Depression and Melancholia," *Philosophy, Psychiatry, and Psychology* 10, 1 (2003) 53–5; Jennifer Hanson, "Listening to People or Listening to Prozac? Another Consideration of Causal Classifications," *Philosophy, Psychiatry, and Psychology* 10, 1 (2003) 57–62; Jennifer Radden, "The Pragmatics of Psychiatry and the Psychiatry of Cross-Cultural Suffering," *Philosophy, Psychiatry, and Psychology* 10, 1 (2003) 63–6.

11 See, for example, Aubrey Lewis, "Melancholia: A Historical Review," *Journal of Mental Science* 80 (January, 1934) 1–42; J. J. López Ibor, "Masked Depressions," *British Journal of Psychiatry* 120 (1972) 245–58.

12 Depressed mood with psychotic delusion can, in contemporary nosology, also be a sign of schizoaffective disorder, which differs

from psychotic depression in that it needs to be treated as a psychosis, rather than as an affective disorder that can be treated primarily by addressing the mood.

13 See also Lawrence Babb, *The Elizabethan Malady: A Study of Melancholia in English Literature from 1580 to 1642* (East Lansing: Michigan State College Press, 1951), 30.

14 This has been shown by a number of people, and argued most closely in Juliana Schiesari, *The Gendering of Melancholia: Feminism, Psychoanalysis, and the Symbolics of Loss in Renaissance Literature* (Ithaca: Cornell University Press, 1992). See also Jennifer Radden, *Moody Minds Distempered: Essays in Melancholy and Depression* (Oxford: Oxford University Press, 2009), 47–62, and Bell, *Melancholia*, ch. 3.

15 H. C. Erik Midelfort, *A History of Madness in Sixteenth-Century Germany* (Stanford: Stanford University Press, 1999), 6–7; Michael MacDonald, *Mystical Bedlam: Madness, Anxiety, and Healing in Seventeenth-Century England* (Cambridge: Cambridge University Press, 1981), 150.

16 Schiesari, *The Gendering of Melancholia*, 93–5.

17 See Jadhav, "The Cultural Construction of Western Depression," 44. The separation is often called "Cartesian." While the philosopher René Descartes voiced an influential version of it, it has a longer history and can be found in philosophers of antiquity and the Middle Ages.

18 One classic treatment is Nancy Scheper-Hughes and Margaret Lock, "'The Mindful Body: A Prolegomenon to Future Work in Medical Anthropology," *Medical Anthropology Quarterly* New Series 1, 1 (March 1987), 6–41.

19 See Radden, "Is This Dame Melancholy?".

20 I do not attempt here to survey every writer on melancholia, not only because of space limitations, but also because accounts like that start to read like a catalogue, and get dull. Many of the works I reference here contain more comprehensive surveys.

21 See chapter 5.

22 Before Galen, humoralism was one paradigm of medicine and the body, but did not have the dominance it came to have with his influence.

23 Babb, *The Elizabethan Malady*, 6.

24 Clark Lawlor, *From Melancholia to Prozac: A History of Depression* (Oxford: Oxford University Press, 2012), 29.

25 Vivian Nutton, "Galenic Madness," in W. V. Harris, ed., *Mental Disorders in the Classical World* (London: Brill, 2013), 122; Mark Grant, *Galen on Food and Diet* (London: Routledge, 2000), 21–4. The quote from Galen appears on p. 22.

26 Jackson, *Melancholia and Depression*; Chiara Thumiger, "The Early Greek Medical Vocabulary of Insanity," in Harris, *Mental Disorders in the Classical World*, 65.

27 Raymond Klibansky, Erwin Panofsky, and Fritz Saxl, *Saturn and Melancholy: Studies in the History of Natural Philosophy, Religions, and Art* (London: Thomas Nelson, 1964), 1.

28 Peter Toohey, *Melancholy, Love, and Time: Boundaries of the Self in Ancient Literature* (Ann Arbor: University of Michigan Press, 2004).

29 Stanley W. Jackson, "Acedia the Sin and Its Relationship to Sorrow and Melancholia," in Arthur Kleinman and Byron Good, eds., *Culture and Depression: Studies in the Anthropology and Cross-cultural Psychiatry of Affect and Disorder* (Berkeley: University of California Press), 43–4.

30 Jackson, *Melancholia and Depression*, 31–6.

31 Radden, *Moody Minds Distempered*, 5; Jacques Joanna, "The Terminology and Aetiology of Madness in Ancient Greek Medical and Philosophical Writing," in Harris, *Mental Disorders in the Classical World*, 99.

32 Toohey, *Melancholy, Love, and Time*, 28.

33 Rufus's work survives only in fragments, and much of it is known from the authors who cited him. Rufus of Ephesus, *On Melancholy* (Peter E. Pormann, ed., Tübingen: Mohr Siebeck, 2008).

34 Peter Pormann, introduction to Rufus of Ephesus, *On Melancholy*, 3.

35 Ibid., 3.

36 Rufus of Ephesus, *On Melancholy*, 47.

37 Peter Pormann, introduction to Rufus of Ephesus, *On Melancholy*, 6.

38 Peter Toohey, "Rufus of Ephesus and the Tradition of the Melancholy Thinker" in Rufus of Ephesus, *On Melancholy*, 221.

39 Peter Pormann, introduction to Rufus of Ephesus, *On Melancholy*, 9.

40 Jackson, *Melancholia and Depression*, 34; George Rosen, *Madness in Society: Chapters in the Historical Sociology of Mental Illness* (Chicago: University of Chicago Press, 1968), 98.

41 Jackson, *Melancholia and Depression*, 51.

42 Lawlor, *From Melancholia to Prozac*, 25.

43 Jackson, *Melancholia and Depression*, 39–40; Rosen, *Madness in Society*, 132.

44 Thumiger, "Ancient Greek and Roman Traditions," 51; Jackson, *Melancholia and Depression*, 33.

45 Jackson, *Melancholia and Depression*, 41–5.

46 Rufus of Ephesus, *On Melancholy*, 63.

47 This was Constantinus Africanus. Jackson, *Melancholia and Depression*, 61. Also see p. 51 on Oribasius of Pergamon, and p. 56 on Paul of Aegina.

48 Jackson, *Melancholia and Depression*, 53.

49 Radden, *Moody Minds Distempered*, 6; Peter Pormann, "Melancholy in the Medieval World," in Rufus of Ephesus, *On Melancholy*, 179.

50 Jackson, "Acedia the Sin," 48.

51 Toohey, *Melancholy, Love, and Time*, 137.

52 Quoted in Pormann, "Melancholy in the Medieval World," 181. See also Jackson, "Acedia the Sin," 44.

53 Toohey, *Melancholy, Love, and Time*, 139.

54 Jackson, "Acedia the Sin," 44–5.

55 Pormann, "Melancholy in the Medieval World," 185–8.

56 Hildegard of Bingen, *On Natural Philosophy and Medicine: Selections from Cause et cure* (Margret Berger, trans., Suffolk: Athenaeum Press, 1999).

57 Pormann, "Melancholy in the Medieval World," 183–5.

58 Hildegard of Bingen, *On Natural Philosophy and Medicine*, 61.

59 Ibid., 60.

60 Claire Trenery and Peregrine Horden, "Madness in the Middle Ages," in Greg Eghigian, ed., *The Routledge History of Madness and Mental Health* (New York: Routledge, 2017).

61 Ibid., 63; see also in the same volume Elizabeth Mellyn, "Healers and Healing in the Early Modern Health Care Market," 86.

62 Jackson, *Melancholia and Depression*, 71; Jackson, "Acedia the Sin," 54.

63 Quoted in H. C. Erik Midelfort, *A History of Madness in Sixteenth-Century Germany* (Stanford: Stanford University Press, 1999), 104.

64 Mellyn, "Healers and Healing in the Early Modern Health Care Market."

65 Midelfort, *A History of Madness in Sixteenth-Century Germany*, 37. See also Jean Delameau, *Sin and Fear: The Emergence of a Western Guilt Culture in the 13th–18th Centuries* (Eric Nicholson, trans., New York: St. Martin's Press, 1990, originally published 1983), 168–9.

66 Babb, *The Elizabethan Malady*; Delameau, *Sin and Fear*, 176.

67 Marsilio Ficino, *The Book of Life* (Charles Boer, trans., Dallas: Spring Publications, 1980), iii, vii, xiii, xv.

68 Ibid., 6–7.

69 Ibid., 18–19.

70 Ibid., 25–6.

71 Ibid., 18–19.

72 My discussion is based on Midelfort, *A History of Madness in Sixteenth-Century Germany*, ch. 2.

73 Ibid., 86–9.

74 Ibid., 81.

75 Babb, *The Elizabethan Malady*, 51; MacDonald, *Mystical Bedlam*, 150.

76 Gowland, *Worlds of Renaissance Melancholy*, 2.

77 Robert Burton, *The Anatomy of Melancholy* (New York: New York Review Books, 2001), introduction by William H. Gass, xiv.

78 Diane E. Dreher, "Abnormal Psychology in the Renaissance," in Thomas G. Plante, ed. *Abnormal Psychology Across the Ages: Volume One, History and Conceptualizations* (Santa Barbara: Praeger, 2013), 41.

79 Burton, *The Anatomy of Melancholy*, first partition, 143–4.

80 Ibid., 178–202.

81 Ibid., 172.

82 Ibid., 217–25.

83 In my readings of Burton, I found no prohibition against eating chicken, but I might have missed it.

84 Burton, *The Anatomy of Melancholy*, first partition, 225.

85 Ibid., 237–9.

86 Ibid., 240–1.

87 Ibid., 241.

88 Dreher, "Abnormal Psychology in the Renaissance."

89 Burton, *The Anatomy of Melancholy*, first partition, 339–70.

90 Ibid., 287.

91 Ibid., 300.

92 Burton, *The Anatomy of Melancholy*, second partition, 11, 21, 61, 69, 115.

93 Gowland, *Worlds of Renaissance Melancholy*, 76.

94 Jackson, *Melancholia and Depression*, 97.

95 Burton, *The Anatomy of Melancholy*, first partition, 259–60.

96 Ibid., 262, 269, 271, 282, 292.

97 Ibid., 250.

98 Andrew Wear, "Early Modern Medicine," in Lawrence I. Conrad, Michael Neve, Vivian Nutton, Roy Porter, and Andrew Wear, *The Western Medical Tradition 800 B.C. to AD 1800* (Cambridge: Cambridge University Press, 1995).

99 Jackson, *Melancholia and Depression*, 112.

100 Ibid., 142–5.

101 Ibid., 130.

102 Ibid., 166–7.

103 Lawlor, *From Melancholia to Prozac*, 111; Jackson, *Melancholia and Depression*, 147.

104 As, for example, in the work of Swiss psychiatrist Richard von Krafft-Ebing. See Jackson, *Melancholia and Depression*, 174.

105 Jackson, *Melancholia and Depression*, 153.

106 David G. Schuster, *Neurasthenic Nation: America's Search for Health, Happiness, and Comfort, 1869–1920* (New Brunswick: Rutgers University Press, 2011), 11.

107 Lawlor, *From Melancholia to Prozac*, 131.

108 Ulrike May, "Abraham's Discovery of the 'Bad Mother': A Contribution to the History of the Theory of Depression," *International Journal of Psychoanalysis* 82, 263 (2001) 284.

109 Lawlor, *From Melancholia to Prozac*, 136–42.

110 Ibid., 138.

111 Radden, *Moody Minds Distempered*, 7.

112 Eunice Winters, ed., *The Collected Papers of Adolph Meyer: Volume II, Psychiatry* (Baltimore: The Johns Hopkins Press, 1951), 566–9; Jackson, *Melancholia and Depression*, 198.

113 See, for example, G. A. Foulds, T. M. Caine, and M. A. Creasy, "Aspects of Extra- and Intropunitive Expression in Mental Illness," *Journal of Mental Science* 106, 443 (April 1960) 599–610. Edward Shorter has lamented the erasure of the concept of the melancholic depression: "The original concept of two depressions, melancholia and nonmelancholia, as different from each other as chalk and cheese, became clouded . . ." Edward Shorter, *Before Prozac: The Troubled History of Mood Disorders in Psychiatry* (Oxford: Oxford University Press, 2009), 10. I do not think the distinction was traditionally so neat.

114 Andreasen, *The Broken Brain*, 38.

115 Jackson says that guilty feelings appear in accounts of melancholia starting in the sixteenth century. Jackson, "Acedia the Sin," 44.

116 The classic account is Ruth Benedict, *The Chrysanthemum and the Sword: Patterns in Japanese Culture* (New York: Mariner Books, 2005, originally published 1946), which contrasts the United States as a "guilt culture" and Japan as a "shame culture." Benedict's detractors have accused her of exaggerating the differences between cultures, and also of writing about the Japanese in a way that was implicitly negative. Her defenders have said she was speaking about tendencies, not totalities, of the cultures, and intended no value judgments in the distinction. See Millie R. Creighton, "Revisiting Shame and Guilt Cultures: A Forty-Year Pilgrimage," *Ethos* 18, 3 (September 1990) 279–307 and Judith Modell, "The Wall of Shame: Ruth Benedict's Accomplishment in *The Chrysanthemum and the Sword*," *Dialectical Anthropology* 24 (1999) 193–215. Many who read her at the time thought she was making a value judgment, and many other Western authors of the twentieth century – including Freud – valorized guilt as an emotion of cultivation and civilization.

117 Delameau, *Sin and Fear*. Delameau, a historian of the Catholic Church, places special blame on the Protestant Reformation, a view that may surprise many Catholics.

118 Jackson, "Acedia the Sin," 49.

119 Jadhav, "The Cultural Construction of Western Depression," 48.

120 Trenery and Horden, "Madness in the Middle Ages," 62.

121 H. B. M. Murphy, "The Advent of Guilt Feelings as a Common Depressive Symptom: A Historical Comparison on Two Continents," *Psychiatry* 41, 3 (1978) 229–42.

122 See John Orley and John K. Wing, "Psychiatric Disorders in Two African Villages," *Archives of General Psychiatry* 36 (May 1979) 513–20, for an explicit refutation of Carothers on the point.

123 Margaret Field, *Search for Security: An Ethno-Psychiatric Study of Rural Ghana* (London: Northwestern University Press, 1960) 149–200. S. Kirson Weinberg argued, in "Cultural Aspects of Manic-Depression in West Africa," *Journal of Health and Human Behavior* 6, 4 (Winter 1965) 247–53, that self-accusation was more common in Ghanaian culture than other West African cultures, but gave no explanation or evidence. Ghana is, like all of West Africa, multicultural and religiously plural. Ayo Binitie, "A Factor Analysis of Depression Across Cultures (African and European)," *British Journal of Psychiatry* 127 (1975) 559–63, also found little guilt in African depression.

124 MacDonald, *Mystical Bedlam*, 155. A report from a hospital in Tanganyika around the same time as Field's work stated that guilty feelings were rare in the patients there – but then went on to say that the depressives in the hospital believed that the bewitchment that caused their illness had been brought on by themselves; see C. G. F. Smartt, "Mental Maladjustment in the African."

125 B. B. Sethi, S. S. Nathawat, and S. C. Gupta, "Depression in India," *The Journal of Social Psychology* 91 (1973) 3–13.

126 Ibid., 11.

127 J. S. Teja, R. L. Narang, and A. K. Aggarwal, "Depression Across Cultures," *British Journal of Psychiatry* 119 (1971) 253–60.

128 This was observed in K. Singer, "Depressive Disorders from a Transcultural Perspective," *Social Science and Medicine* 9 (1975) 296.

129 Frantz Fanon, *The Wretched of the Earth* (New York: Grove Press, 1963), 296–310. See also Schiesari, *The Gendering of Melancholy*, 236.

130 Much recent clinical science of depression accommodates multi-causal analysis; see chapter 5. In a recent book on Burton, Radden points out that he anticipated this, in his different idiom. She also notes that the search for a single cause of depression remains powerful in contemporary science. Jennifer Radden, *Melancholy Habits: Burton's Anatomy and the Mind Sciences* (Oxford: Oxford University Press, 2017), 39, 102.

Chapter 3: Turned Inward

1 Pierre Janet, "Fear of Action as an Essential Element in the Sentiment of Melancholia," in Martin L. Reymert, ed., *Feelings and Emotions: The Wittenberg Symposium by Thirty-Four Psychologists* (Worcester: Clark University Press, 1928).

2 On the critique that psychoanalysis was not scientific, see Adolf Grünbaum, *The Foundations of Psychoanalysis* (Berkeley: University of California Press, 1984). On the role of managed care, see T. M. Luhrmann, *Of Two Minds: An Anthropologist Looks at American Psychiatry* (New York: Random House, 2001). On the role of drugs, see David Healy, *The Antidepressant Era* (Cambridge: Harvard University Press, 1997), ch. 7. Jonathan Metzl has argued that sexist assumptions and practices that characterized psychoanalysis survived into drug treatment; see Jonathan Metzl, *Prozac on the Couch: Prescribing Gender in the Era of Wonder Drugs* (Durham: Duke University Press, 2003).

3 Julia Segal, *Melanie Klein* (London: Sage Publications, 1992), 117.

4 See George Makari, *Revolution in Mind: The Creation of Psychoanalysis* (New York: HarperCollins, 2008), ch. 3.

5 Karen Horney, *Feminine Psychology* (New York: W. W. Norton, 1993).

6 This can be seen in many histories of the psychoanalytic movement, but Makari, *Revolution in Mind*, is especially strong on this point.

7 Similarly, sociologist Stanley Cohen has shown that while cognitive science often claims to have dislodged, if not eviscerated, psychoanalysis, it will at times use the same concepts while giving them different names. Stanley Cohen, *States of Denial: Knowing*

about Atrocities and Suffering (Cambridge: Polity Books, 2001), 43–5.

8 Mark Solms, "The Scientific Standing of Psychoanalysis," *BJPsych International* 15, 1 (February 2018), 5–8; Jonathan Shedler, "The Efficacy of Psychodynamic Therapy," *American Psychologist* 65, 2 (February/March 2010), 98–109. More empirical research on the efficacy of psychodynamic treatment is cited in chapter 4.

9 Meri Nana-Ama Danquah, *Willow, Weep for Me: A Black Woman's Journey Through Depression* (New York: Ballantine Publishing Group, 1998), 34–5.

10 This has been shown in compelling detail in Anna Bentick van Schoonheten's *Karl Abraham; Life and Work, a Biography* (Liz Waters, trans., London: Karnac Books, 2016, originally published 2013). This book is a principal source on Abraham's life, and his contributions on depression. Also important (and used by Bentick van Schoonheten) is May, "Abraham's Discovery of the 'Bad Mother.'"

11 Bentick van Schoonheten, *Karl Abraham*, 255.

12 Abraham's idea, discussed below, that parental absence, neglect, or lack of warmth is important in the genesis of depression, has empirical support. See Bentick van Schoonheten, *Karl Abraham*, 327; Fredric N. Busch, Marie Rudden, and Theodore Shapiro, *Psychodynamic Treatment of Depression* (Arlington: American Psychiatric Publishing, 2004), 24. To the extent this idea appears in Freud's work on depression, it is vague and undeveloped.

13 May, "Abraham's Discovery of the 'Bad Mother'", 284.

14 On Stekel, see ibid., 286.

15 Abraham's analysands also included two other prominent early women analysts, Ella Sharpe and Helene Deutsch, as well as Edward and James Glover, and Sandor Radó, all of whom were important in the spread of psychoanalysis. See James Lieberman, *Acts of Will: The Life and Work of Otto Rank* (New York: The Free Press, 1985), 166.

16 May, "Abraham's Discovery of the 'Bad Mother,'" 287.

17 Bentick van Schoonheten, *Karl Abraham*, 82.

18 Ibid., 82–3; Karl Abraham, "Giovanni Segantini: A Psychoanalytic Study" (1911) in *Clinical Papers and Essays on Psychoanalysis* (London:

Maresfield Reprints, 1955). My discussion of Abraham also draws directly on Karl Abraham, "Notes on the Psycho-Analytic Investigation and Treatment of Manic-Depressive Insanity and Allied Conditions," in Ernest Jones, ed., *Selected Papers of Karl Abraham, M.D.* (London: Hogarth Press, 1927). Despite the title, the paper was also about unipolar depression. Abraham considered manic-depressive and unipolar depressive illness to be two types of the same illness.

19 Bentick van Schoonheten, *Karl Abraham*, 353.

20 Ulrike May, "In Conversation: Freud, Abraham and Ferenczi on 'Mourning and Melancholia' (1915–1918)," *The International Journal of Psychoanalysis* 100, 1 (2019) 77–98.

21 Darian Leader, *The New Black: Mourning, Melancholia and Depression* (Minneapolis: Graywolf Press, 2008), 61.

22 Karl Abraham, "A Short Study of the Development of the Libido," in Ernest Jones, ed., *Selected Papers of Karl Abraham, M.D.* (London: Hogarth Press, 1927), 479.

23 "Mourning and Melancholia" is frequently cited by psychoanalysts as one of Freud's greatest achievements; see, for example, Priscilla Roth, "Melancholia, Mourning, and the Countertransference," in Leticia Fiorini, Thierry Bokanowski, and Sergio Lewkowicz, eds., *On Freud's "Mourning and Melancholia"* (London: Karnac Books, 2009, originally published 2007).

24 Sigmund Freud, "Mourning and Melancholia," in Sigmund Freud, *On Murder, Mourning, and Melancholia* (Shaun Whiteside, ed., London: Penguin Books, 2005).

25 Freud, "Mourning and Melancholia," 206.

26 May, "In Conversation," 79.

27 See Sadowsky, *Electroconvulsive Therapy in America*, ch. 4.

28 Freud, "Mourning and Melancholia," 203; Jackson, *Melancholia and Depression*, 226.

29 May, "Abraham's Discovery of the 'Bad Mother,'" 297. May notes that Freud had also told Stekel and Victor Tausk that they would eventually come around to his views. He made this prediction with Jung as well; it proved inaccurate.

30 Abraham, "A Short Study of the Development of the Libido," 433.

31 As Klein put it, "These anxiety contents and defence mechanisms form the basis of paranoia. In the infantile dread of magicians, witches, evil beasts, etc., we detect something of this anxiety . . ." Melanie Klein, "A Contribution to The Psychogenesis of Manic-Depressive States," in Juliet Mitchell, ed., *The Selected Melanie Klein* (New York: The Free Press, 1986), 117.

32 Dina Rosenbluth, "The Kleinian Theory of Depression," *Journal of Child Psychotherapy* 1, 3 (1965) 20–5.

33 Melanie Klein, "Mourning and Its Relation to Manic-Depressive States," in Mitchell, ed, *The Selected Melanie Klein*, 147–8.

34 Rosenbluth, "The Kleinian Theory of Depression," 22.

35 Klein, "Mourning and Its Relation to Manic-Depressive States," 149.

36 Ibid., 155.

37 Herbert Rosenfeld, "An Investigation into the Psychoanalytic Theory of Depression," *International Journal of Psychoanalysis* 40 (1959), 105–29.

38 Otto Fenichel, *The Psychoanalytic Theory of Neurosis* (New York: W. W. Norton & Company, 1945).

39 Ibid., 403. Fenichel thought the likelihood of a hereditary factor was particularly likely in manic depression.

40 André Green, *On Private Madness* (London: H. Karnak Books, 1997, originally published 1986). See also Gregorio Kohon, ed., *The Dead Mother: The Work of André Green* (London: Routledge, 1999).

41 Green, *On Private Madness*, 146.

42 Alice Miller, *The Drama of the Gifted Child: The Search for the True Self* (Ruth Ward, trans., New York: Basic Books, 2007, originally published 1979).

43 Sharon O'Brien, *The Family Silver: A Memoir of Depression and Inheritance* (Chicago: University of Chicago Press, 2004), 32.

44 Sandor Radó, "The Problem of Melancholia," *The International Journal of Psychoanalysis* 9 (1928) 420–38. Radó's ideas found a place in Fenichel's outline of depression in *The Psychoanalytic Theory of the Neuroses*.

45 Edward Bibring, "The Mechanism of Depression," in Phyllis Greenacre, ed., *Affective Disorders: Psychoanalytic Contributions to*

Their Study (New York: International Universities Press, 1953); David Rapaport, "Edward Bibring's Theory of Depression," in James C. Coyne, ed., *Essential Papers on Depression* (New York: New York University Press, 1986).

46 Martin Seligman, "A Learned Helplessness Model of Depression," in Jennifer Radden, ed., *The Nature of Melancholy* (Oxford: Oxford University Press), 311–16.

47 See his memoir, Martin Seligman, *The Hope Circuit: A Psychologist's Journey from Helplessness to Optimism* (New York: Public Affairs, 2018), ch. 7.

48 Biography of Jacobson is drawn from Brenda Maddox, *Freud's Wizard: Ernest Jones and the Transformation of Psychoanalysis* (Cambridge: Da Capo Press, 2007, originally published 2006), 224–5. On the increasing depth of clinical experience with depression in Jacobson's generation and after, see Arieti and Bemporad, *Severe and Mild Depression*, 54–5.

49 Edith Jacobson, *Depression: Comparative Studies of Normal, Neurotic, and Psychotic Conditions* (Madison: International Universities Press, 1971).

50 Rosenfeld, "An Investigation into the Psychoanalytic Theory of Depression," 114.

51 There are numerous accounts of the Freud/Jung relationship. One of the best recent discussions is in George Makari's *Revolution in Mind: The Creation of Psychoanalysis*.

52 There is no book or essay by Jung devoted exclusively to depression. References to it are scattered in his writings. My summary relies heavily on W. Steinberg, "Depression: A Discussion of Jung's Ideas," *Journal of Analytical Psychology* 34 (1989) 339–52.

53 David Karp, *Is It Me or My Meds?: Living with Antidepressants* (Cambridge: Harvard University Press, 2006), 196.

54 Gary Greenberg, *Manufacturing Depression: The Secret History of a Modern Disease* (New York: Simon and Schuster, 2010), 149–50.

55 Elliot S. Valenstein, *Blaming the Brain: The Truth About Drugs and Mental Health* (New York: The Free Press, 1998), 11.

56 Silvano Arieti and Jules Bemporad, "The Psychological Organization of Depression," *American Journal of Psychiatry* 137, 11 (November 1980) 1360–5.

57 Nancy McWilliams, *Psychoanalytic Diagnosis: Understanding Personality Structure in the Clinical Process* (New York: The Guilford Press, 1994), 229; also see 240. Her book meant to supplement *DSM-III*, whose atheoretical nature she welcomed because it allowed for standardization across psychiatry. Historians have sometimes written as though psychoanalysts all reviled DSM-III; McWilliams' endorsement of it is on p. vii. For another example of psychoanalytic recognition of the value of medication, see Busch et al., *Psychodynamic Treatment of Depression*.

58 John Bowlby, *Attachment and Loss, Volume III: Loss* (New York: Basic Books, 1980), 261.

59 Ibid., 247-8.

60 Silvano Arieti and Jules Bemporad, *Severe and Mild Depression: The Psychotherapeutic Approach* (New York: Basic Books, 1978), 4-5.

61 Ibid., 128.

62 Busch et al., *Psychodynamic Treatment of Depression*, 3-5.

63 Julia Kristeva, *Black Sun: Depression and Melancholia* (New York: Leon S. Roudiez, trans., Columbia University Press, 1989, originally published 1987), 3-94.

64 I will look at these problems in detail in chapter 4.

65 McWilliams, *Psychoanalytic Diagnosis*, 239.

66 Kristeva has been accused of being a spy for the Bulgarian Communist government, a charge she denies. I have not looked at the evidence carefully or comprehensively, but what I have seen is short of conclusive.

67 Schiesari provides a critical exposition of Kristeva's theory of depression in *The Gendering of Melancholia*, 77-93. Schiesari sees Kristeva's work as mother-blaming and therefore anti-feminist, a reading I do not share. Schiesari also considers Kristeva's advocacy of lithium "disturbing," but does not say why (*The Gendering of Melancholia*, 78).

68 Mark Solms, *The Brain and the Inner World: An Introduction to the Neuroscience of the Subjective Experience* (New York: Other Press, 2003).

69 Margaret R. Zellner, Douglas F. Watt, Mark Solms, and Jaak Panskepp, "Affective Neuroscientific and Neuropsychoanalytic Approaches to Two Intractable Problems: Why Depression

Feels So Bad and What Addicts Really Want," *Neuroscience and Biobehavioral Reviews* 35 (2011) 2000–8.

70 Otto F. Kernberg, "An Integrated Theory of Depression," *Neuropsychoanalysis* 11 (2009) 76–80.

71 Anne Harrington says the tricyclics helped, Gail Hornstein claims the medication had little effect. Harrington, *Mind Fixers*, 197; Gail A. Hornstein, *To Redeem One Person is to Redeem the World: The Life of Frieda Fromm-Reichmann* (New York: The Free Press, 2000), 384.

72 Sandra G. Boodman, "A Horrible Place, A Wonderful Place," *The Washington Post*, October 8, 1989, https://www.washingtonpost.com/archive/lifestyle/magazine/1989/10/08/a-horrible-place-a-wonderful-place/ee4d7572-7ac0-4159-baf8-e8112a983e50/, accessed October 9, 2019.

73 Harrington, *Mind Fixers*, 197.

74 Peter D. Kramer, *Ordinarily Well: The Case for Antidepressants* (New York: Farrar, Straus and Giroux, 2016), 44–5.

75 According to Hornstein, the overall atmosphere of treatment was more humane at Silver Hill. Hornstein, *To Redeem One Person is to Redeem the World*, 384–5.

76 Daniel Barron, "The Rise of Evidence-Based Psychiatry," *Scientific American* on-line, February 28, 2017, https://blogs.scientificamerican.com/guest-blog/the-rise-of-evidence-based-psychiatry/, accessed May 8, 2019.

77 Hornstein, *To Redeem One Person is to Redeem the World*, 386; Healy, *The Antidepressant Era*, 246–8.

78 Hornstein, *To Redeem One Person is to Redeem the World*, 385–6.

Chapter 4: A Diagnosis in Ascent

1 Derek Summerfield, "Afterword: Against 'Global Mental Health,'" *Transcultural Psychiatry* 49, 3–4 (2012) 519–30.

2 Andreasen, *The Broken Brain*, 41.

3 Biographical information on Rothko is from James E. B. Breslin, *Mark Rothko: A Biography* (Chicago: University of Chicago Press, 1993).

4 The friend was the poet Stanley Kunitz. Breslin, *Mark Rothko*, 267.

5 Hilarie M. Sheets, "Mark Rothko's Dark Palette Illuminated,"

The New York Times, November 2, 2016. I am grateful to Carolyn Slebodnik for this reference, and for educating me about Rothko more generally.

6 Edward Shorter, *A Historical Dictionary of Psychiatry* (Oxford: Oxford University Press, 2005), 155.

7 Breslin, *Mark Rothko*, 533.

8 See, for example, J. Alexander Bodkin and Jessica L. Green, "Not Obsolete: Continuing Roles for TCAs and MAOIs," *Psychiatric Times* 10, 24 (September 15, 2007).

9 Kline prescribed the tricyclic Sinequan without consulting Rothko's other doctors. At least one of them thought it was an ill-advised choice in Rothko's case, because it could cause changes in heart rhythm, and seemed to actually worsen Rothko's mood. Breslin, *Mark Rothko*, 534.

10 William Styron, *Darkness Visible: A Memoir of Madness* (New York: Vintage Books, 1990), 7, 37.

11 As late as the 1950s, though, some clinicians were still using melancholia to refer to what we now call depression. See Theodore T. Stone, "Melancholia: Clinical Study of Fifty Selected Cases," *Journal of the American Medical Association* 142, 3 (1950) 165–8.

12 Laura D. Hirshbein, *American Melancholy: Constructions of Depression in the Twentieth Century* (New Brunswick: Rutgers University Press, 2014), 68.

13 John T. MacCurdy, *The Psychology of the Emotions: Morbid and Normal* (New York: Harcourt, Brace & Company, 1925), 337–79. Texts like this make me wonder why it has become so common among historians to insist that current medical usage of the term depression is so new.

14 MacCurdy, *The Psychology of the Emotions*, 342.

15 On Kraepelin's changing classification systems, see Berrios, *The History of Mental Symptoms*, 300–13. Kraepelin's classification system is sometimes hailed as a major – perhaps the major – contribution to modern psychiatry. His classifications kept changing, though, and many of them are no longer in use. As Berrios says, he may have created as many problems as he solved. Kraepelin's reputation for being the pivotal creator of modern

psychiatry also seems to leave out something: he made no major contribution to therapeutics.

16 Shorter, *A Historical Dictionary*, 82.

17 Kraepelin himself abandoned involutional melancholia and switched to "depression." Shorter, *A Historical Dictionary*, 175.

18 Shorter argues that endogenous depression is basically what was once called melancholia. Edward Shorter, *Before Prozac*, 14–15.

19 Teja et al., "Depression Across Cultures."

20 See, for example, V. A. Kral, "Masked Depression in Middle Aged Men," *Canadian Medical Association Journal* 79, 1 (July 1, 1958) 1–5; Arieti and Bemporad, *Severe and Mild Depression*, 58. The endogenous/reactive distinction was held on to longer in Britain than in the United States, and according to at least one American psychiatrist's critique in the 1960s, never had an empirical basis; see Hirshbein, *American Melancholy*, 35. Some psychiatrists still use the distinction. An ECT provider once told me that ECT should not be used for people with reactive depressions.

21 Radden, *Melancholy Habits*, 104.

22 Abraham Myerson, *When Life Loses its Zest* (Boston: Little, Brown, and Company, 1925), 1–5.

23 Ibid., 6.

24 Ibid., 162.

25 Paul H. Hoch and Joseph Zubin, eds., *Depression* (New York: Grune and Stratton, 1954).

26 Per Bach and Alec Coppen, eds., *The Hamilton Scales* (Berlin: Springer Verlag, 1990).

27 M. Roth, "Max Hamilton: A Life Devoted to Science," in Bach and Coppen, eds., *The Hamilton Scales*, 2.

28 Callahan and Berrios, *Reinventing Depression*, 130.

29 C.B. Pull, "French Experience with the Hamilton Scales," in Bach and Coppen, eds., *The Hamilton Scales*, 36.

30 Roth, "Max Hamilton," 4.

31 Take, for example, the subtitle of a popular introduction to cognitive therapy by a student of Beck's: David D. Burns, *Feeling Good: The New Mood Therapy* (New York: Signet, 1980).

32 Rachael I. Rosner, "Manualizing Psychotherapy: Aaron T. Beck

and the Origins of *Cognitive Therapy of Depression*," *European Journal of Psychotherapy and Counseling* 20, 1 (2018) 25–47.

33 Burns, *Feeling Good* details how cognitive therapy works in practice.

34 Rachael I. Rosner, "The 'Splendid Isolation' of Aaron T. Beck," *Isis* 105 (2014) 734–58.

35 Rosner, "Manualizing Psychotherapy." The Beck quote is from Barry L. Duncan and Scott Miller, "Treatment Manuals Do Not Improve Outcomes," https://www.scottdmiller.com/wp-content/uploads/Treatment_Manuals.pdf, accessed February 17, 2020.

36 Rosner, "The 'Splendid Isolation' of Aaron T. Beck."

37 William Davies, *The Happiness Industry: How the Government and Big Business Sold Us Well-Being* (London: Verso, 2015), 111.

38 I am drawing here on the concept of "therapeutic discipline" which was given thoughtful expression in Joel Braslow's *Mental Ills and Bodily Cures: Psychiatric Treatment in the First Half of the Twentieth Century* (Berkeley: University of California Press, 1997); I elaborated on Braslow's idea in ch. 3 of *Electroconvulsive Therapy in America*.

39 Kramer, *Ordinarily Well*, 120.

40 Marie-Luise Schermuly-Haupt, Michael Linden, and A. John Rush, "Unwanted Events and Side Effects in Cognitive Behavior Therapy," *Cognitive Therapy and Research* 42, 3 (June 2018) 219–29.

41 Tracy Thompson, *The Beast: A Journey Through Depression* (New York: Penguin Books, 1996), 145–6.

42 Scott Stuart, "Interpersonal Psychotherapy: A Guide to the Basics," *Psychiatric Annals* 36, 8 (2006) 542–50.

43 Shorter, *A Historical Dictionary*, 154.

44 Myrna Weissman, "A Brief History of Interpersonal Psychotherapy," *Psychiatric Annals* 36, 8 (2006) 553–7.

45 Ibid.

46 Davies, *The Happiness Industry*.

47 Arthur Brooks, "Choose to be Grateful. It Will Make You Happier," *New York Times*, November 21, 2015.

48 Myrna M. Weissman, "The Psychological Treatment of Depression: Evidence for the Efficacy of Psychotherapy Alone, in Comparison with, and in Combination with Pharmacotherapy,"

Archives of General Psychiatry 36 (1979) 1261–9; Jürgen Barth, Thomas Munder, Heike Gerger, Eveline Nüesch, Sven Trelle, Hansjörg Znoj, Peter Jüni, and Pim Cuijpers, "Comparative Efficacy of Seven Psychotherapeutic Interventions for Patients with Depression: A Network Meta-Analysis," *PLoS Med* 10, 5 (May 2010) e1001454; Irving Kirsch, *The Emperor's New Drugs: Exploding the Antidepressant Myth* (New York: Basic Books, 2010), 158–63.

49 Mary Lee Smith, Gene V. Glass, and Thomas I. Miller, *The Benefits of Psychotherapy* (Baltimore: The Johns Hopkins University Press, 1980).

50 Lotte H. J. M. Lemans, Suzanne C. van Brunswick, Frenk Peeters, Arnoud Arntz, Steven D. Hollon, and Marcus J. H. Huibers, "Long-term Outcomes of Acute Treatment with Cognitive Therapy v. Interpersonal Psychotherapy for Adult Depression: Follow-up of a Randomized Controlled Trial," *Psychological Medicine* 49 (May 24, 2018) 465–73.

51 Pim Cuijpers, Steven D. Hollon, Annemieke van Straten, Claudi Bockting, Matthias Berking, and Gerhard Andersson, "Does Cognitive Behaviour Therapy Have an Enduring Effect that is Superior to Keeping Patients on Continuation Pharmacotherapy? A Meta-Analysis," *BMJ Open* 3 (2013) e002542; Kirsch, *The Emperor's New Drugs*, 161.

52 Kirsch, *The Emperor's New Drugs*, 162–3.

53 Christiane Steinert, Thomas Munder, Sven Rabung, Jürgen Hoyer, and Falk Leichsenring, "Psychodynamic Therapy: As Efficacious as Other Empirically Supported Treatments? A Meta-Analysis Testing Equivalence of Outcomes," *American Journal of Psychiatry* (May, 2017); Barth et al., "Comparative Efficacy of Seven Psychotherapeutic Interventions for Patients with Depression." See also studies cited in Busch et al., *Psychodynamic Treatment of Depression*, 4. Smith et al.'s 1980 overview *The Benefits of Psychotherapy* also included psychodynamic therapy among those found to work.

54 Barth et al., "Comparative Efficacy of Seven Psychotherapeutic Interventions for Patients with Depression."

55 Busch et al., *Psychodynamic Treatment of Depression*, 100.

56 Jonathan Metzl, *The Protest Psychosis: How Schizophrenia Became a Black Disease* (Boston: Beacon Press, 2009).

57 Charles Mingus, *Beneath the Underdog* (New York: Vintage Books, 1971), 328–9.

58 Gene Santoro, *Myself When I Am Real: The Life and Music of Charles Mingus* (New York: Oxford University Press, 2000), 268.

59 http://aln2.albumlinernotes.com/The_Black_Saint.html, accessed May 1, 2020.

60 Mingus, *Beneath the Underdog*, 6.

61 Anne Stevenson, *Bitter Fame: A Life of Sylvia Plath* (Boston: Houghton Mifflin, 1989), 15.

62 See my discussions of Plath in Sadowsky, *Electroconvulsive Therapy in America*.

63 Levinson and Nichols, "Genetics of Depression," 303.

64 While women predominate in depression diagnoses, they do not seem to suffer from more mental illness overall. Dena T. Smith, Dawne M. Mouzon, and Marta Elliott, "Reviewing the Assumptions about Men's Mental Health: An Exploration of the Gender Binary," *American Journal of Men's Health* 12, 1 (2018) 78–89.

65 S. Seedat, K. M. Scott, M. C. Angermeyer et al., "Cross-National Associations between Gender and Mental Disorders in the WHO World Mental Health Surveys," *Archives of General Psychiatry* 66, 7 (July 2009) 785–95. Research on class, race, and gender in Bahia, Brazil, found that gender was the strongest predictor of depression. Naomar Almeida-Filho, Ines Lessa, Lucélia Magalhães, Maria Jenny Araujo, Estela Aquino, Sherman A. James, and Ichiro Kawachi, "Social Inequality and Depressive Disorders in Bahia, Brazil: Interactions of Gender, Ethnicity, and Social Class," *Social Science and Medicine* 59 (2004) 1339–53.

66 Some of the possibilities outlined below are assessed in Marta Elliott, "Gender Differences in the Determinants of Distress, Alcohol Misuse, and Related Psychiatric Disorders," *Sociology and Mental Health* 3, 2 (2013) 96–113.

67 Jill M. Goldstein, L. Holsen, S. Cherkerzian, M. Misra, and R. J. Handra, "Neuroendocrine Mechanisms of Depression," in Charney et al., *Charney and Nestler's Neurobiology of Mental Illness*.

68 Sarah Rosenfield and Dawne Mouzon, "Gender and Mental Health," in Carol S. Aneshensel, Jo C. Phelan, and Alex Bierman, eds., *Handbook of the Sociology of Mental Health* (2nd edn, Dordrecht: Springer, 2013), 282–3.

69 Hirshbein has developed this argument extensively. She argues that the gender ratio is an artifact of a circularity: mental health workers – often with the best intentions of helping women – defined depression as a women's problem, which then inclined them to see depression in women. She also points out that many studies of depression were done with exclusively female patients, but were used to generalize about the illness. Hirshbein, *American Melancholy*, ch. 4.

70 Junko Kitanaka, *Depression in Japan: Psychiatric Cures for a Society in Distress* (Princeton: Princeton University Press, 2012), 129–30.

71 Radden, *Moody Minds*, 47.

72 Schiesari, *The Gendering of Melancholia*.

73 This is intersectionality, which also stresses that identities are mutually constitutive. Intersectionality is only beginning to get a lot of attention in the study of illness, but see Olena Hankivsky, "Women's Health, Men's Health, and Gender and Health: Implications of Intersectionality," *Social Science and Medicine* 74 (2012) 1712–20.

74 G. E. Kraus, J. O'Loughlin, I. Karp, N. C. Low, "High Depressive Symptoms during Adolescence Increases the Effect of Stressful Life Events on Depression in a Population-based Sample of Young Adults," *Comprehensive Psychiatry* 54, 8 (2013) e25.

75 Jutta Lindert, Ondine von Ehrenstein, and Marc Weisskopf, "Long Term Effects of Abuse in Early Life on Depression and Anxiety over the Life Course," *Comprehensive Psychiatry* 54, 8 (2013) e28.

76 Walter Forrest, Ben Edwards, and Galina Daraganova, "The Intergenerational Consequences of War: Anxiety, Depression, Suicidality, and Mental Health among the Children of War Veterans," *International Journal of Epidemiology* 47, 4 (2018) 1060–7.

77 José M. Salguero, Pablo Fernández-Berrocal, Itiar Iruarrizaga, Antonio Cano-Vindel, and Sandro Galea, "Major Depressive

Disorder following Terrorist Attacks: A Systematic Review of Prevalence, Course, and Correlates," *BMC Psychiatry* 11, 96 (2011) 1–16.

78 Andrew Solomon, *The Noonday Demon: An Atlas of Depression* (2nd edn, New York: Scribner, 2015, originally published 2001), 187.

79 Janis H. Jenkins, Arthur Kleinman, and Byron Good, "Cross-cultural Studies of Depression," in Becker and Kleinman, *Psychosocial Studies of Depression*, 81; I. Ba and R. S. Bhopal, "Physical, Mental and Social Consequences in Civilians Who Have Experienced War-Related Sexual Violence: A Systematic Review (1981–2014)," *Public Health* 142 (2017) 121–35. This study found Post-Traumatic Stress Disorder to be even more likely than major depression.

80 Kraus et al. "High Depressive Symptoms during Adolescence."

81 I am using class in a loose sense, to refer to position in an economic hierarchy. Most sociology of mental illness uses the term "socioeconomic status" (SES) which refers to a cluster of things that include income, prestige, and educational level. Tamar Wohlfarth has suggested that class, understood in a more Marxist sense as relationship to the means of production, has particular effects on the distribution of several mental disorders, including depression, and that these effects are distinct from those of SES. She further argues that one reason may be that class used in this precise sense is a stronger predictor of the amount of control one feels in life, which could be quite different from one's prestige or income. But the literature on mental illness and class defined this way remains undeveloped. Tamar Wohlfarth, "Socioeconomic Inequality and Psychopathology: Are Socioeconomic Status and Social Class Interchangeable?," *Social Science and Medicine* 45, 3 (1997) 399–410.

82 Andrew Solomon, "Depression, The Secret We Share," https://www.ted.com/talks/andrew_solomon_depression_the_secret_we_share?language=en, accessed May 16, 2019.

83 Becker and Kleinman, *Psychosocial Aspects of Depression*, xi.

84 A 2005 meta-analysis, for example, concluded (for mental illness generally) that there was "a remarkably strong and consistent negative correlation between socioeconomic conditions and mental illness, one that cannot be accounted for by geographic or economic

downward mobility." Gregory G. Hudson, "Socioeconomic Status and Mental Illness: Tests of the Social Causation and Selection Hypothesis," *American Journal of Orthopsychiatry* 75, 1 (2005) 3–18, quote is on p. 16.

85 George W. Brown and Tirril Harris, *Social Origins of Depression: A Study of Psychiatric Disorder in Women* (New York: The Free Press, 1978), 276–7.

86 V. Lorant. D. Deliège, W. Eaton, A. Robert, P. Philippot, and M. Ansseau, "Socioeconomic Inequalities in Depression: A Meta-Analysis," *American Journal of Epidemiology* 157, 2 (2003) 98–112.

87 Aislinne Freeman, Stefanos Tyrovolas, Ai Koyanagi et al., "The Role of Socio-Economic Status in Depression: Results from the COURAGE (aging survey in Europe)," *BMC Public Health* 16 (2016) 1098.

88 Stephanie A. Riolo, Tuan Anh Nguyen, John F. Greden, and Cheryl A. King, "Prevalence of Depression by Race/Ethnicity: Findings from the National Health and Nutrition Examination Survey III," *American Journal of Public Health* 95, 6 (June 2005) 998–1000.

89 Marti Loring and Brian Powell, "Gender, Race, and DSM-III: A Study of the Objectivity of Psychiatric Behavior," *Journal of Health and Social Behavior* 29, 1 (March 1988) 1–22; Sarah Rosenfield, "Race Differences in Involuntary Hospitalization: Psychiatric vs. Labeling Perspectives," *Journal of Health and Social Behavior* 25 (March 1984) 14–23; Metzl, *The Protest Psychosis*.

90 David B. Williams, Hector M. Gonzales, Harold Neighbors et al., "Prevalence and Distribution of Major Depressive Disorder in African Americans, Caribbean Blacks, and Non-Hispanic Whites: Results from the National Survey of American Life," *Archives of General Psychiatry* 64 (March 2007) 305–15; Dorothy D. Dunlop, Jing Song, John S. Lyons, Larry Manheim, and Rowland W. Chang, "Racial/Ethnic Differences in Depression Among Preretirement Adults," *American Journal of Public Health* 93, 11 (November 2003) 1945–52. This last was a community study that did not depend on treatment rates.

91 Igda E. Martinez Pincay and Peter J. Guarnaccia, "'It's Like Going Through an Earthquake': Anthropological Perspectives on

Depression among Latino Immigrants," *Journal of Immigrant and Minority Health* 9, 17 (2007) 17–28.

92 Leopoldo J. Cabassa, Rebecca Lester, and Luis H. Zayas, "'It's Like Being in a Labyrinth': Hispanic Immigrants' Perceptions of Depression and Attitudes Toward Treatments," *Journal of Immigrant and Minority Health* 9, 1 (January 2007) 1–16.

93 Theresa DeLeane O'Nell, *Disciplined Hearts: History, Identity, and Depression in an American Indian Community* (Berkeley: University of California Press, 1996), 4.

94 Zornitsa Kalibatseva and Frederick T. L. Leiong, "Depression among Asian Americans: Review and Recommendations," *Depression Research and Treatment* July 2011, Article ID 320902.

95 Megan Sutter and Paul B. Perrin, "Discrimination, Mental Health, and Suicidal Ideation Among LGBT People of Color," *Journal of Counseling Psychology* 63, 1 (2016) 98–105.

96 Brian Mustanski, Rebecca Andrews, and Jae Puckett, "The Effects of Cumulative Victimization on Mental Health among Lesbian, Gay, Bisexual, and Transgender Adolescents and Young Adults," *American Journal of Public Health* 106, 3 (March 2016), 527–33.

97 Sutter and Perrin, "Discrimination, Mental Health, and Suicidal Ideation Among LGBT People of Color," 98.

98 Dianne L. Kerr, Laura Santurri, and Patricia Peters, "A Comparison of Lesbian, Bisexual, and Heterosexual College Undergraduate Women on Selected Mental Health Issues," *Journal of American College Health* 61, 4 (2013) 185–94; Meg John Barker, "Depression and/or Oppression? Bisexuality and Mental Health," *Journal of Bisexuality* 15 (2015) 369–84.

99 Sutter and Perrin, "Discrimination, Mental Health, and Suicidal Ideation Among LGBT People of Color," 102.

100 Simon Denny, Mathijs F. G. Lucassen, Jaimee Stuart et al., "The Association between Supportive High School Environments and Depressive Symptoms and Suicidality Among Sexual Minority Students," *Journal of Clinical Child and Adolescent Psychology* 45, 3 (2016) 248–61.

101 Carmen H. Logie, Ashley Lacombe-Duncan, Tonia Poteat, and Anne C. Wagner, "Syndemic Factors Mediate the Relationship between Sexual Stigma and Depression among Sexual Minority

Women and Gender Minorities," *Women's Health Issues* 217, 5 (2017) 592–9.

102 M. Yadegarfard, Mallika E. Meinhold-Bergmann, and Robert Ho, "Family Rejection, Social Isolation, and Loneliness as Predictors of Negative Health Outcomes (Depression, Suicidal Ideation, and Sexual Risk Behavior) among Thai Male-to-Female Transgender Adolescents," *Journal of LGBT Youth* 11, 4 (2014) 347–63.

103 Tyler Hatchel, Alberto Valido, Kris T. De Pedro, Yuanhong Huang, and Dorothy L. Espelage, "Minority Stress among Transgender Adolescents: The Role of Peer Victimization, School Belonging, and Ethnicity," *Journal of Child and Family Studies* 28 (2019) 2467–76.

104 Charles P. Hoy-Ellis, and Karen I. Fredriksen-Goldsen, "Depression among Transgender Older Adults: General and Minority Stress," *American Journal of Community Psychology* 59, 3–4 (2017) 295–305.

105 Tiziana Leone, Ernestina Coast, Shilpa Narayanan, and Ama de Graft Aikins, "Diabetes and Depression Comorbidity and Socioeconomic Status in Low and Middle Income Countries (LMICs): A Mapping of the Evidence," *Globalization and Health* 8, 39 (2012) 1–10; Emily Mendenhall, *Syndemic Suffering: Social Distress, Depression, and Diabetes among Mexican Immigrant Women* (London: Routledge, 2012); David W. Kissane, Mario Maj, and Norman Sartorius, eds., *Depression and Cancer* (Oxford: Wiley-Blackwell, 2011); Alexander Glassman, Mario Maj, and Norman Sartorius, eds., *Depression and Heart Disease* (Oxford: Wiley-Blackwell, 2011).

106 Leone et al. "Diabetes and Depression Comorbidity and Socioeconomic Status in Low and Middle Income Countries," 1.

107 Ibid., 6–8.

108 Marco Piccinelli and Greg Wilkinson, "Gender Differences in Depression," *British Journal of Psychiatry* 177 (2000) 486–92. Piccinelli and Wilkinson support adversity as a cause of the gender disparity – in part, because they find the evidence favoring some of the other explanations to be even weaker.

109 This has been found in studies going back at least to the 1970s; for a recent source, see Elliott, "Gender Differences in the Determinants of Distress." The protective effect of marriage for

men shows some variation across cultures; see Almeida-Filho et al., "Social Inequality and Depressive Disorders in Bahia, Brazil," 1350.

110 Jenkins et al., "Cross-cultural Studies of Depression," 79.

111 S. Seedat et al., "Cross-National Associations between Gender and Mental Disorders in the WHO World Mental Health Surveys."

112 Elliott, "Gender Differences in the Determinants of Distress."

113 Carol Emslie, Damien Ridge, Sue Ziebland, and Kate Hunt, "Men's Accounts of Depression: Reconstructing or Resisting Hegemonic Masculinity?" *Social Science & Medicine* 62 (2006) 2246–57.

114 Smith, Mouzon, and Elliott, "Reviewing the Assumptions about Men's Mental Health."

115 Ann Cvetkovich, *Depression: A Public Feeling* (Durham: Duke University Press, 2012).

116 O'Nell, *Disciplined Hearts.*

117 This included the influential Karl Menninger. Hannah S. Decker, *The Making of DSM-III: A Diagnostic Manual's Conquest of American Psychiatry* (Oxford: Oxford University Press, 2013).

118 Harrington, *Mind Fixers*, 43.

119 Allen Frances, *Saving Normal: An Insider's Revolt Against Out-of-Control Psychiatric Diagnosis, DSM-V, Big Pharma, and the Medicalization of Ordinary Life* (New York: William Morrow, 2013), 61–2.

120 Harrington, *Mind Fixers*, 127.

121 D. L. Rosenhan, "On Being Sane in Insane Places," *Science* 179, 70 (January 1973), 250–8.

122 Susannah Cahalan, *The Great Pretender: The Undercover Mission That Changed Our Understanding of Madness* (New York: Grand Central Publishing, 2019); Alison Abbott, "On the Troubling Trail of Psychiatry's Pseudopatients Stunt," *Nature*, October 29, 2019.

123 Mark Ruffalo, "The Rosenhan Study Never Proved Anything Anyway," https://www.psychologytoday.com/us/blog/freud-fluoxetine/201911/the-rosenhan-study-never-proved-anything-anyway, accessed March 6, 2020.

124 Decker, *The Making of DSM-III*, 91–2. Reich's fringe ideas included most infamously the "orgone," a sexual life-force. These ideas may

have been symptoms of his own worsening mental health, as he descended into psychosis. Spitzer tested Reich's theories and concluded orgone did not exist.

125 Greenberg, *The Book of Woe*; Kutchins and Kirk, *Making Us Crazy*.

126 Farhad Dalal, *CBT: The Cognitive Behavioural Tsunami* (London: Routledge, 2018), 54; Frances, *Saving Normal*, 64; Greenberg, *The Book of Woe*, 44–5.

127 Kutchins and Kirk, *Making Us Crazy*, 42.

128 I am referring to Spitzer's work on the Research Diagnostic Criteria (RDC); see Hirshbein, *American Melancholy*, 40–1.

129 Ibid., 43.

130 Ibid., 44–5.

131 Frances, *Saving Normal*, 65.

132 Arthur Kleinman, "Culture, Bereavement, and Psychiatry," *The Lancet*, February 18, 2012.

133 Frances, *Saving Normal*, 186.

134 Quoted in Greenberg, *The Book of Woe*, 155.

135 Ibid., 161–3.

136 Ronald W. Pies, "The Bereavement Exclusion and *DSM-5*: An Update and Commentary," *Innovations in Clinical Neuroscience* 11, 7–8 (July–August 2014) 19–22.

137 As Frances acknowledged, "There is no clear line separating those who are experiencing loss in their own necessary and particular way from those who will stay stuck in a depression unless they receive specialized psychiatric help." Frances, *Saving Normal*, 187.

138 Kleinman, "Culture, Bereavement, and Psychiatry."

139 Gordon Parker, Max Fink, Edward Shorter et al., "Issues for DSM-V: Whither Melancholia? The Case for its Classification as a Distinct Mood Disorder," *American Journal of Psychiatry* 167, 7 (July 2010) 745–7; Radden, *Melancholy Habits*, 143–9. Also see Greenberg, *The Book of Woe*, 335–6. Greenberg thinks that the effort failed because having a disorder with a known biology in the DSM would call embarrassing attention to the absence elsewhere, but he's just speculating. It could as easily be because there was no consensus in psychiatry that melancholia constituted a distinct form of depression.

140 Homosexuality had already been removed from DSM-II, but its

status as an illness remained controversial in psychiatry. Decker, *The Making of DSM-III*, 154–61.

141 Andreasen, *The Broken Brain*, 156–61. Andreasen criticized DSM-II for not specifying how many symptoms were needed to make a diagnosis, and for its unreliability – that is, the way different doctors could use the same manual and come up with divergent diagnoses. But she acknowledged that the increased reliability of DSM-III may have come at a cost of validity – that is, the degree to which the diagnoses capture precise illness conditions.

142 Nancy Andreasen, "DSM and the Death of Phenomenology in America: An Example of Unintended Consequences," *Schizophrenia Bulletin* 33, 1 (2007) 108–12.

143 An alienating society is cited in Blazer, *The Age of Melancholy*. Changing social roles is put forth as an explanation in Alain Ehrenberg, *The Weariness of the Self: Diagnosing the History of Depression in the Contemporary Age* (Enrico Caouette, Jacob Homel, David Homel, and Don Winkler, trans., Montreal and Kingston: McGill Queen's University Press, 2010, originally published 1998).

144 Researchers in Britain as late as the 1970s found that women they diagnosed with clinical depression were more likely to refer to their problems as "nerves." Brown and Harris, *Social Origins of Depression*, 22.

145 Andrea Tone, *The Age of Anxiety: America's Turbulent Affair with Tranquilizers* (New York: Basic Books, 2008).

146 Allan V. Horwitz, "How an Age of Anxiety Became an Age of Depression," *The Milbank Quarterly* 88, 1 (2010) 112–38.

147 David Harvey, *A Brief History of Neo-Liberalism* (Oxford: Oxford University Press, 2007), 119.

148 Jean-François Lyotard, *The Postmodern Condition: A Report on Knowledge* (University of Minnesota Press, 1984).

149 Byung-Chul Han, *Psychopolitics: Neoliberalism and the New Technologies of Power* (Erik Butler, trans., London: Verso, 2017), 29.

150 Ibid., 6–7, emphasis in original.

151 Allan Horwitz and Jerome Wakefield, *The Loss of Sadness: How Psychiatry Transformed Normal Sorrow into Depressive Disorder* (New York: Oxford University Press, 2007).

152 Frances, *Saving Normal*, 155–7.

Chapter 5: "Just Chemical"

1 Daphne Merkin, *This Close to Happy: A Reckoning with Depression* (New York: Farrar, Straus and Giroux, 2017), 16.

2 Quoted in Midelfort, *A History of Madness in Sixteenth-Century Germany*, 91.

3 Virginia Woolf, "Mr. Bennett and Mrs. Brown," http://www.columbia.edu/~em36/MrBennettAndMrsBrown.pdf, accessed October 31, 2019, originally published 1924.

4 Mark Ruffalo, "The Story of Prozac: A Landmark Drug in Psychiatry," *Psychology Today* (March 1, 2020).

5 I love this point, but it's not mine, but Katie Kilroy-Marac's.

6 Solomon, *The Noonday Demon*, 22.

7 See, for example, Carol P. Weingarten and Timothy J. Strauman, "Neuroimaging for Psychotherapy Research: Current Trends," *Psychotherapy Research* 25, 2 (March 2015) 185–213.

8 Alison Karasz and Liza Watkins, "Conceptual Models of Treatment in Depressed Hispanic Patients," *Annals of Family Medicine* 4, 6 (November/December 2006) 527–33; Sushrut Jadhav, Mitchell G. Weiss, and Roland Littlewood, "Cultural Experience of Depression among White Britons in London," *Anthropology and Medicine* 8, 1 (2001) 47–69.

9 Sadowsky, *Electroconvulsive Therapy in America*; Sadowsky, "Somatic Treatments."

10 For more on the physical treatments for mental illness that preceded widespread use of psychopharmaceuticals, both those covered here and some others, see Braslow, *Mental Ills and Bodily Cures*; Sadowsky, "Somatic Treatments."

11 Harrington, *Mind Fixers*, 57–9.

12 There is a large historiography of lobotomy. See Elliott S. Valenstein, *Great and Desperate Cures: The Rise and Decline of Psychosurgery and Other Radical Treatments for Mental Illness* (New York: Basic Books, 1986); Braslow, *Mental Ills and Bodily Cures*, chs. 6 and 7; Jack D. Pressman, *Last Resort: Psychosurgery and the Limits of Medicine* (Cambridge: Cambridge University Press, 1998); Mical Raz, *The Lobotomy Letters: The Making of American Psychosurgery* (Rochester: University of Rochester Press, 2013); Jenell Johnson,

American Lobotomy: A Rhetorical History (Ann Arbor: University of Michigan Press, 2014).

13 Nicolas Rasmussen, *On Speed: The Many Lives of Amphetamine* (New York: New York University Press, 2008).

14 The discussion of ECT that follows largely draws on my *Electroconvulsive Therapy in America*. See also Timothy Kneeland and Carol A. B. Warren, *Pushbutton Psychiatry: A History of Electroshock in America* (Westport: Praeger Publishers, 2002) and Edward Shorter and David Healy, *Shock Therapy: A History of Electroconvulsive Treatment in Mental Illness* (New Brunswick: Rutgers University Press, 2007).

15 Karen V. Kukil, ed., *The Unabridged Journals of Sylvia Plath, 1950–1962* (New York: Anchor Books, 2000), 455.

16 Sylvia Plath, *The Bell Jar* (New York: Bantam Books, 1971, originally published 1963), 118.

17 Harrington, *Mind Fixers*, 102.

18 Ibid., 102–4.

19 Malaria Fever Therapy is the only truly curative one.

20 Sheldon Gelman, *Medicating Schizophrenia: A History* (New Brunswick: Rutgers University Press, 1999).

21 More recent research looks at the possibility that abnormalities in the receptors of the neurotransmitters matter, not just the availability of the transmitters. Stephen M. Stahl, *Stahl's Essential Psychopharmacology* (Cambridge: Cambridge University Press), 262–6.

22 The most detailed accounts of the history of psychopharmacology are David Healy's *The Creation of Psychopharmacology* (Cambridge: Harvard University Press, 1992) and *The Anti-Depressant Era* (Cambridge: Harvard University Press, 1997).

23 Harrington, *Mind Fixers*, 191–2.

24 Nathan Kline usually gets most of the credit for the use of MAOIs as antidepressants, but there was some dispute about this. Healy, *The Antidepressant Era*, 68–71.

25 Harrington, *Mind Fixers*, 192–3.

26 Stahl, *Stahl's Essential Psychopharmacology*, 327.

27 Harrington, *Mind Fixers*, 194.

28 Several changes since the early days of MAOIs make them less

risky now, including a patch the patient can wear to mitigate adverse effects.

29 Valenstein, *Blaming the Brain*, 39.

30 Harrington, *Mind Fixers*, 194–5. As with Kline and MAOIs, there is some question as to whether Kuhn deserves all or most of the credit for identifying imipramine as an antidepressant. Healy, *The Antidepressant Era*, 52.

31 Healy, *The Antidepressant Era*, 53.

32 Shorter, *Before Prozac*.

33 J. Alexander and Jessica Gören, "Not Obsolete: Continuing Roles for TCAs and MAOIs," *Psychiatric Times* 24, 10 (September 15, 2007).

34 Ibid.

35 Valenstein, *Blaming the Brain*, 71.

36 Ibid., 72; Alexander and Gören, "Not Obsolete."

37 Alexander and Gören, "Not Obsolete."

38 Joseph Schildkraut, "The Catecholamine Hypothesis of Affective Disorders: A Review of the Supporting Evidence," *American Journal of Psychiatry* 122, 5 (November 1965) 509–22.

39 Joseph J. Schildkraut, "The Catecholamine Hypothesis: Before and Thereafter," http://inhn.org/fileadmin/user_upload/User_Up loads/INHN/FILES/BAN_OF_BULLETIN_14_-_2_THE_CA TECHOLAMINE_HYPOTHESIS__1_.pdf, accessed October 26, 2019.

40 Valenstein, *Blaming the Brain*, 72.

41 Lauren Slater, *Blue Dreams: The Science and the Story of the Drugs That Changed Our Minds* (New York: Little, Brown & Co., 2018), 159.

42 Stahl, *Stahl's Essential Psychopharmacology*, 269; Cathy Spatz Wilson, Kimberly DuMont, and Sally J. Czaja, "A Prospective Investigation of Major Depressive Disorder and Comorbidity in Abused and Neglected Children Grown Up," *Archives of General Psychiatry* 64 (2007) 49–56.

43 Levinson and Nichols, "Genetics of Depression," 301–2; Falk W. Lohoff, "Overview of the Genetics of Major Depressive Disorder," *Current Psychiatry Reports* 12, 6 (2010) 539–46.

44 Douglas F. Levinson, "The Genetics of Depression: A Review," *Biological Psychiatry* 60, 2 (2006) 84–92.

45 Meredith Platt, *Storming the Gates of Bedlam: How Dr. Nathan Kline Transformed the Treatment of Mental Illness* (Dumont, NJ: DePew Publishing, 2012), 8.

46 Jason Schnittker, "An Uncertain Revolution: Why the Rise of a Genetic Model of Mental Illness Has Not Increased Tolerance," *Social Science & Medicine* 67, 9 (November 2008), 1370–81; Patrick W. Corrigan and Amy C. Watson, "At Issue: Stop the Stigma: Call Mental Illness a Brian Disease," *Schizophrenia Bulletin* 30, 3 (2004) 477–9.

47 Peter Kramer, *Listening to Prozac: A Psychiatrist Explores Antidepressant Drugs and the Remaking of the Self* (New York: Penguin Books, 1993), xiv.

48 Callahan and Berrios, *Reinventing Depression*, 147.

49 Eric J. Nestler, "New Approaches for Treating Depression," in Charney et al., *Charney and Nestler's Neurobiology of Mental Illness*, 378.

50 For work in this vein, see Ian Dowbiggin, *The Quest for Mental Health* (Cambridge: Cambridge University Press, 2011), and some of the essays in Carl Elliott and Tod Chambers, eds., *Prozac As A Way of Life* (Chapel Hill: University of North Carolina Press, 2004).

51 Laurie Zoloth, "Care of the Dying in America," in Elliott and Chambers, *Prozac As A Way of Life*.

52 Valenstein, *Blaming the Brain*, 96.

53 See for example, Kelli Maria Korducki, "It's Not Just a Chemical Imbalance," *The New York Times* July 27, 2019, https://www.nytimes.com/2019/07/27/opinion/sunday/its-not-just-a-chemical-imbalance.html?action=click&module=Opinion&pgtype=Homepage, accessed July 28, 2019.

54 Erick H. Turner, Annette M. Matthews, Eftihia Linardatos, Robert A. Tell, and Robert Rosenthal, "Selective Publication of Antidepressant Trials and Its Influence on Apparent Efficacy," *New England Journal of Medicine* 358 (January 17, 2008) 252–60.

55 Hirshbein, *American Melancholy*, 37.

56 Greenberg, *Manufacturing Depression*, 215–26.

57 Joanna Moncrieff, *The Myth of the Chemical Cure: A Critique of Psychiatric Drug Treatment* (Houndmills: Palgrave Macmillan, 2008), 139. See also Greenberg, *Manufacturing Depression*, 8.

58 Moncrieff, *Myth of the Chemical Cure*, 20, 138.

59 Stahl, *Stahl's Essential Psychopharmacology*, 285.

60 B. Timothy Walsh, Stuart N. Seidman, Robyn Sysko, and Madelyn Gould, "Placebo Response in Studies of Major Depression: Variable, Substantial, and Growing," *Journal of the American Medical Association* 287, 14 (April 10, 2002) 1840–7.

61 Personal Communication, August 14, 2019.

62 These are the animating questions of Irving Kirsch, *The Emperor's New Drugs*, in my view one of the smartest critiques of antidepressant trials, though much of Kirsch's book is devoted to showing that the placebo effect is real, which I don't think is in serious question.

63 In *The Emperor's New Drugs*, Kirsch concedes that the tailoring effect might explain this gap, but counters reasonably that it is the job of the drug producers to prove that their products work, not his to prove beyond doubt that they do not. Clinical trials rarely test individual patients on a series of different drugs. A large study called STAR*D tracked patients on different medications, and found that patients with more treatment-resistant depression can improve if different treatments are tried or added on. The odds of success declined with every additional treatment strategy, though. Some depressions are just hard to treat. https://www.nimh.nih.gov/funding/clinical-research/practical/stard/allmedicationlevels.shtml, accessed October 14, 2019.

64 Peter Kramer makes these arguments in *Ordinarily Well: The Case for Antidepressants*. He also points out that other researchers did their own analyses of Kirsch's data and had different results. Kirsch included trials of the drug Serzone, which fared poorly and is not used now. Kramer agrees that the placebo effect complicates the picture, and says we need more studies with active placebos – placebos that have effects, but are not antidepressants.

65 This point is also stressed in Shorter, *Before Prozac*, but only to support the use of MAOIs and tricyclics, not SSRIs.

66 Kramer, *Ordinarily Well*, 167.
67 Vieda Skultans, "From Damaged Nerves to Masked Depression: Inevitability and Hope in Latvian Psychiatric Narratives," *Social Science and Medicine* 56 (2003) 2421–31.
68 Healy, *The Creation of Psychopharmacology*, 66, quote on p. 372.
69 Corina Dubos, "Psychiatry and Ideology: The Emergence of 'Asthenic Neurosis' in Communist Romania," in Sarah Marks and Mat Savelli, eds., *Psychiatry in Communist Europe* (London: Palgrave Macmillan, 2015).
70 My account is based on Skultans, "From Damaged Nerves to Masked Depression." Mat Savelli and Sarah Marks note that Soviet psychiatry was anti-Freudian, avoiding stress on early childhood, and placing emphasis on social and physical environment. Sarah Marks and Mat Savelli, "Communist Europe and Transnational Psychiatry," in Marks and Savelli, eds., *Psychiatry in Communist Europe*.
71 Orkideh Behrouzan, *Prozak Diaries: Psychiatry and Generational Memory in Iran* (Stanford: Stanford University Press, 2016).
72 Except where noted, my account of Japan is based on Kitanaka, *Depression in Japan*.
73 Akihito Suzuki, "Global Theory, Local Practice: Shock Therapies in Japanese Psychiatry, 1920–1945," in Waltraud Ernst and Thomas Mueller, eds., *Transnational Psychiatries: Social and Cultural Histories of Psychiatry in Comparative Perspective, c. 1800–2000* (Newcastle upon Tyne: Cambridge Scholars Publishing, 2010).
74 Healy, *The Creation of Psychopharmacology*, 66.
75 Waltraud Ernst, "Practicing 'Colonial' or 'Modern' Psychiatry in British India? Treatments at the Indian Mental Hospital at Ranchi, 1925–1940," in Ernst and Mueller, eds., *Transnational Psychiatries*.
76 Kramer, *Ordinarily Well*, 67–8.
77 Stefan Ecks, *Eating Drugs: Psychopharmaceutical Pluralism in India* (New York: New York University Press, 2014).
78 Claudia Lang and Eva Jansen, "Appropriating Depression: Biomedicalizing Ayurvedic Psychiatry in Kerala, India," *Medical Anthropology* 32, 1 (2013) 25–45.
79 Jadhav, "The Cultural Construction of Western Depression," 42.

80 Caroline Ménard, Madeline L. Pfau, Georgia E. Hodes, and Scott J. Russo, "Immune Mechanisms of Depression," in Charney et al., *Charney and Nestler's Neurobiology of Mental Illness*; Jill M. Goldstein, L. Holsen, S. Cherkerzian, M. Misra, and R. J. Handra, "Neuroendocrine Mechanisms of Depression" in Charney et al., *Charney and Nestler's Neurobiology of Mental Illness*.

81 See Sarah H. Lisanby, ed., *Brain Stimulation in Psychiatric Treatment* (Washington, DC: American Psychiatric Publishing, 2004).

82 Jamilah R. George, Timothy I. Michaels, Jae Sevelius, and Monica T. Williams, "The Psychedelic Renaissance and the Limitations of a White-dominant Medical Framework: A Call for Indigenous and Ethnic Minority Inclusion," *Journal of Psychedelic Studies* 4, 1 (2020) 4–15.

83 "LSD Alters Perception Via Serotonin Receptors," *Science News*, January 26, 2017, https://www.sciencedaily.com/releases/2017/01/170126123127.htm, accessed October 30, 2019. Links between LSD and the serotonin system have been known for decades; see Healy, *The Creation of Psychopharmacology*, 106.

84 Franz X. Vollenweider and Michael Kometer, "The Neurobiology of Psychedelic Drugs: Implications for the Treatment of Mood Disorders," *Nature Reviews, Neuroscience* 11 (2010) 642–51.

85 Ibid. On the medicinal origins of LSD, see Erica Dyck, *Psychedelic Psychiatry: LSD from Clinic to Campus* (Baltimore: The Johns Hopkins University Press, 2008).

86 William Ralston, "Has Eskatamine Been Vastly Overhyped?" *Gentleman's Quarterly*, July 20, 2019.

87 Vollenweider and Kometer, "The Neurobiology of Psychedelic Drugs."

88 Erick H. Turner, "Eskatamine for Treatment-Resistant Depression: Seven Concerns about Efficacy and FDA Approval," *The Lancet*, October 31, 2019.

89 Moncrieff, *Myth of the Chemical Cure;* Johann Hari, *Lost Connections: Uncovering the Real Causes of Depression – And the Unexpected Solutions* (New York: Bloomsbury, 2018).

Chapter 6: Darkness Legible

1 Kitanaka, *Depression in Japan*, 97.
2 Bruce Springsteen, *Born to Run* (New York: Simon and Schuster, 2016), 499.
3 Definition taken from the Merriam Webster app.
4 Sylvia Plath, *The Bell Jar* (New York: Bantam Books, 1971, originally published 1963), 152.
5 Ibid., 193.
6 William Styron, *Darkness Visible: A Memoir of Madness* (New York: Vintage Books, 1990).
7 Arthur Frank, *The Wounded Storyteller* (Chicago: University of Chicago Press, 1995). See also Brenda Dyer, "Winter Tales: Comedy and Romance Story-Types in Narratives of Depression," in Hilary Clark, ed., *Depression and Narrative: Telling the Dark* (Albany: State University of New York Press, 2008). Frank acknowledges that many narratives will not fit neatly into just one of the types he identifies. See also Jette Westerbeek and Karen Mutsaers, "Depression Narratives: How the Self Became a Problem," *Literature and Medicine* 21, 1 (2008) 25–55.
8 Norman S. Endler, *Holiday of Darkness: A Psychologist's Personal Journey Out of His Depression* (Toronto: John Wiley & Sons, 1982).
9 For similar restitution accounts with ECT treatment, see Frank Kimball, "Hope for Tired Minds," *Hygeia* (December 1946) 906–7 and 946, (January 1947) 36–7, 66–9; and Leon Rosenberg, "Brainsick: A Physician's Journey to the Brink," *Cerebrum* 4 (2002) 43–60, for a similar account.
10 Styron, *Darkness Visible*, 7. See also Lewis Wolpert, *Malignant Sadness: The Anatomy of Depression* (London: Faber and Faber, 1999), 1.
11 Styron, *Darkness Visible*, 17.
12 Leader, *The New Black*, 187–8.
13 Lauren Slater, *Prozac Diary* (New York: Penguin Books, 1998), 16. On the incommunicability of depression, see also David A. Karp, *Speaking of Sadness: Depression, Disconnection, and the Meanings of Illness* (Oxford: Oxford University Press, 1996) 40–2.
14 Kimberly K. Emmons has drawn attention to gendered language in Styron and others, including making this observation about

Styron's gendered use of the word itself. See her *Black Dogs and Blue Words: Depression and Gender in the Age of Self-Care* (New Brunswick: Rutgers University Press, 2010), 5.

15 Tracy Thompson, *The Beast: A Journey Through Depression* (New York: Penguin Books, 1996), 189.

16 Styron, *Darkness Visible*, 37.

17 Wurtzel, *Prozac Nation*, 68.

18 Merkin, *This Close to Happy*.

19 Merkin anticipated my students' displeasure, noting that the presence of money in a person's life provokes an envy that can block sympathy. This pre-emptive observation had little impact on my students. See also Matt Haig, *Reasons to Stay Alive* (New York: Penguin Books, 2015).

20 Wurtzel, *Prozac Nation*, 22. Merkin also describes *Darkness Visible* as "strangely contextless." Merkin, *This Close to Happy*, 12.

21 Wurtzel, *Prozac Nation*, 22.

22 Lora Inman, *Running Uphill: A Memoir of Surviving Depressive Illness* (Jacksonville Beach: High-Pitched Hum Publishing, 2007), 113.

23 Merkin, *This Close to Happy*, 16. The perceptions of memoirists that many people (1) regard depression as a failure of will, and (2) do not realize that one can look well to others even when suffering from the illness, are borne out in research. Shoji Yokoya, Takami Maeno, Naoto Sakamoto, Ryohei Goto, and Tetsuhiro Maeno, "A Brief Survey of Public Knowledge and Stigma Towards Depression," *Journal of Clinical Medicine Research* 10, 3 (March 2010) 202–9; thanks to Kevin Parvizi for this reference.

24 Merkin, *This Close to Happy*, 10.

25 On the themes in this paragraph, see also O'Brien, *The Family Silver*, 105, and Jeffrey Smith, *Where the Roots Reach for Water: A Personal and Natural History of Melancholia* (New York: North Point Press, 1999), 7.

26 Thanks to Marnie Nichole for suggesting this to me.

27 Thompson, *The Beast*, 161.

28 Jenny Diski, *Skating to Antarctica* (London: Virago, 2014, originally published 1997). Thompson says the same in *The Beast*, 52.

29 Gillian Marchenko, *Still Life: A Memoir of Living Fully with Depression* (Downers Grove: IVP Books, 2016), 13–14.

30 Sally Brampton, *Shoot the Damn Dog: A Memoir of Depression* (New York: W. W. Norton & Co., 2008), 63. Brampton tried many medications and more than one psychotherapy, but her depression was deeply resistant to treatment. Tragically, she died by suicide.

31 Styron, *Darkness Visible*, 9.

32 Meri Nana-Ama Danquah, *Willow, Weep for Me: A Black Woman's Journey Through Depression* (New York: Ballantine Publishing Group, 1998), 21; see also pp. 18–20.

33 Ibid., 247.

34 Inman, *Running Uphill*, 63.

35 Thompson, *The Beast*, 187.

36 Wurtzel, *Prozac Nation*, 341.

37 On worries about the damage to career, see also Karp, *Is It Me or My Meds?*, 162–3.

38 Thompson, *The Beast*, 7. See also Styron, *Darkness Visible*, 34; Lewis Wolpert, *Malignant Sadness: The Anatomy of Depression* (New York: The Free Press, 2000), viii.

39 Tim Lott, *The Scent of Dried Roses* (London: Penguin, 1996), 34.

40 Sadowsky, *Electroconvulsive Therapy in America*, 1–2, 86, 99.

41 Greenberg, *Manufacturing Depression*, 43.

42 Slater, *Prozac Diary*, 107

43 Inman, *Running Uphill*, 2.

44 Linda Gask, *The Other Side of Silence: A Psychiatrist's Memoir of Depression* (Chichester: Summersdale Publishers, 2015).

45 Marchenko, *Still Life*, 19.

46 Wurtzel, *Prozac Nation*, 50.

47 Ibid., 193.

48 Judith Kruger, *My Fight for Sanity* (Greenwich: Crest Books, 1959). I look at Kruger's narrative in more detail in Sadowsky, *Electroconvulsive Therapy in America*, 82–3.

49 Wurtzel, *Prozac Nation*, 345.

50 Styron, *Darkness Visible*, 56.

51 Wurtzel, *Prozac Nation*, 29.

52 Danquah, *Willow, Weep for Me*, 34–5.

53 Brampton, *Shoot the Damn Dog*, 158.

54 Ibid., 148.
55 Slater, *Prozac Diary*, 21.
56 Stevenson, *Bitter Fame*, 7–10.
57 Thompson, *The Beast*, 25.
58 Inman, *Running Uphill*, 26.
59 Diski, *Skating to Antarctica*, 109–11.
60 Ibid., 192.
61 Merkin, *This Close to Happy*, 85.
62 Slater, *Prozac Diary*, 82–3.
63 Ibid., 142.
64 Brampton, *Shoot the Damn Dog*, 34, 251.
65 Karp, *Speaking of Sadness*, 7.
66 Danquah, *Willow, Weep for Me*, 22.
67 O'Brien, *The Family Silver*, 89.
68 Merkin, *This Close to Happy*, 12.
69 Jeffrey Smith, *Where the Roots Reach for Water: A Personal and Natural History of Melancholia* (New York: North Point Press, 1999), 5 and 72.
70 Marchenko, *Still Life*, 29.
71 Brampton, *Shoot the Damn Dog*, 123.
72 O'Brien, *The Family Silver*, 219.
73 Springsteen, *Born to Run*, 498–9.
74 Inman, *Running Uphill*, 2.
75 Diski, *Skating to Antarctica*, 131.
76 Ibid., 60–1.
77 Martha Manning, *Undercurrents: A Life Beneath the Surface* (New York: HarperSanFrancisco, 1994), 89.
78 Karp, *Speaking of Sadness*, 4–5.
79 Smith, *Where Roots Reach for Water*, 14.
80 Brampton, *Shoot the Damn Dog*, 29.
81 Ibid., 31
82 Merkin, *This Close to Happy*, 97–8.
83 Thompson, *The Beast*, 35, 51.
84 Marchenko, *Still Life*, 159–60.
85 Brampton, *Shoot the Damn Dog*, 29.
86 Marchenko, *Still Life*, 50.
87 Diski, *Skating to Antarctica*, 225.

88 Haig, *Reasons to Stay Alive*, 11.

89 See also Solomon, *The Noonday Demon*, 244.

90 As Karp says, "The power of antidepressants seems most incontrovertible when relief occurs precisely on the time schedule predicted and is experienced as a complete cure." Karp, *Is It Me or My Meds?*, 53.

91 Slater, *Prozac Diary*, 29–44.

92 Slater, *Prozac Diary*, 103.

93 Kitty Dukakis and Larry Tye, *Shock: The Healing Power of Electroconvulsive Therapy* (New York: Penguin, 2006); Carrie Fisher, *Shockaholic* (New York: Simon and Schuster, 2011).

94 Manning, *Undercurrents*, 138.

95 Manning, *Undercurrents*, 165–6. Endler was also asked by a friend why he allowed "them" to do that to him; Endler, *Holiday of Darkness*, 76.

96 Judith Kruger, *My Fight for Sanity* (Greenwich: Crest Books, 1959).

97 Anne B. Donahue, "Electroconvulsive Therapy and Memory Loss: A Personal Journey," *The Journal of ECT* 16, 2 (2000) 133–43, quote is on p. 138.

98 Sherwin Nuland, *Lost in America: A Journey with My Father* (New York: Alfred A. Knopf, 2003), 7–8. Clinical science has not found a correlation between memory loss and symptom remission in ECT, so it is unlikely that the memory loss is the reason for efficacy.

99 See Sadowsky, *Electroconvulsive Therapy in America*, ch. 6.

100 Springsteen, *Born to Run*, 487.

101 Slater, *Prozac Diary*, 154.

102 Ibid., 10–11.

103 Rasmussen, *On Speed*.

104 Dyck, *Psychedelic Psychiatry*.

105 Wurtzel, *Prozac Nation*, 17.

106 David Lazarus, "Hi, I'm David. I'm a Drug Addict," *Los Angeles Times* (September 6, 2019).

107 Merkin, *This Close to Happy*, 126.

108 This theme is explored at length in Sadowsky, *Electroconvulsive Therapy in America*, ch. 6.

109 Brampton, *Shoot the Damn Dog*, 28, 219; see also Karp, *Speaking of Sadness*, 27.

110 Smith, *Where the Roots Reach for Water*, 22.

111 Inman, *Running Uphill*, 92.

112 Brampton, *Shoot the Damn Dog*, 199.

113 Ibid., 195–8.

114 Wurtzel, *Prozac Nation*, 342.

115 Wurtzel, *Prozac Nation*, 326–7.

116 Thompson, *The Beast*, 167.

117 Gask, *The Other Side of Silence*, 182.

118 Cvetkovich, *Depression: A Public Feeling*. Hari makes similar arguments in *Lost Connections*.

119 Smith, *Where Roots Reach for Water*.

120 http://bookslive.co.za/blog/2015/03/13/i-felt-violated-chimamanda-ngozi-adichie-reveals-her-anger-at-the-guardian-over-article-on-depression/, accessed October 25, 2019.

121 For example, O'Nell, *Disciplined Hearts*.

122 Susan Lamb, *Adolf Meyer: Pathologist of the Mind* (Baltimore: The Johns Hopkins University Press, 2014).

Epilogue: Depression's Past and Future

1 Foreword by Judith N. Shklar in Wolf Lepenies, *Melancholy and Society* (Jeremy Gaines and Doris Jones, eds., Cambridge: Harvard University Press, 1992), xvi.

2 Brampton, *Shoot the Damn Dog*, 84.

3 Pim Cuijpers, Aartan T. F. Beekman, and Charles Reynolds, "Preventing Depression: A Global Priority," *Journal of the American Medical Association* 301, 10 (March 2012) 1033–4.

4 These last two sentences are drawn from my review of Ian Dowbiggin's *The Quest for Mental Health*. My review is in the *Bulletin of the History of Medicine* 86, 2 (Summer, 2012).

Note on the Historiography

1 Janet Oppenheim, *"Shattered Nerves": Doctors, Patients and Depression in Victorian England* (New York: Oxford University Press, 1991).

Partial Bibliography

This list is partial since it does not list every work cited in the footnotes – and also, because I learned a lot from them, it lists books I am partial to. It includes books I broadly agree with and others I have strong disagreements with. It is annotated – but only partially.

General Works on the History and Philosophy of Depression and Melancholia

Stanley Jackson's erudite work has been foundational for all later historical scholarship. Jennifer Radden's work brings exceptional clarity to many of the issues. Andrew Solomon's book is a remarkable look at depression from multiple perspectives.

Callahan, Christopher M. and German E. Berrios, *Reinventing Depression: A History of the Treatment of Depression in Primary Care, 1940–2004* (Oxford: Oxford University Press, 2005).

Greenberg, Gary. *Manufacturing Depression: The Secret History of a Modern Disease* (New York: Simon and Schuster, 2010).

Hirshbein, Laura D. *American Melancholy: Constructions of Depression in the Twentieth Century* (New Brunswick, NJ: Rutgers University Press, 2014).

Jackson, Stanley. *Melancholia and Depression: From Hippocratic Times to Modern Times* (New Haven, CT: Yale University Press, 1986).

Lawlor, Clark. *From Melancholia to Prozac: A History of Depression* (Oxford: Oxford University Press, 2012).

Radden, Jennifer. *Moody Minds Distempered: Essays in Melancholy and Depression* (Oxford: Oxford University Press, 2009).

Radden, Jennifer. *Melancholy Habits: Burton's Anatomy and the Mind Sciences* (Oxford: Oxford University Press, 2017).

Solomon, Andrew. *The Noonday Demon: An Atlas of Depression* (2nd edition, New York: Scribner, 2015, originally published 2001).

Anthropology of Depression and Related Issues

Kleinman's pioneering work in this area remains valuable, and the subtlety of his arguments is often missed. The listed ethnographies of antidepressant use – Behrouzan, Ecks, Kitanaka – are excellent.

Behrouzan, Orkideh. *Prozak Diaries: Psychiatry and Generational Memory in Iran* (Stanford, CA: Stanford University Press, 2016).

Ecks, Stefan. *Eating Drugs: Psychopharmaceutical Pluralism in India* (New York: New York University Press, 2014).

Field, Margaret. *Search for Security: An Ethno-Psychiatric Study of Rural Ghana* (Evanston, IL: Northwestern University Press, 1960).

Kitanaka, Junko. *Depression in Japan: Psychiatric Cures for a Society in Distress* (Princeton, NJ: Princeton University Press, 2012).

Kleinman, Arthur. *Social Origins of Distress and Disease: Depression, Neurasthenia, and Pain in Modern China* (New Haven, CT: Yale University Press, 1986).

Kleinman, Arthur. *Rethinking Psychiatry: From Cultural Category to Personal Experience* (New York: The Free Press, 1991).

Kleinman, Arthur and Byron Good, eds., *Culture and Depression: Studies in the Anthropology and Cross-Cultural Psychiatry of Affect and Disorder* (Berkeley, CA: University of California Press, 1985).

O'Nell, Theresa DeLeane. *Disciplined Hearts: History, Identity, and Depression in an American Indian Community* (Berkeley, CA: University of California Press, 1996).

Psychoanalysis

Some historians of medicine and psychiatry think that psychoanalysis has received too much attention. Many who say that are also the ones who don't like psychoanalysis much. I think psychoanalysis has enduring value, but even if you disagree, its historical importance is unquestionably huge. Really good new books – fresh, smart, original – on the history of psychoanalysis come out every year. I've only listed ones I used for this book. George Makari's book is about as good an introduction to the history of the movement as one could hope for. Julia Segal's book on Klein is an unusually clear introduction to a difficult thinker. The Solms book is a good overview of neuropsychoanalysis.

Abraham, Karl. *Clinical Papers and Essays on Psychoanalysis* (London: Maresfield Reprints, 1955).

Bentick van Schoonheten, Anna. *Karl Abraham; Life and Work, a Biography* (Liz Waters, trans., London: Karnac Books, 2016, originally published 2013).

Busch, Fredric N., Marie Rudden, and Theodore Shapiro, *Psychodynamic Treatment of Depression* (Arlington, VA: American Psychiatric Publishing, 2004).

Fiorini, Leticia, Thierry Bokanowski, and Sergio Lewkowicz, eds., *On Freud's "Mourning and Melancholia"* (London: Karnac Books, 2009, originally published 2007).

Freud, Sigmund. *On Murder, Mourning, and Melancholia* (Shaun Whiteside, ed., London: Penguin Books, 2005).

Green, André. *On Private Madness* (London: Karnak Books, 1997, originally published 1986).

Jacobson, Edith. *Depression: Comparative Studies of Normal, Neurotic, and Psychotic Conditions* (Madison, CT: International Universities Press, 1971).

Kristeva, Julia. *Black Sun: Depression and Melancholia* (Leon S. Roudiez, trans., New York: Columbia University Press, 1989, originally published 1987).

Leader, Darian. *The New Black: Mourning, Melancholia and Depression* (Minneapolis, MN: Graywolf Press, 2008).

Makari, George. *Revolution in Mind: The Creation of Psychoanalysis* (New York: HarperCollins, 2008).

Miller, Alice. *The Drama of the Gifted Child: The Search for the True Self* (Ruth Ward, trans., New York: Basic Books, 2007, originally published 1979).

Mitchell, Juliet, ed., *The Selected Melanie Klein* (New York: The Free Press, 1986).

Segal, Julia. *Melanie Klein* (London: Sage Publications, 1992).

Solms, Mark. *The Brain and the Inner World: An Introduction to the Neuroscience of the Subjective Experience* (New York: Other Press, 2003).

Politics, Social Identity, and Inequality

Study of the politics and demographics of depression has given most attention to gender. There is still more to do on this subject, but there is also a lot of research waiting to be done on depression and other forms of inequality and injustice. Some of the books below are more about other aspects of psychiatry or medicine, not depression. I've not listed articles in this bibliography, but much of the sociology and epidemiology on inequality and depression is in journals; see the footnotes to chapter 4. The historical literature on depression and social inequality is thin, and awaiting researchers.

Brown, George W. and Tirril Harris, *Social Origins of Depression: A Study of Psychiatric Disorder in Women* (New York: The Free Press, 1978).

Cvetkovich, Ann. *Depression: A Public Feeling* (Durham, NC: Duke University Press, 2012).

Davies, William. *The Happiness Industry: How the Government and Big Business Sold Us Well-Being* (London: Verso, 2015).

Emmons, Kimberly K. *Black Dogs and Blue Words: Depression and Gender in the Age of Self-Care* (New Brunswick, NJ: Rutgers University Press, 2010).

Fanon, Frantz. *The Wretched of the Earth* (New York: Grove Press, 1963).

Han, Byung-Chul. *Psychopolitics: Neoliberalism and the New Technologies of Power* (Erik Butler, trans., London: Verso, 2017).

Metzl, Jonathan. *Prozac on the Couch: Prescribing Gender in the Era of Wonder Drugs* (Durham, NC: Duke University Press, 2003).

Metzl, Jonathan. *The Protest Psychosis: How Schizophrenia Became a Black Disease* (Boston, MA: Beacon Press, 2009).

Mustakeem, Sowande' M. *Slavery at Sea: Terror, Sex, and Sickness in the Middle Passage* (Urbana, IL: University of Illinois Press, 2016).

Schiesari, Juliana. *The Gendering of Melancholia: Feminism, Psychoanalysis, and the Symbolics of Loss in Renaissance Literature* (Ithaca, NY: Cornell University Press, 1992).

The DSM

All of these books are worth reading, but in my opinion the one by Hannah Decker is the best.

Decker, Hannah S. *The Making of DSM-III: A Diagnostic Manual's Conquest of American Psychiatry* (Oxford: Oxford University Press, 2013).

Frances, Allen. *Saving Normal: An Insider's Revolt Against Out-of-Control Psychiatric Diagnosis, DSM-V, Big Pharma, and the Medicalization of Ordinary Life* (New York: William Morrow, 2013).

Greenberg, Gary. *The Book of Woe: The DSM and the Unmaking of Psychiatry* (New York: Plume, 2013).

Kutchins, Herb and Stuart A. Kirk. *Making Us Crazy: DSM: The Psychiatric Bible and the Creation of Mental Disorders* (New York: The Free Press, 1997).

Biological Psychiatry and Pharmaceuticals

For thoroughness on the history of psychopharmacology, David Healy's work remains unsurpassed. In the spirit of listing books that I am partial towards, I have listed my own book on ECT; see Kneeland and Warren for a less favorable take on ECT than mine, and Shorter and Healy for a more favorable one than mine. Many of the treatments that preceded the antidepressant era are ably examined in Joel Braslow's even-handed book. Anne Harrington's book is a recent and lucid overview of biological psychiatry in general.

Andreasen, Nancy C. *The Broken Brain: The Biological Revolution in Psychiatry* (New York: Harper and Row, 1984).

Braslow, Joel. *Mental Ills and Bodily Cures: Psychiatric Treatment in the First Half of the Twentieth Century* (Berkeley, CA: University of California Press, 1997).

Elliott, Carl and Tod Chambers, eds. *Prozac as a Way of Life* (Chapel Hill, NC: University of North Carolina Press, 2004).

Harrington, Anne. *Mind Fixers: Psychiatry's Troubled Search for the Biology of Mental Illness* (New York: W.W. Norton and Company, 2019).

Healy, David. *The Anti-Depressant Era* (Cambridge, MA: Harvard University Press, 1997).

Healy, David. *The Creation of Psychopharmacology* (Cambridge, MA: Harvard University Press, 1992).

Karp, David A. *Is It Me or My Meds?: Living with Antidepressants* (Cambridge, MA: Harvard University Press, 2006).

Kirsch, Irving. *The Emperor's New Drugs: Exploding the Antidepressant Myth* (New York: Basic Books, 2010).

Kneeland, Timothy and Carol A. B. Warren, *Pushbutton Psychiatry: A History of Electroshock in America* (Westport, CT: Praeger Publishers, 2002).

Kramer, Peter. *Listening to Prozac: A Psychiatrist Explores Antidepressant Drugs and the Remaking of the Self* (New York: Penguin Books, 1993).

Kramer, Peter. *Ordinarily Well: The Case for Antidepressants* (New York: Farrar, Straus and Giroux, 2016).

Moncrieff, Joanna. *The Myth of the Chemical Cure: A Critique of Psychiatric Drug Treatment* (Houndmills: Palgrave Macmillan, 2008).

Rasmussen, Nicolas. *On Speed: The Many Lives of Amphetamine* (New York: New York University Press, 2008).

Sadowsky, Jonathan. *Electroconvulsive Therapy in America* (New York: Routledge, 2006).

Shorter, Edward. *Before Prozac: The Troubled History of Mood Disorders in Psychiatry* (Oxford: Oxford University Press, 2009).

Shorter, Edward and David Healy, *Shock Therapy: A History of Electroconvulsive Treatment in Mental Illness* (New Brunswick, NJ: Rutgers University Press, 2007).

Valenstein, Elliot S. *Blaming the Brain: The Truth About Drugs and Mental Health* (New York: The Free Press, 1998).

Memoir and Narrative

I believe deeply that while other experts obviously matter, no one can understand any illness state without an immersive reckoning with the words of people who have had it. This is why I devoted substantial attention here to patients' voices, as I did in my previous books. The list below features my personal favorites. The books by Jamison and Saks are about other mental illnesses, but they are incredible and should be read by anyone trying to understand mental illness and psychiatry.

Danquah, Meri Nana-Ama. *Willow, Weep for Me: A Black Woman's Journey Through Depression* (New York: Ballantine Publishing Group, 1998).

Diski, Jenny. *Skating to Antarctica* (London: Virago, 2014, originally published 1997).

Fisher, Carrie. *Shockaholic* (New York: Simon and Schuster, 2011).

Frank, Arthur. *The Wounded Storyteller* (Chicago, IL: University of Chicago Press, 1995).

Gask, Linda. *The Other Side of Silence: A Psychiatrist's Memoir of Depression* (Chichester: Sommersdale Publishers, 2015).

Jamison, Kay Redfield. *An Unquiet Mind: A Memoir of Moods and Madness* (New York: Vintage Books, 2011, originally published 1995).

Manning, Martha. *Undercurrents: A Life Beneath the Surface* (New York: HarperSanFrancisco, 1994).

Merkin, Daphne. *This Close to Happy: A Reckoning with Depression* (New York: Farrar, Straus and Giroux, 2017).

Saks, Elyn R. *The Center Cannot Hold: My Journey Through Madness* (New York: Hachette Books, 2007).

Slater, Lauren. *Prozac Diary* (New York: Penguin Books, 1998).

Springsteen, Bruce. *Born to Run* (New York: Simon and Schuster, 2016).

Styron, William. *Darkness Visible: A Memoir of Madness* (New York: Vintage Books, 1990).

Thompson, Tracy. *The Beast: A Journey Through Depression* (New York: Penguin Books, 1996).

Wurtzel, Elizabeth. *Prozac Nation: Young and Depressed in America* (New York: Riverhead Books, 1994).

Index

Page numbers in *italic* refer to figures.